IMAGES
of America

BOSTON'S NORTH END

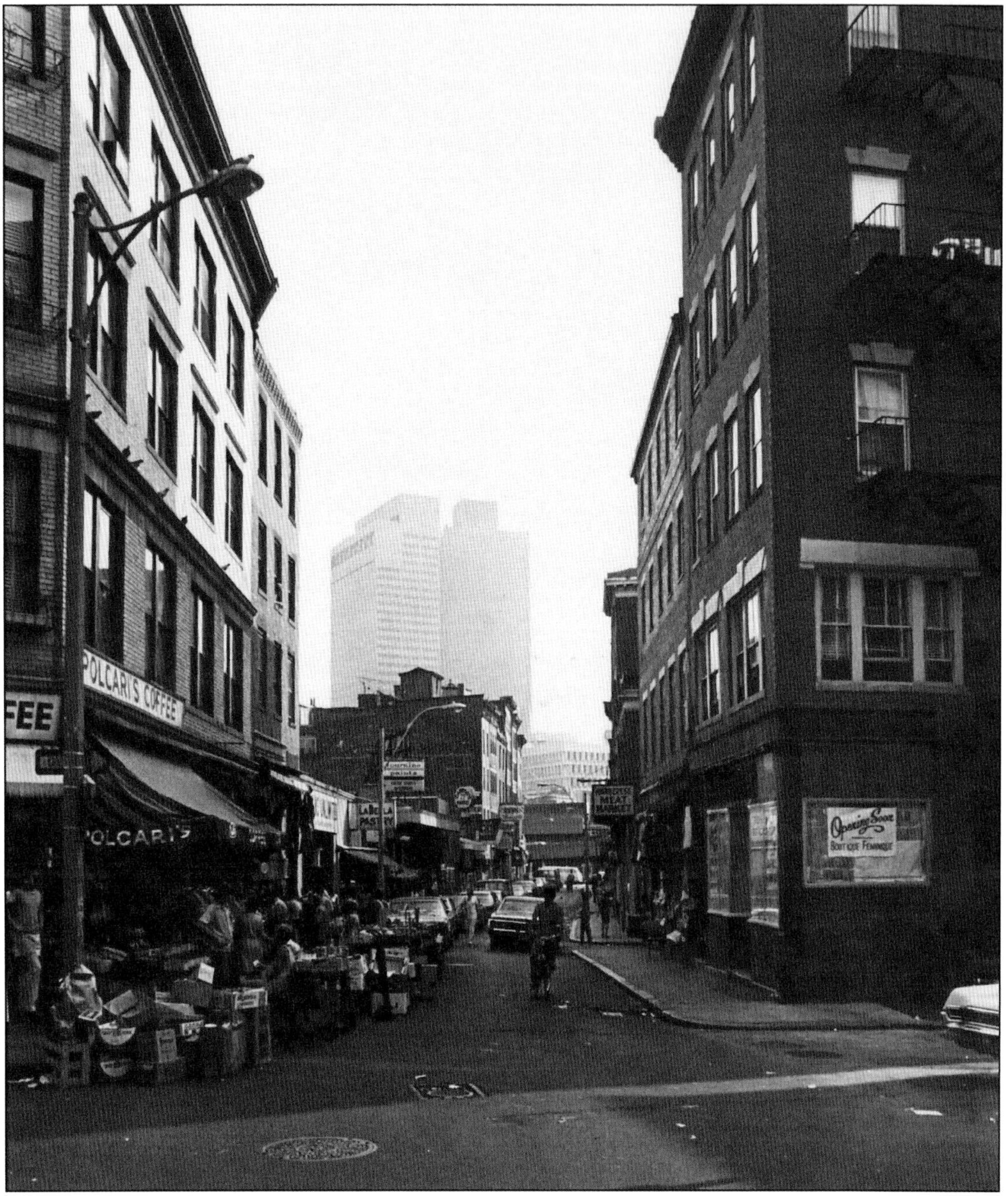

This view of the Boston skyscrapers from Salem Street offers the quintessential aspect of the North End. With street vendors displaying their goods along the sidewalks and shops with apartments above, the appeal of this densely settled and vibrant neighborhood remains unchanged by the passage of time. (Courtesy of the North End Branch of the Boston Public Library, hereinafter referred to as the BPL)

IMAGES
of America

BOSTON'S NORTH END

Anthony Mitchell Sammarco

ARCADIA
PUBLISHING

ISBN 978-0-7385-3469-5

Published by Arcadia Publishing
Charleston, South Carolina

Printed in the United States of America

For all general information contact Arcadia Publishing at:
Telephone 843-853-2070
Fax 843-853-0044
E-Mail sales@arcadiapublishing.com
For customer service and orders:
Toll-Free 1-888-313-2665

Visit us on the Internet at www.arcadiapublishing.com

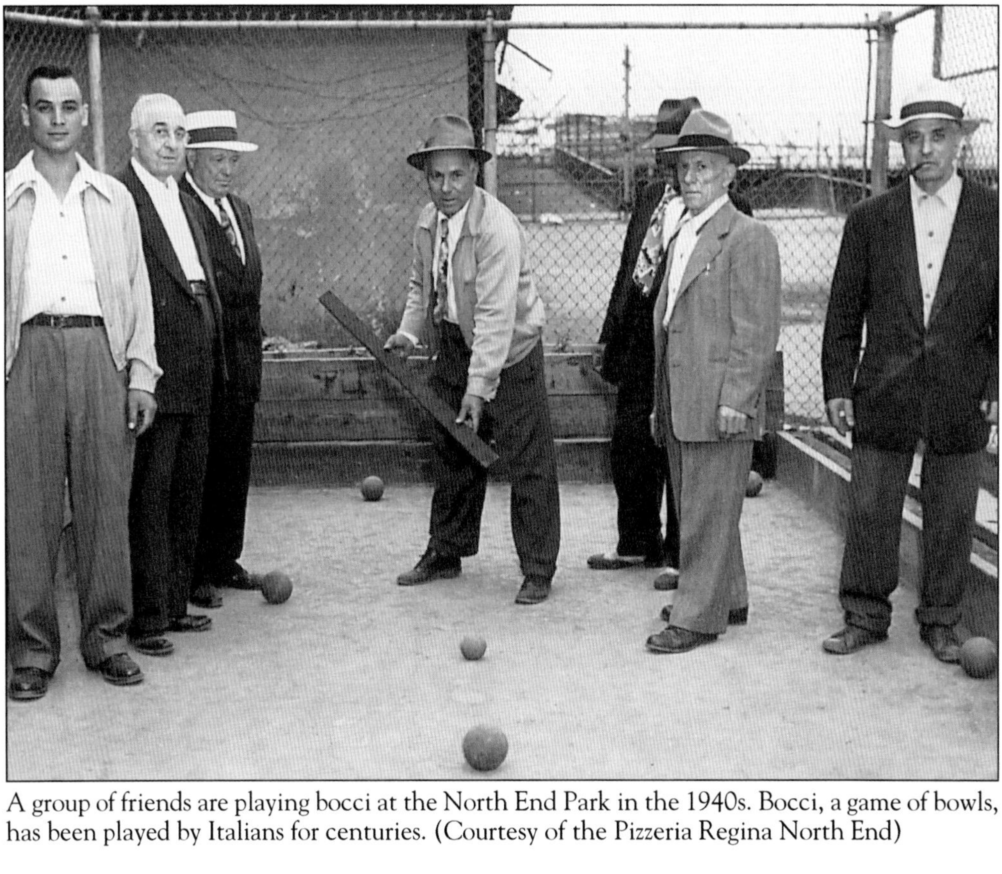

A group of friends are playing bocci at the North End Park in the 1940s. Bocci, a game of bowls, has been played by Italians for centuries. (Courtesy of the Pizzeria Regina North End)

Contents

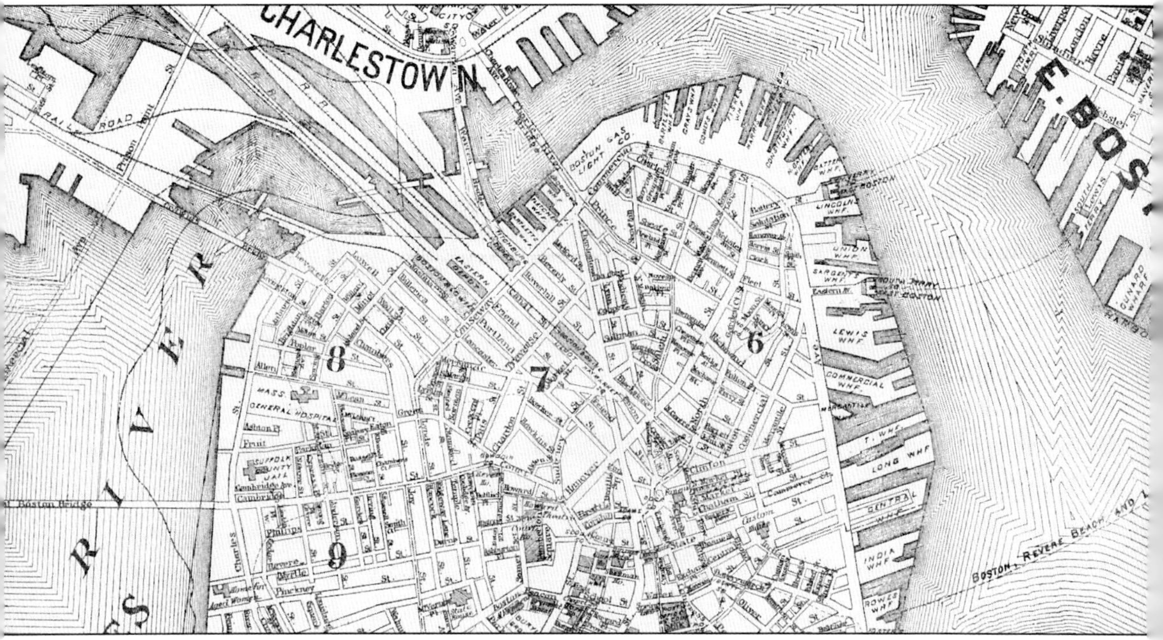
CHARLESTOWN
E. BOS
RIVER
BOSTON GAS LIGHT CO.
LINCOLN WHF.
UNION WHF.
LEWIS WHF.
COMMERCIAL WHF.
LONG WHF
CENTRAL WHF.
INDIA WHF.
ROWES WHF
CUNARD WHARF
MASS. GENERAL HOSPITAL
SUFFOLK COUNTY JAIL
BOSTON, REVERE BEACH, AND L
8
7
6
9

Introduction

The North End of Boston is not only the oldest neighborhood of the city of Boston, but a thriving nexus of cultures that offers a glimpse of what an ethnic neighborhood truly represents. With streets, alleys, and ways that are among the oldest in the city, this densely settled area retains a colonial history, along with the cultures of nineteenth and early-twentieth-century immigrants. Beginning with the Irish and including German, Russian, and Polish Jews, Azoreans, and Italians, the North End has been home to almost every immigrant group to pass through Boston. Today it retains its distinctly Italian flavor, especially during the feasts which honor various saints and culminate with reverent processions through the streets.

The North End has also been an area of commerce, with the merchants and artisans of the eighteenth century having established a thriving economy that included building ships (the USS *Constitution* was built on Constitution Wharf), silversmithing, goldsmithing, copper manufacturing, and bell casting. The nineteenth century would lead to an expansion of business that included massive landfill projects along the waterfront and at Dock Square, where Quincy Market was built between 1824 and 1826. As the century progressed, the Port of Boston attracted hundreds of ships, bringing sailors who patronized the dance halls and taverns in the North End. To stem this "evil influence," the Port of Boston established the Mariner's House in North Square and Father Taylor held forth at the Seamen's Bethel.

By the mid-nineteenth century, the North End had attracted many new immigrants, who lived in rapidly built tenements and the once elegant mansions of North End merchants. By 1860, one half of Boston's residents were foreign born and a diverse group of immigrants called the North End home. Realizing that the immigrants needed assistance, the North Bennet Street School was founded in 1884 to instruct immigrants in vocational training. The Relief Station at Haymarket Square offered medical care, the North End Mission offered assistance, and the North End Branch of the Boston Public Library offered Americanization programs to assimilate the immigrants to American culture and ways.

Today, the North End retains a distinctly Italian flavor, and the streets still teem with activity from the Haymarket on weekends to the many pastry shops, bread bakeries, and restaurants offering both delicious foods and specialty items. The North End isn't just the former home of Paul Revere, but a neighborhood of residents who strive to make it a welcoming and inviting part of Boston.

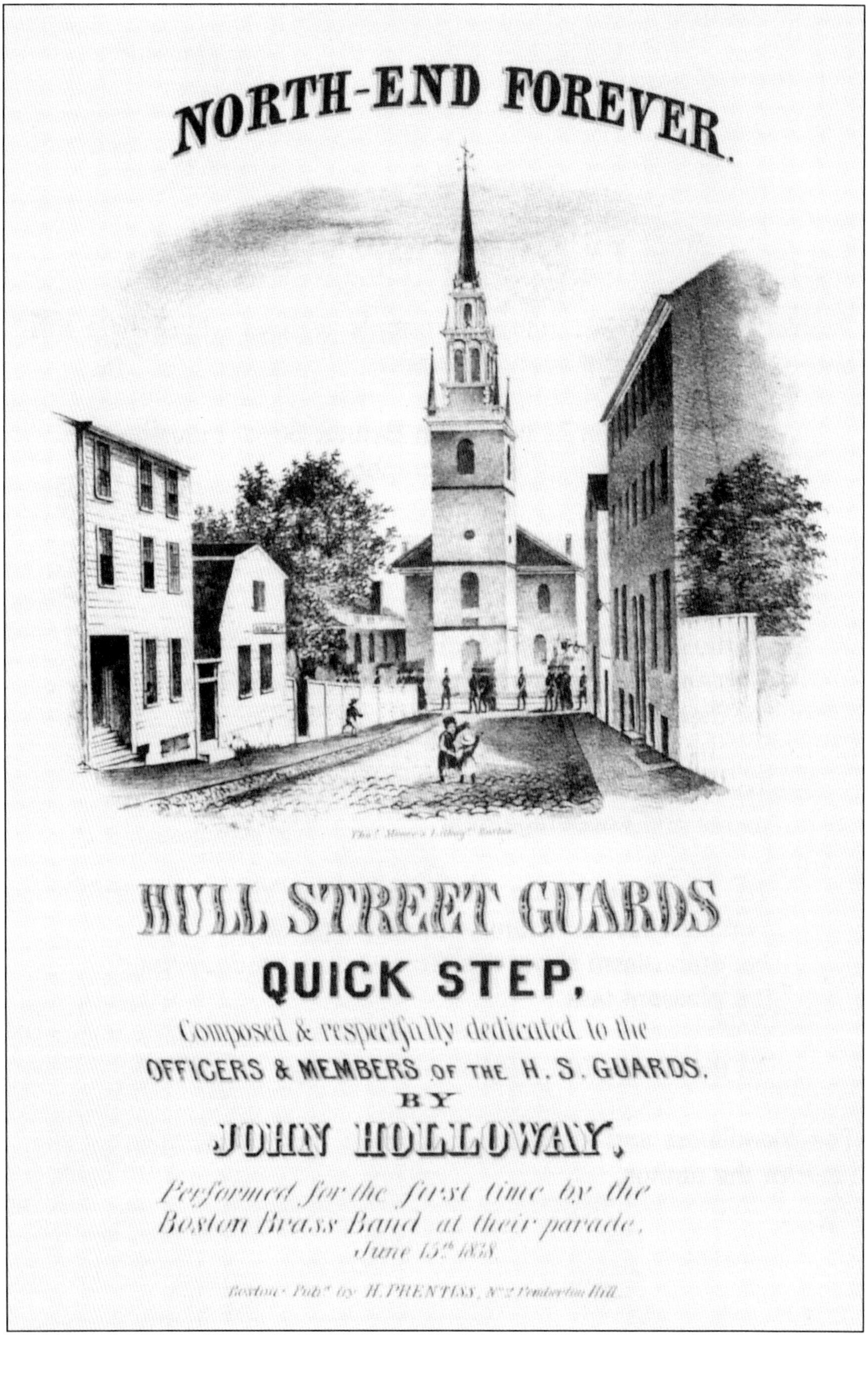
NORTH-END FOREVER.
HULL STREET GUARDS
QUICK STEP,
Composed & respectfully dedicated to the
OFFICERS & MEMBERS OF THE H. S. GUARDS.
BY
JOHN HOLLOWAY,
Performed for the first time by the
Boston Brass Band at their parade,
June 15th 1838.
Boston. Pubd by H. PRENTISS, No. 2 Pemberton Hill

One

The Colonial North End

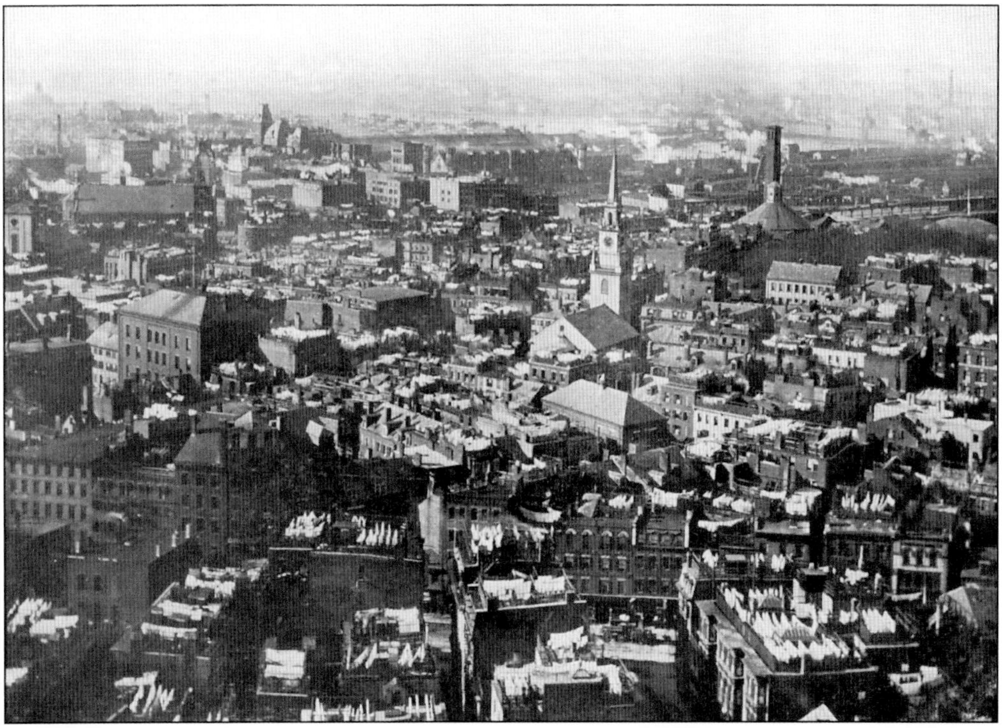

A panoramic view of the North End from the top of the Lincoln Wharf Power House chimney at the turn of the century shows the densely settled neighborhood around the Old North Church on Salem Street.

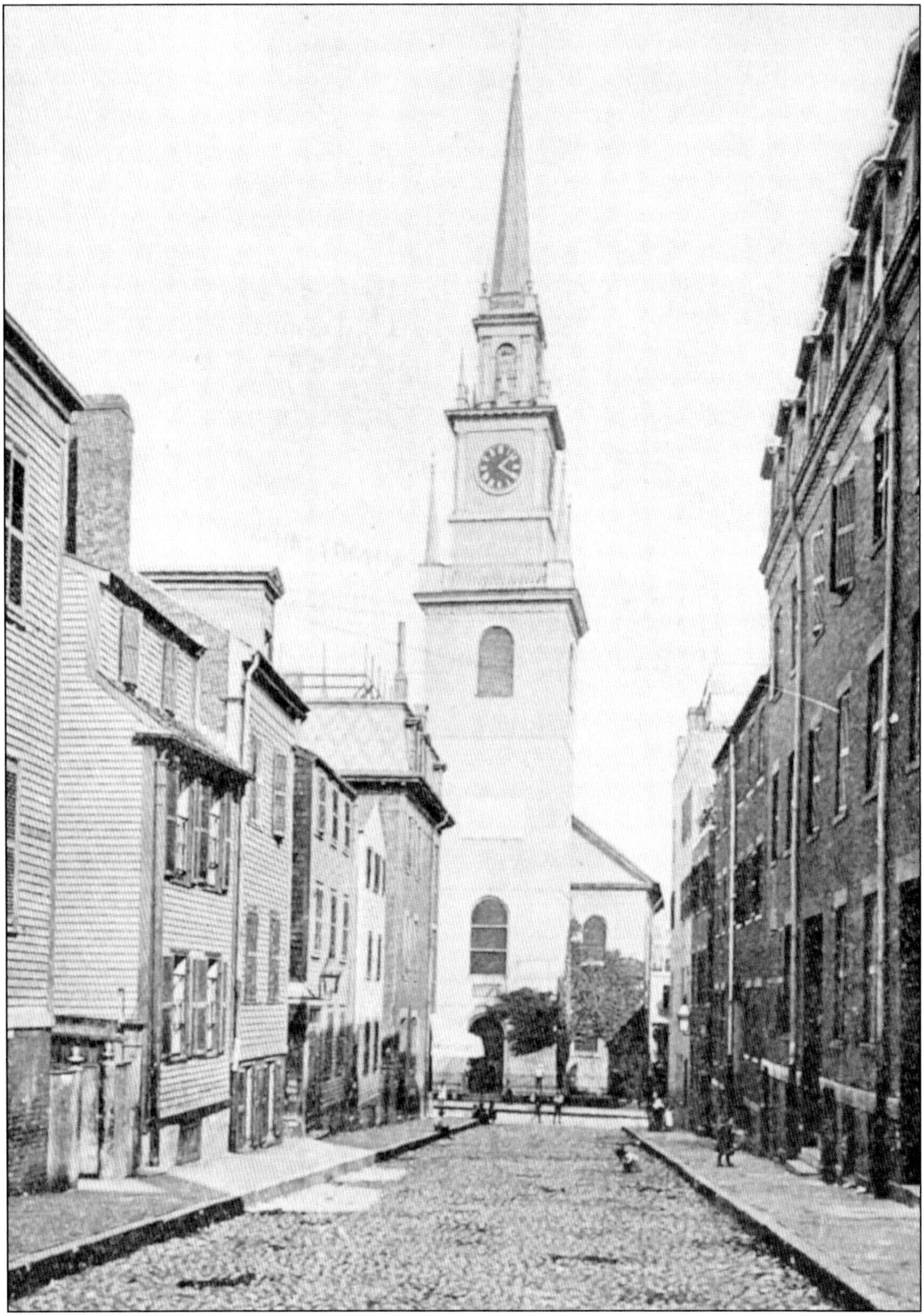

The Old North Church was built in 1723 and is today the oldest church building in Boston. Christ Church, its actual name, was built on Salem Street opposite Hull Street by former parishioners of King's Chapel. The brick church is 75 feet long, 50 feet wide, and the spire rises to a height of 175 feet.

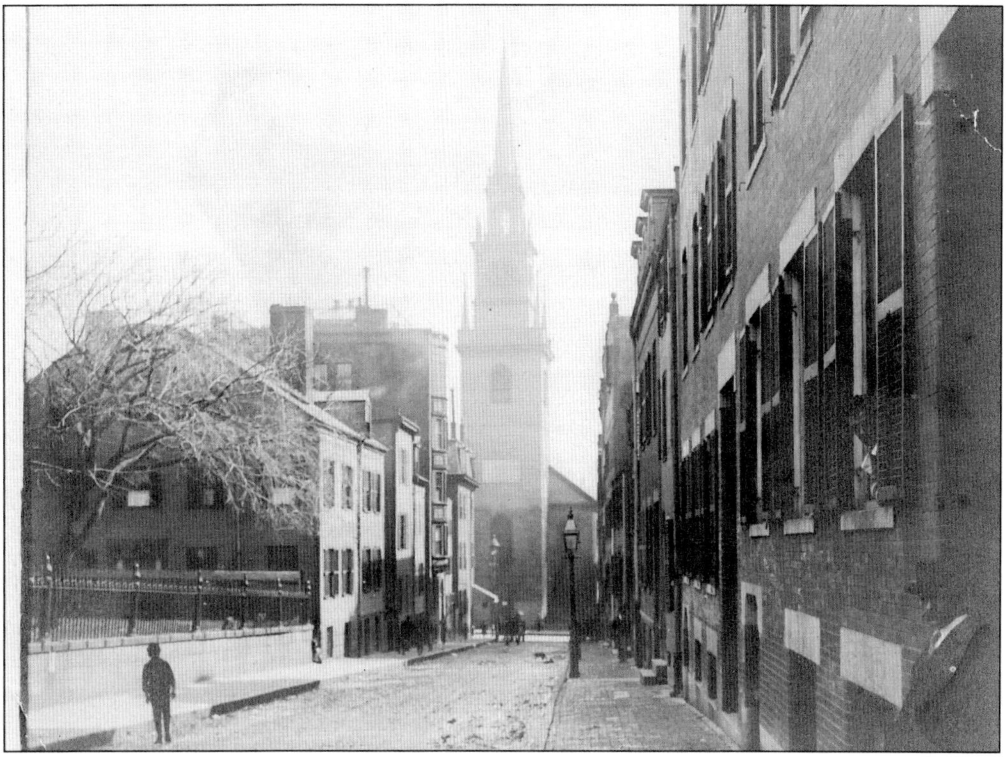

The Old North Church, at the turn of the century, was closed in by tenements and apartment buildings on all sides. Looking from Hull Street, the granite wall of the Copp's Hill Burying Ground can be seen on the left. The present spire was replaced after being blown down in 1954 by Hurricane Carol.

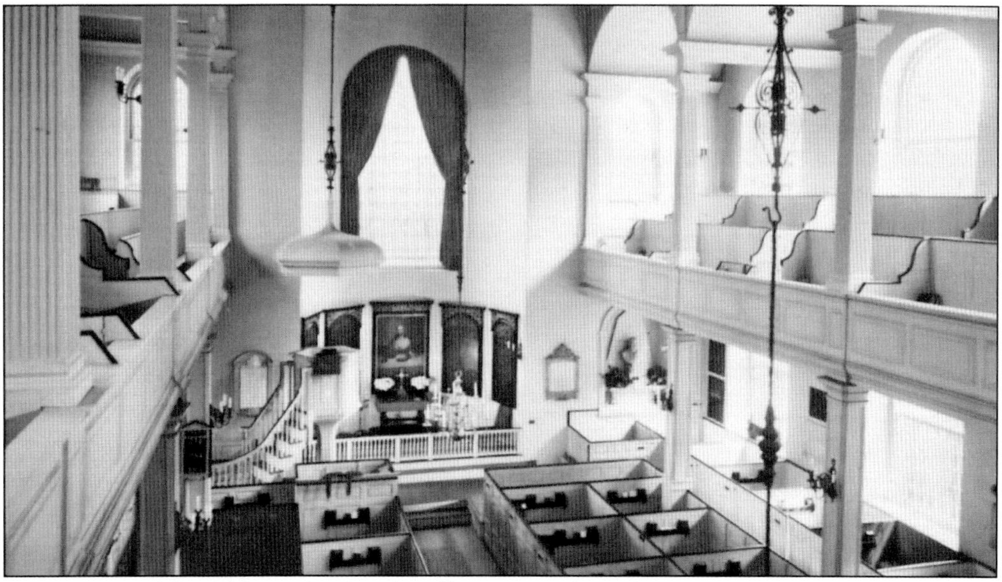

The interior of the Old North Church still retains its long slip pews and a gallery supported by Doric columns. A large painting by artist John Ritto Penniman of the Last Supper hangs above the altar.

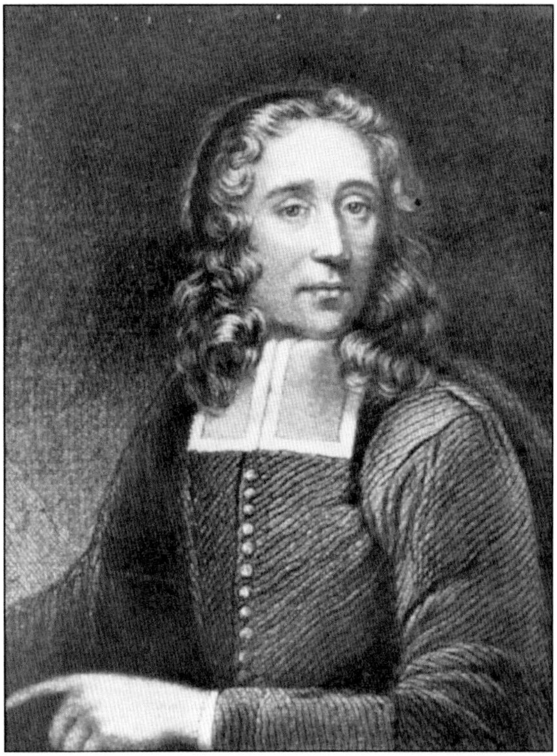

Increase Mather (1639–1723) was the son of Reverend Richard Mather of Dorchester. A clergyman of wide knowledge and repute, he was pastor of the Second Church in North Square, later serving as president of Harvard College. His sermon, *The Wicked Man's Portion*, printed by John Foster in 1675, was the first book printed in Boston.

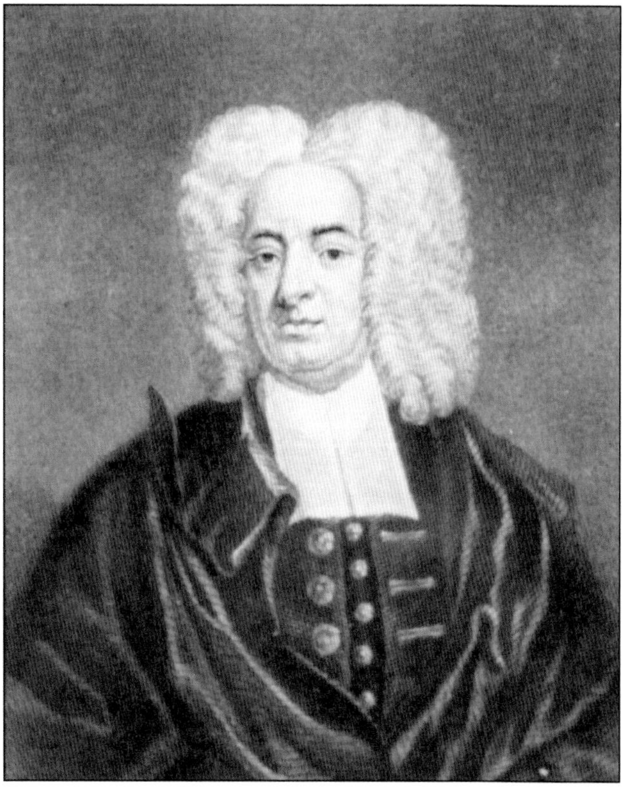

Cotton Mather (1663–1728) was the son of Increase Mather and the namesake of his maternal grandfather, Reverend John Cotton. Reverend Cotton had been the rector of Saint Botolph's Church in Boston, England, prior to his arrival in Boston, Massachusetts, in 1633. Cotton Mather, a noted clergyman, succeeded his father at the Second Church, was a fellow of the Royal Society, and was one of the most prolific writers in American literary history. *Magnalia Christi Americana* is considered his finest effort.

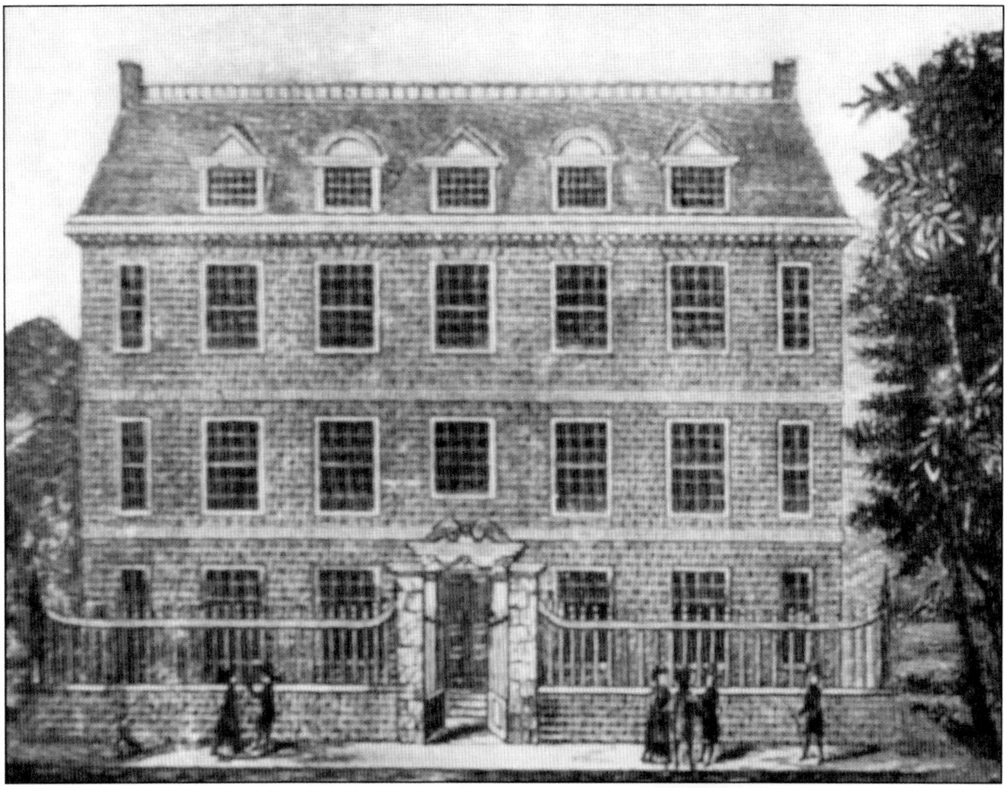

The Clarke-Frankland House was a three-story mansion at the corner of Garden Court and Bell Alley (North Street). In Bynner's *Agnes Surriage*, the house was described as being "plain to severity . . . but this was merely an architectural mask, a Puritan cloak, as it were, covering the swashing bravery of a Royalist and courtier." Sir Harry Frankland was collector of customs and had married his servant, Agnes Surriage, after she had nursed him back to health.

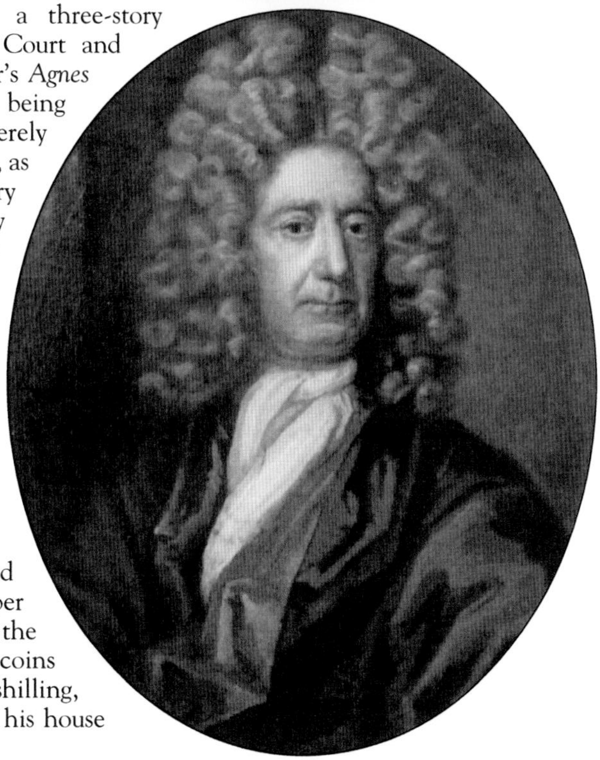

John Cony (1655–1722) was a noted silversmith who engraved the copper plate for the first paper money of the Massachusetts Bay Colony. The first coins minted in Boston, the "Pine Tree" shilling, were struck by John Hull in 1652 at his house on Sheafe Street.

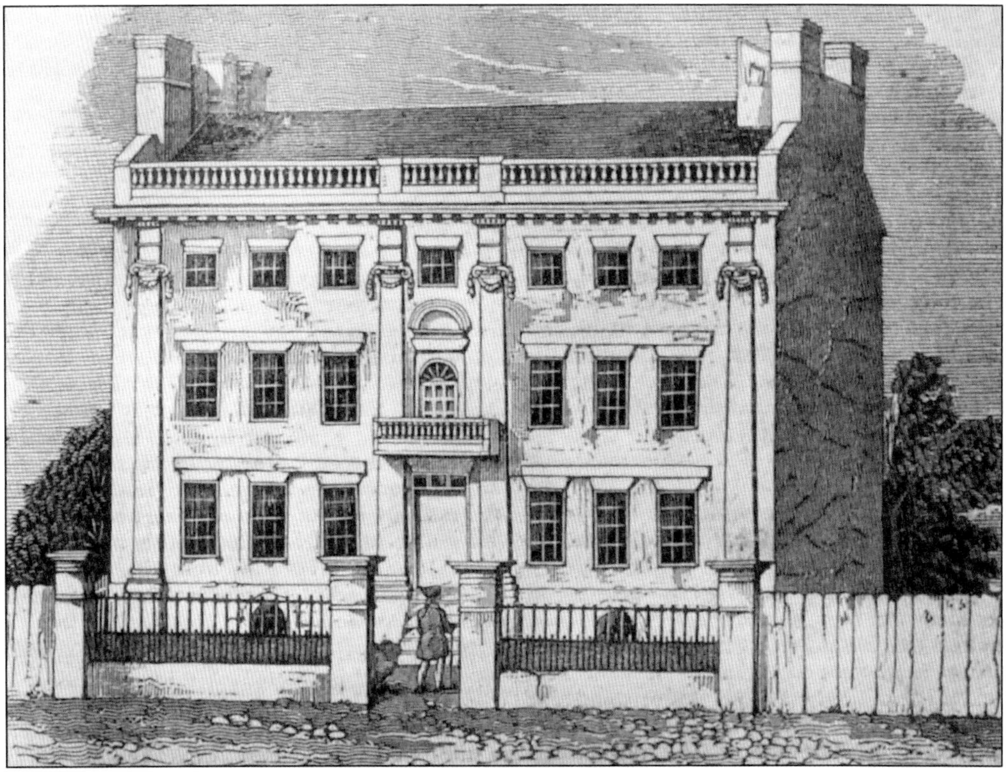

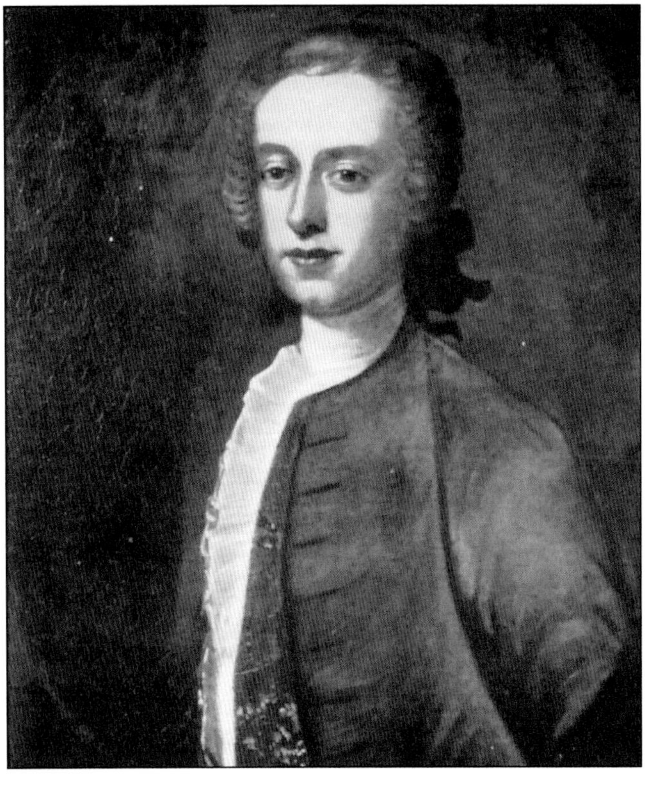

The Hutchinson House stood next to the Clarke-Frankland House at the corner of Garden Court and Fleet Street. Built in 1711, it was the first house in Boston to utilize classical details. The mansion was the home of Thomas Hutchinson, the last Royal Governor of Massachusetts, and was sacked by a mob in 1765 in retaliation for the Stamp Act.

Thomas Hutchinson (1711–1780) had a distinguished career, serving as a representative in the General Court of the Province of Massachusetts, a judge of probate, the lieutenant governor, and the last Royal Governor of Massachusetts. He was also an able historian and the author of *The History of Massachusetts Bay*.

Paul Revere lived in this house, which was built in 1680 and is considered the oldest house in Boston proper. A group of men pose in front of the home of the patriot in 1895.

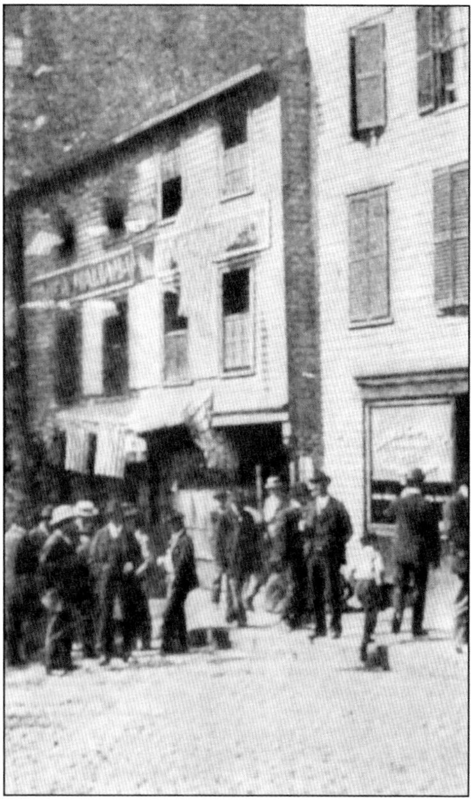

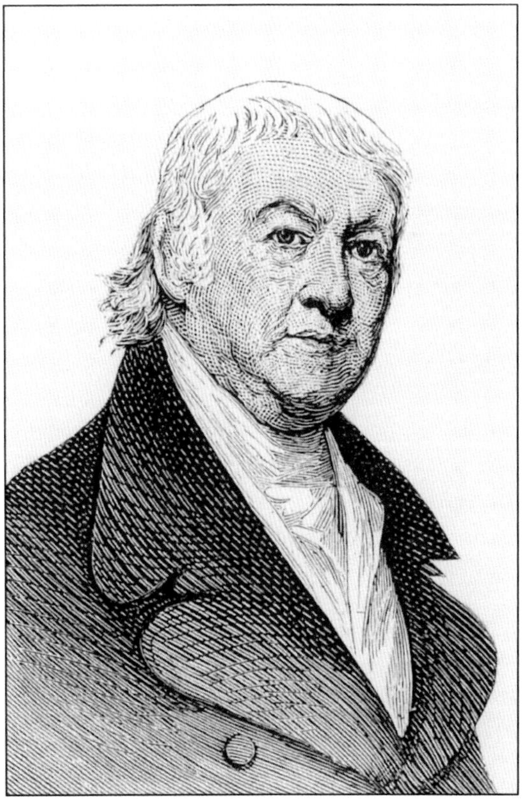

Paul Revere (1735–1818) followed in his father's footsteps as a silversmith but also became a noted goldsmith and engraver, in addition to owning a cannon and bell foundry and a copper mill. His historic horse ride from Charlestown to Lexington, where he was halted by the British, was immortalized in a poem by Longfellow and the shout "The British are coming!" is replayed every Patriot's Day.

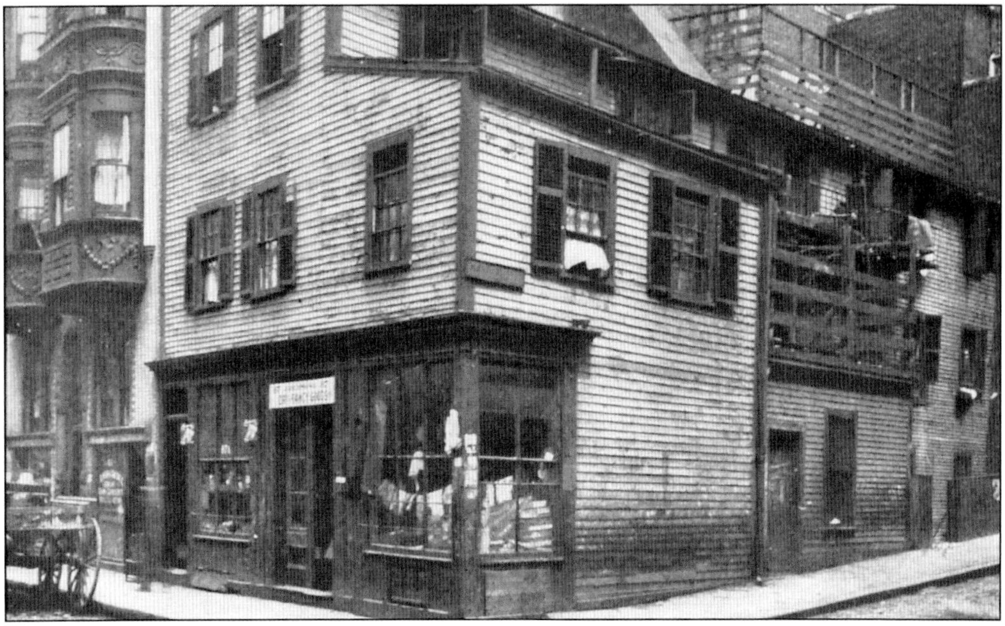

The house of Master John Tileston (1735–1826) still stands at the corner of Margaret and Prince Streets. Tileston, known as "the father of good writing," was a noted master of the North Grammar School in the North End; he held that position for eighty years as the town continued his salary until the day of his death.

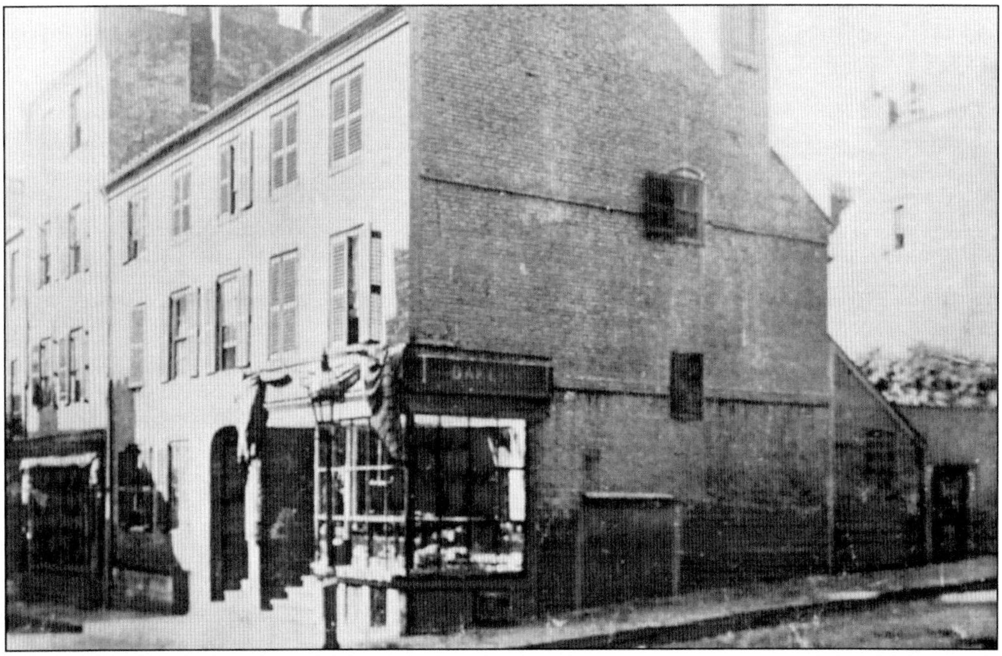

The house of brothers Robert Newman (the sexton of Christ Church during the Revolution) and John Newman (the organist at Christ Church) stood until 1889 at the corner of Salem and Sheafe Streets. A bakery was located on the first floor for much of the nineteenth century. When the house was demolished, an old tombstone of the Greenough family dated 1674 was found in the foundation. (Courtesy of the BPL)

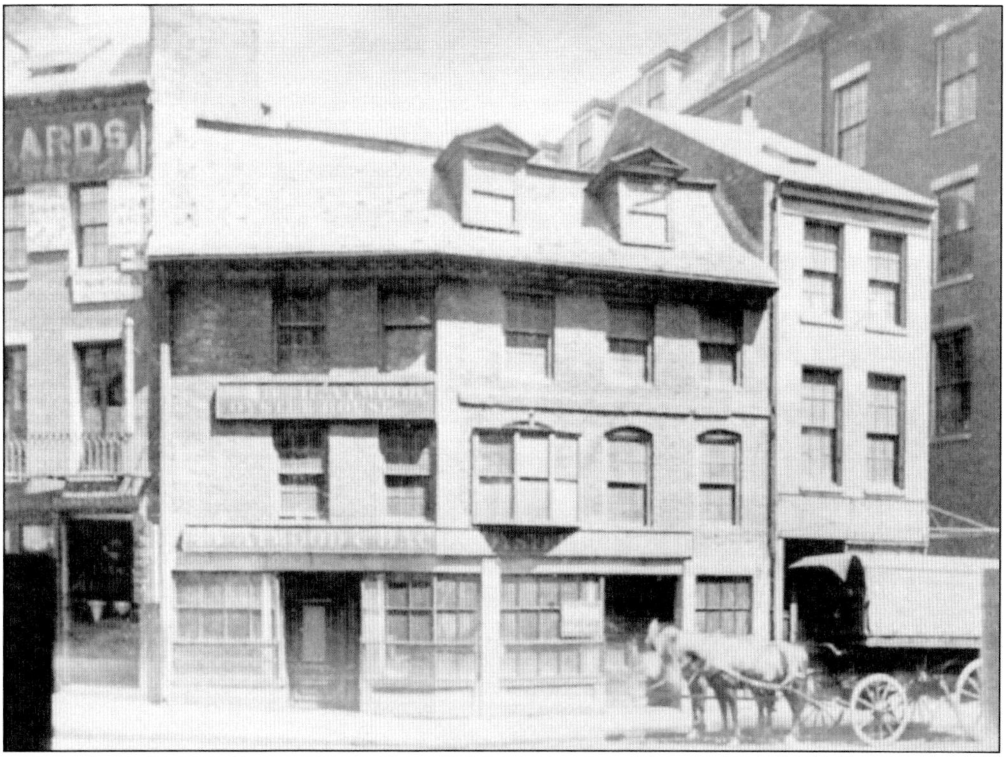

The brick building at the corner of Union and Marshall Streets has been an oyster house since 1826. A horse-drawn wagon stops in front of Atwood & Bacon's Oyster House, predecessor of the Union Oyster House. (Courtesy of the BPL)

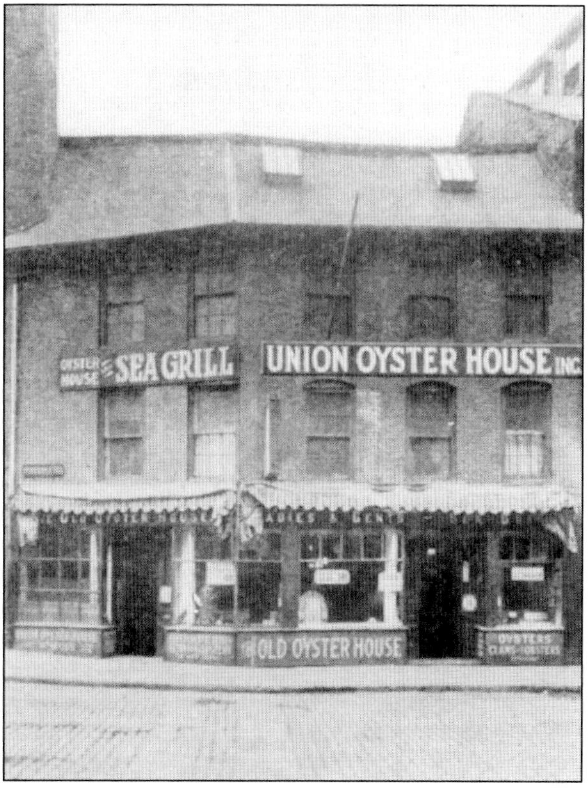

The Union Oyster House, with the stalls and oyster bar in their original positions, has become a Boston landmark. Originally built by Hopestill Capen, it was here "At the Sign of the Cornfields" that silks and fancy dress goods were sold. During the early 1770s the *Massachusetts Spy* was printed in rooms above by Isaiah Thomas, prior to his removal to Worcester. Louis Phillipe, future King of France, lived here while in exile after the French Revolution.

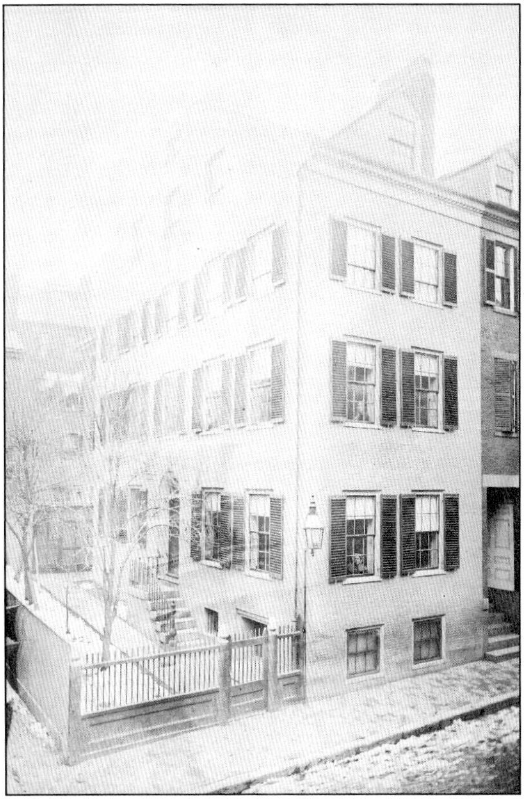

The Dodd House was built, c. 1804, at 190 Salem Street and was home of Timothy Dodd, a wholesale furrier on Milk Street in Boston. The Dodd family moved to the North End from Boylston Street and lived here until the death of the last family member in 1912. (Courtesy of Robert Bayard Severy)

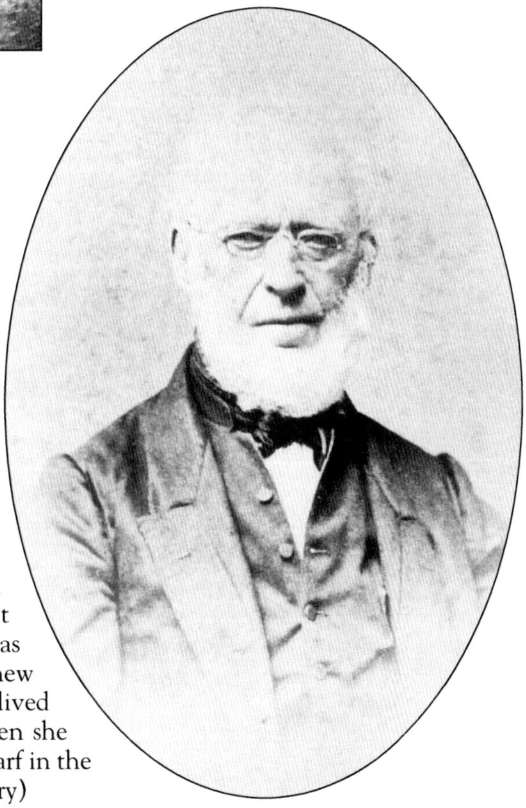

Timothy Dodd (1780–1876) was considered, at the time of his death, the oldest merchant in active service in the United States. He was an apprentice of Governor Hancock's nephew on Long Wharf in 1795, and was the longest-lived of the men aboard the USS *Constitution* when she was launched in 1797 from Constitution Wharf in the North End. (Courtesy of Robert Bayard Severy)

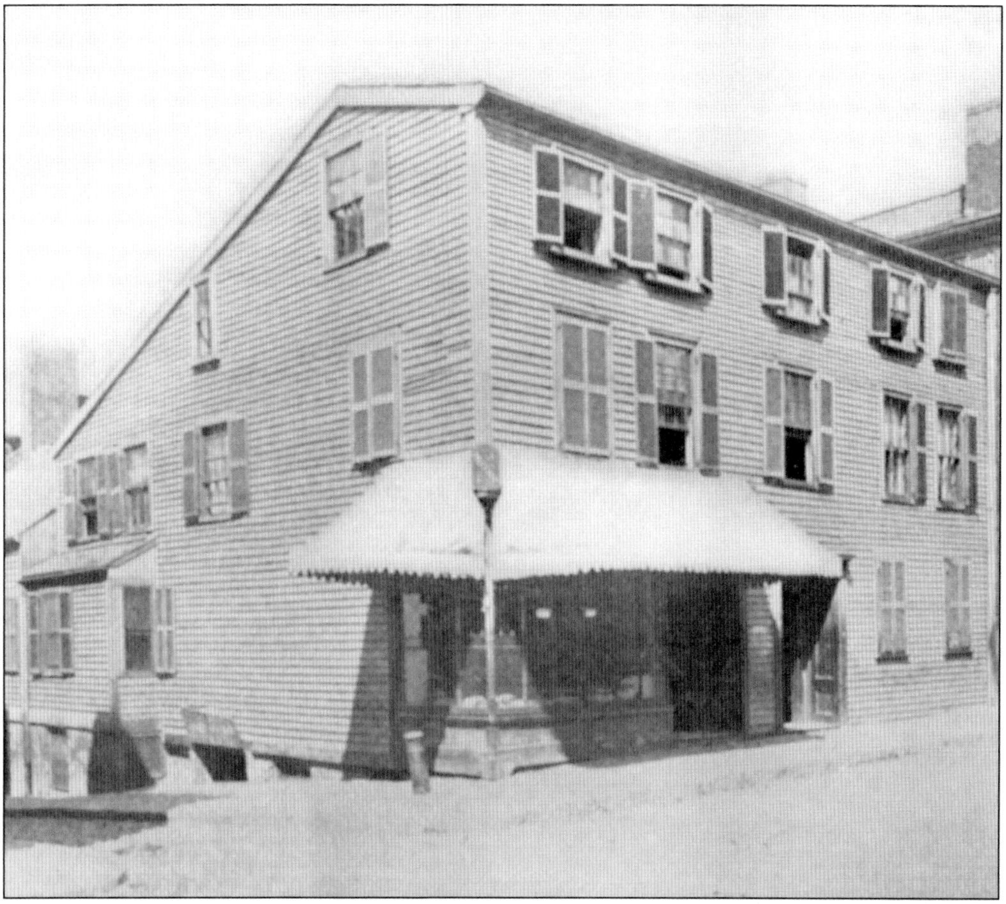

The Gray House, at the corner of Prince Street and Lafayette Avenue, was built in 1770; it was used as a British Hospital in 1775 for those wounded at the Battle of Bunker Hill. (Courtesy of the BPL)

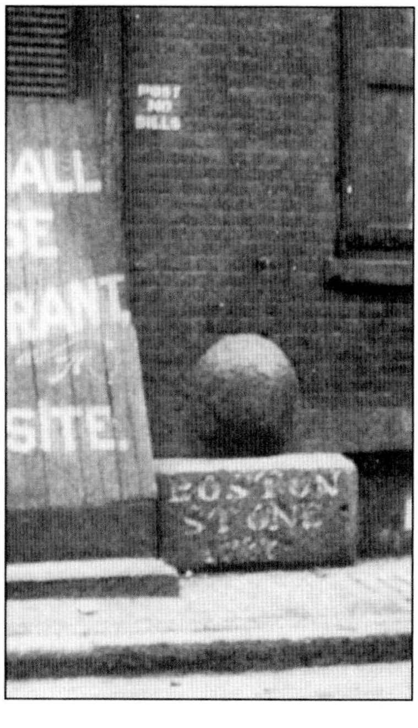

The Boston Stone is embedded in a wall on Marshall Street and is from where all distances from Boston are measured. Brought from England about 1700, it was originally used as a paint grinder, the brown sandstone ball being used to grind the paint in the muller. They were embedded in the wall by Joseph Howe in 1737 in imitation of the London Stone in front of Saint Swithin's Church in London, England.

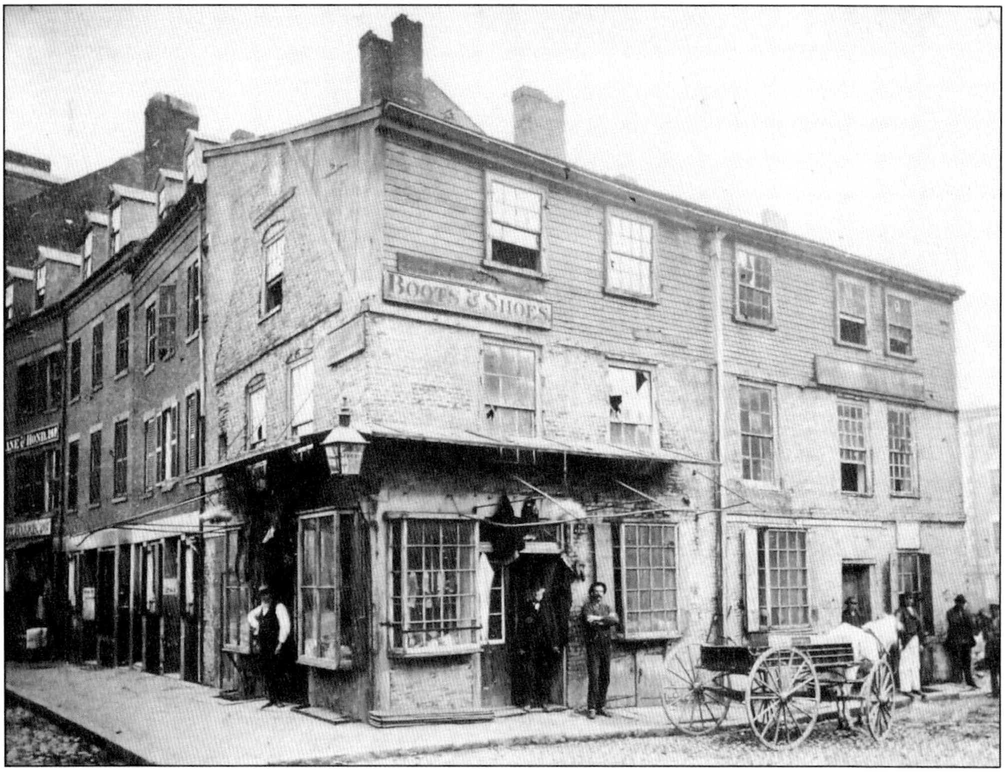

Men stand in the doorways to a boot and shoe shop at the corner of Lewis and North Streets in 1860. (Courtesy of the BPL)

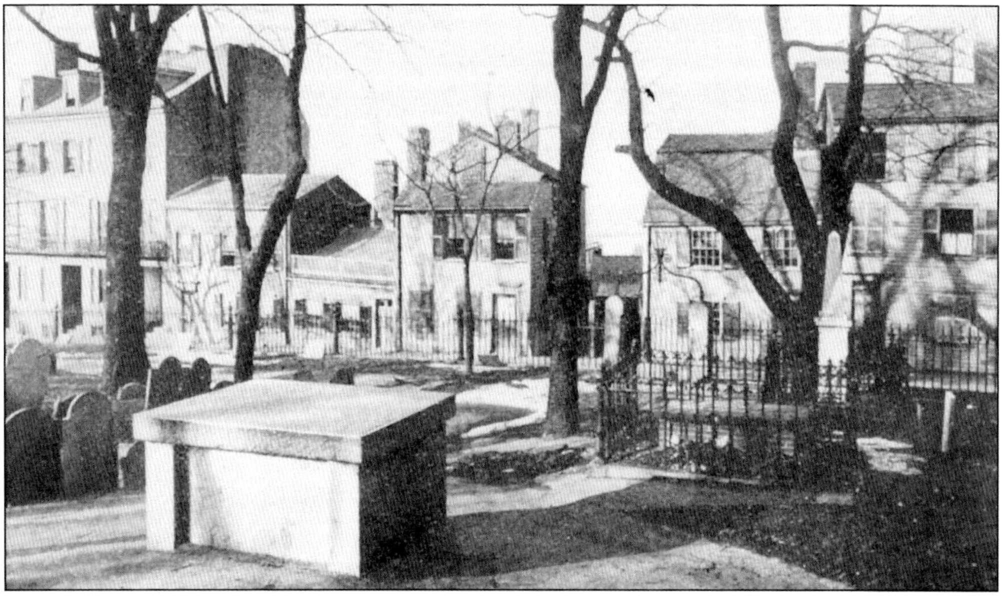

Copp's Hill Burying Ground is bounded by Hull, Charter, and Snowhill Streets. Originally known as Windmill Hill (the first windmill in Boston was built here), it was renamed Copp's Hill, after William Copp. In the foreground are both table tombs and slate headstones in a cemetery that was filled to capacity by the early nineteenth century.

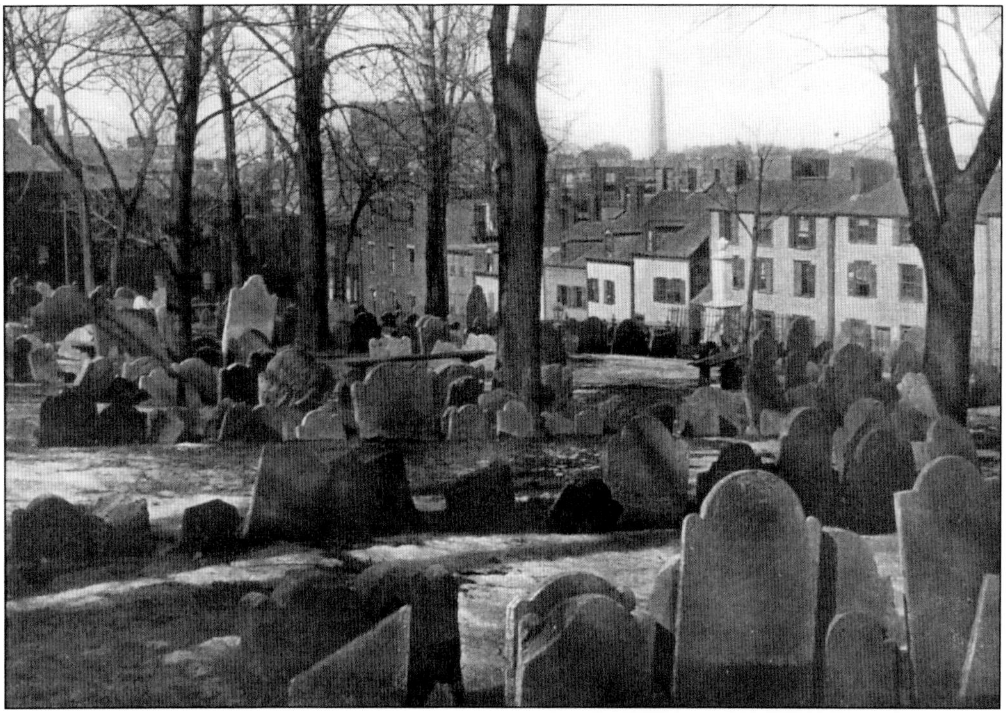

Looking north from the Copp's Hill Burying Ground, the Bunker Hill Monument rises above houses closely built along the Hull Street side of the cemetery. On this ground the British batteries were erected that destroyed Charlestown on June 17, 1775.

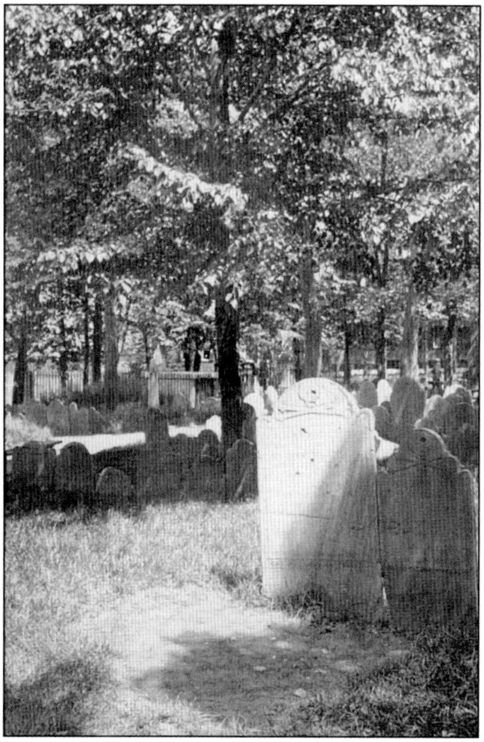

The headstone of Captain Daniel Malcom (1725–1769) was used for target practice by British soldiers who were probably enraged by its inscription: "A true Son of Liberty a Friend to the Publick, An Enemy to Oppression and One of the foremost in opposing the Revenue Acts on America."

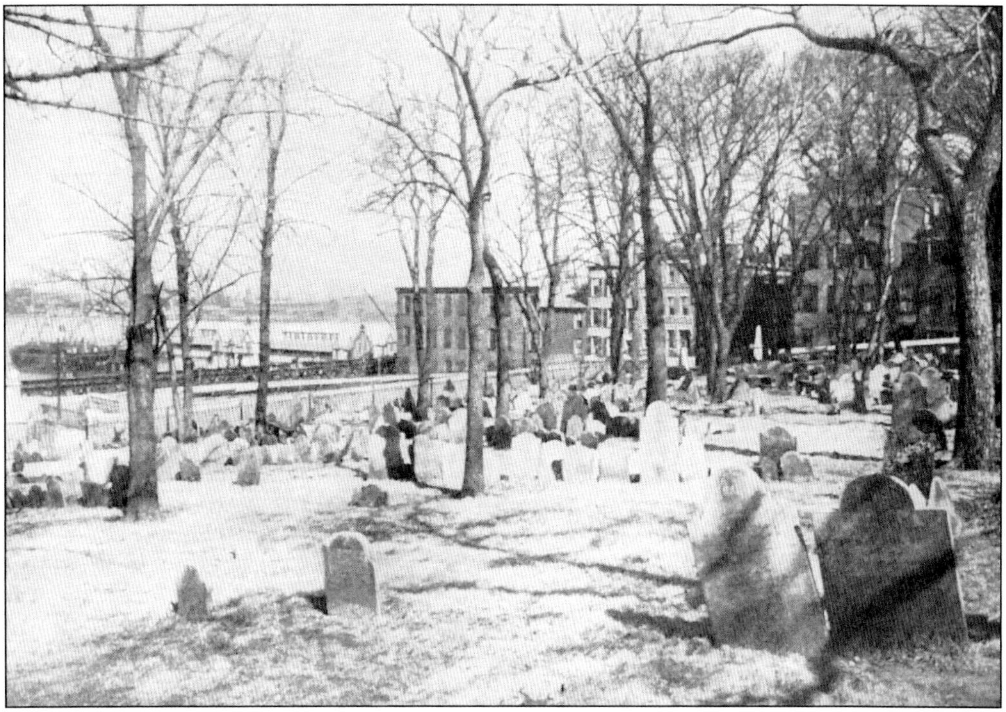

The Copp's Hill Burying Ground has been part of the ever-evolving history of the North End since it was laid out in 1660. Once four independent burial grounds, it is today under the direction of the Historic Burying Ground Initiative of Boston.

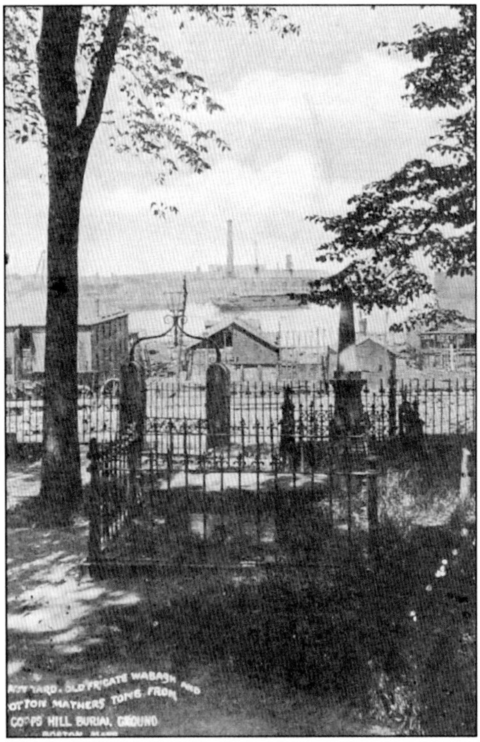

Looking toward Charlestown, Massachusetts, from the Copp's Hill Burying Ground, the Boston Navy Yard and the frigate *Wabash* can be seen in the distance.

Two

Faneuil Hall and Quincy Market

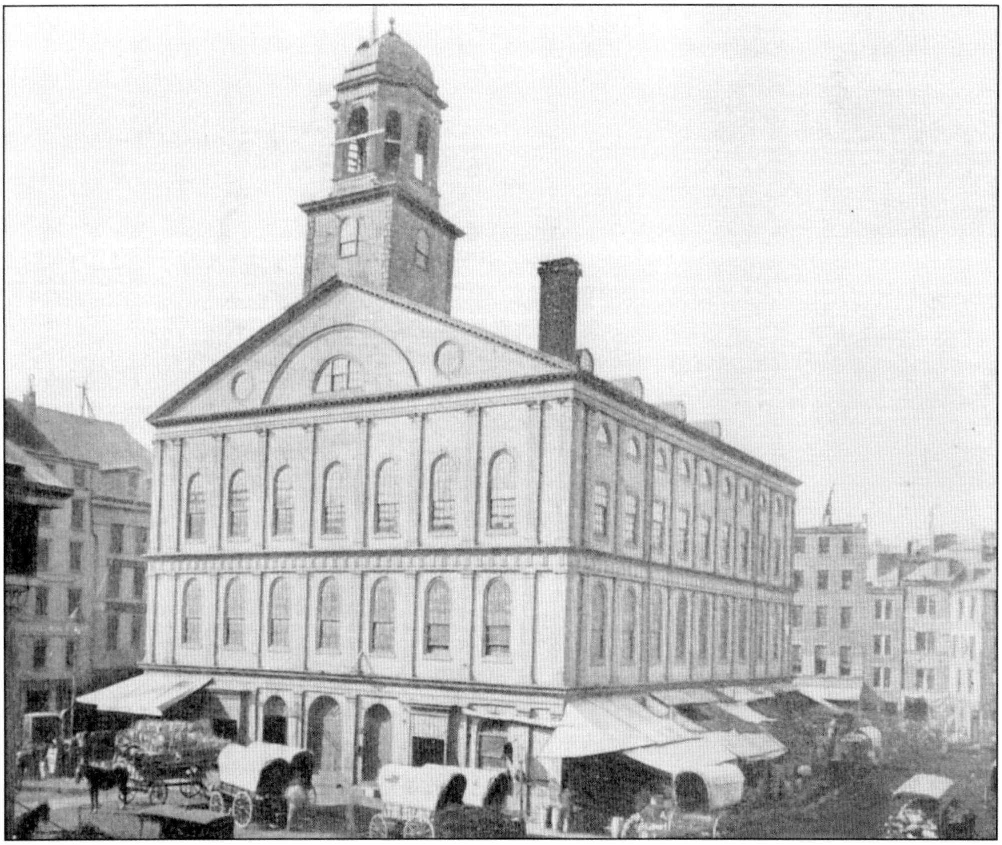

Faneuil Hall, donated to the Town of Boston in 1742 by Peter Faneuil, is known as the "Cradle of Liberty." Burned in 1761 and rebuilt in 1763, it has been used as a public market and a place of popular assembly for over two centuries, and is today a popular tourist attraction. Atop the cupola is a copper weather vane in the shape of a grasshopper that was wrought by Deacon Shem Drowne in 1742.

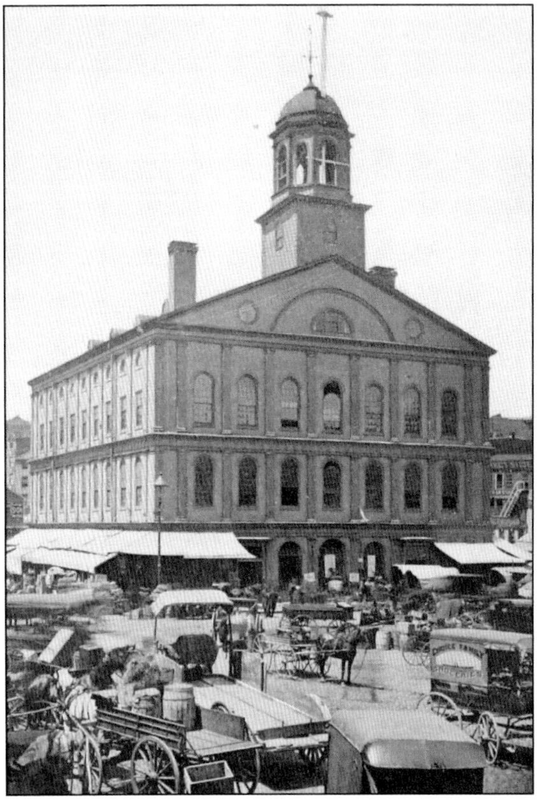

Faneuil Hall, designed by portrait painter John Smibert and built in 1742, had a market on the first floor and an assembly hall on the second floor. Horse-drawn wagons are shown here delivering fresh produce to the market at the turn of the century.

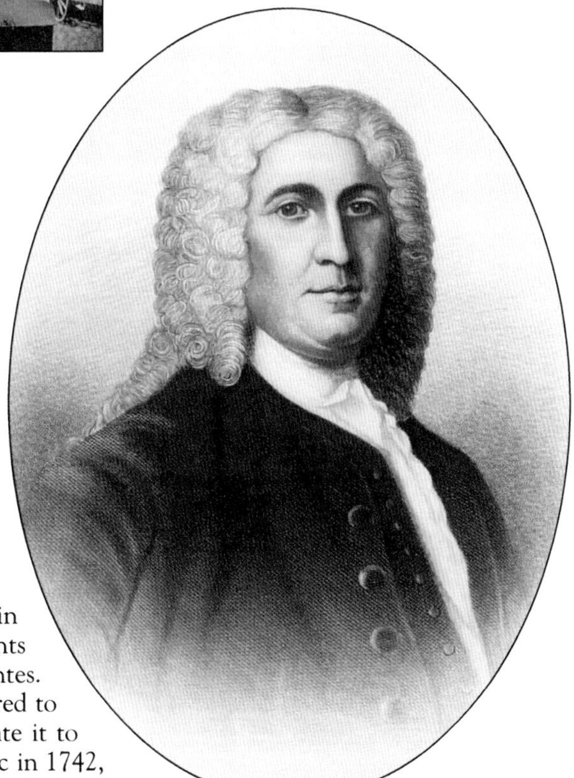

Peter Faneuil (1700–1743) was born in New Rochelle, New York, after his parents left France following the Edict of Nantes. A prosperous Boston merchant, he offered to build a market house in 1740 and donate it to the town. The hall, opened to the public in 1742, was named in his honor.

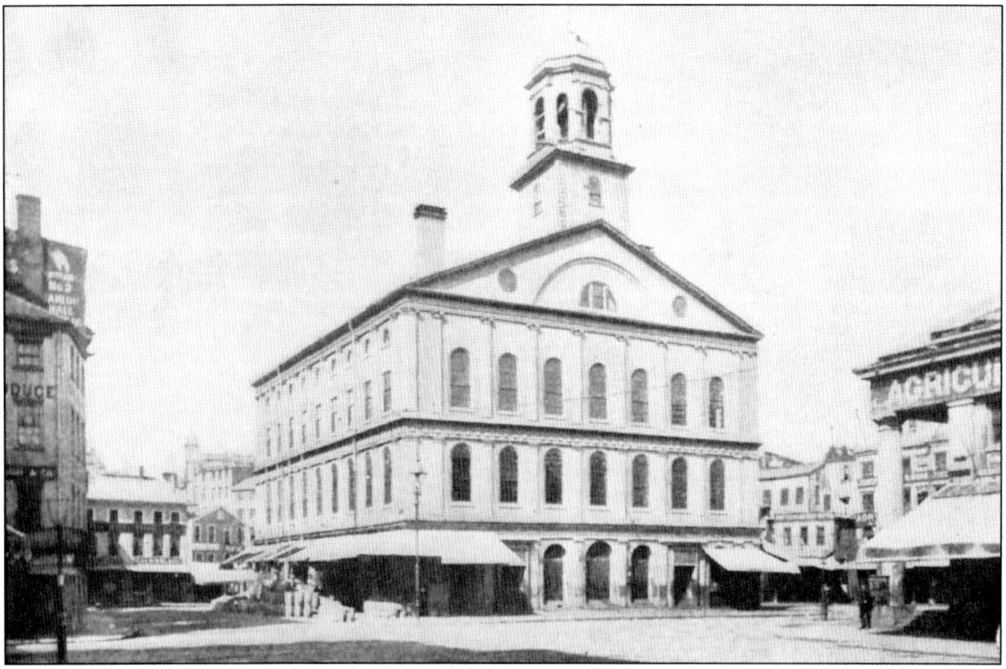

Faneuil Hall was doubled in size in 1806 by architect Charles Bulfinch to accommodate an increasing need for a larger town hall and market. The first floor remained an open stall market until the early 1970s; the top floor became the headquarters of the Ancient and Honorable Artillery Company, the oldest military organization in the country.

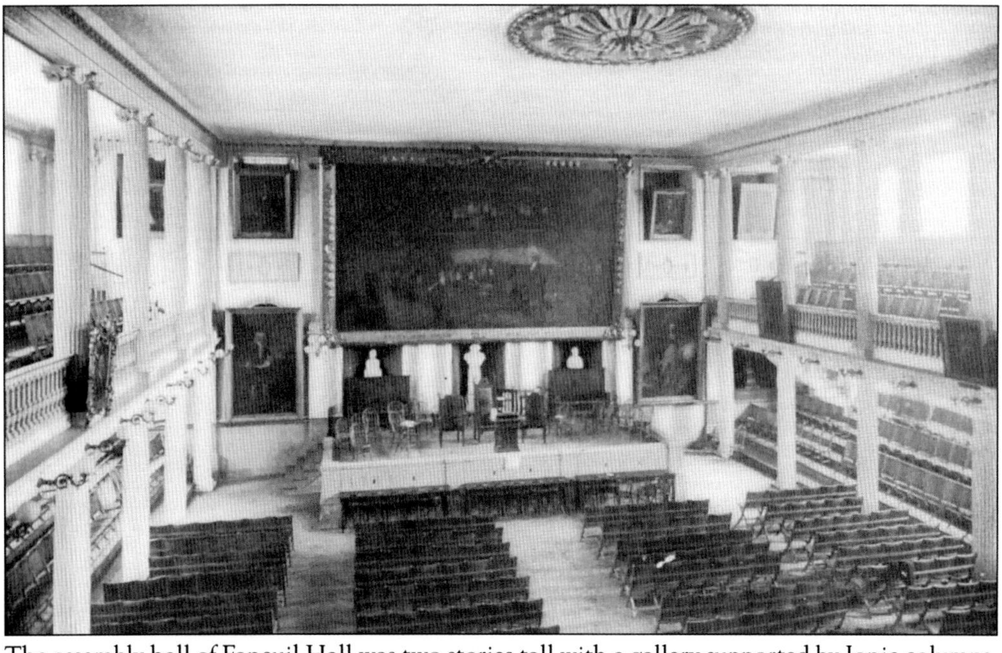

The assembly hall of Faneuil Hall was two stories tall with a gallery supported by Ionic columns. With portraits of prominent Bostonians, including benefactor Peter Faneuil, adorning the walls, the monumental painting *Daniel Webster replying to Hayne in the Senate* has a place of honor. It was in this hall that the voters of Boston incorporated the city on March 4, 1822.

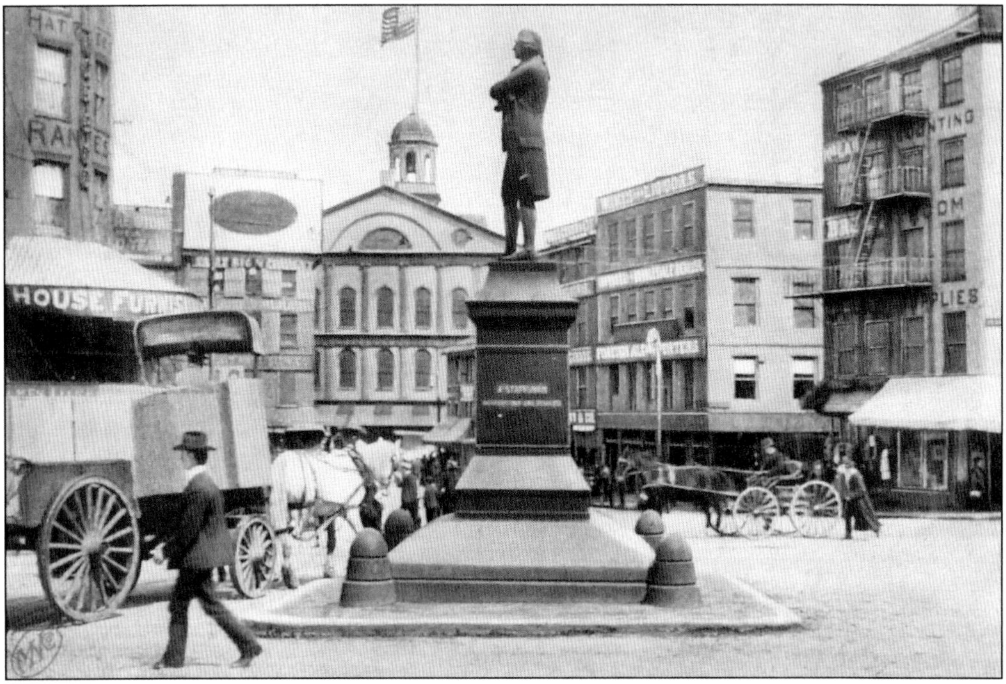

A statue of Samuel Adams was placed in Adams Square in front of Faneuil Hall. Adams (1722–1803) was called the "Pioneer in Propaganda" during the Revolution and later served as governor of Massachusetts from 1794 to 1798. Sculpted by Anne Whitney, the statue echoes the statement engraved on the plinth base: "A Statesman incomparable and fearless."

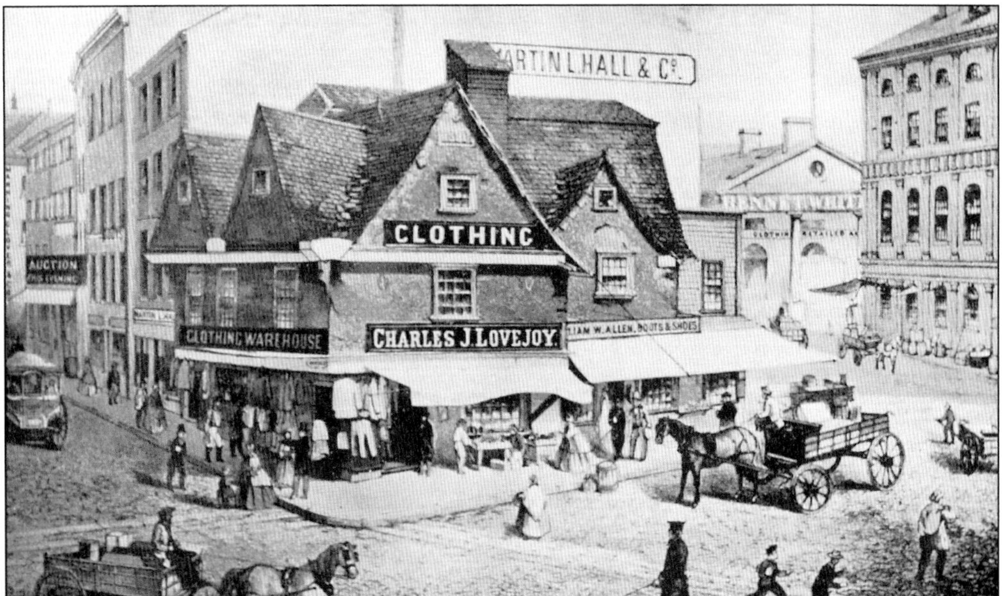

The Old Feather Store was at the corner of Dock Square and North Street. Built by Thomas Stanbury in 1680, this multi-gabled house became the clothing warehouse of Charles J. Lovejoy and the boot and shoe shop of William W. Allen prior to its demolition in 1860. (Courtesy of the BPL)

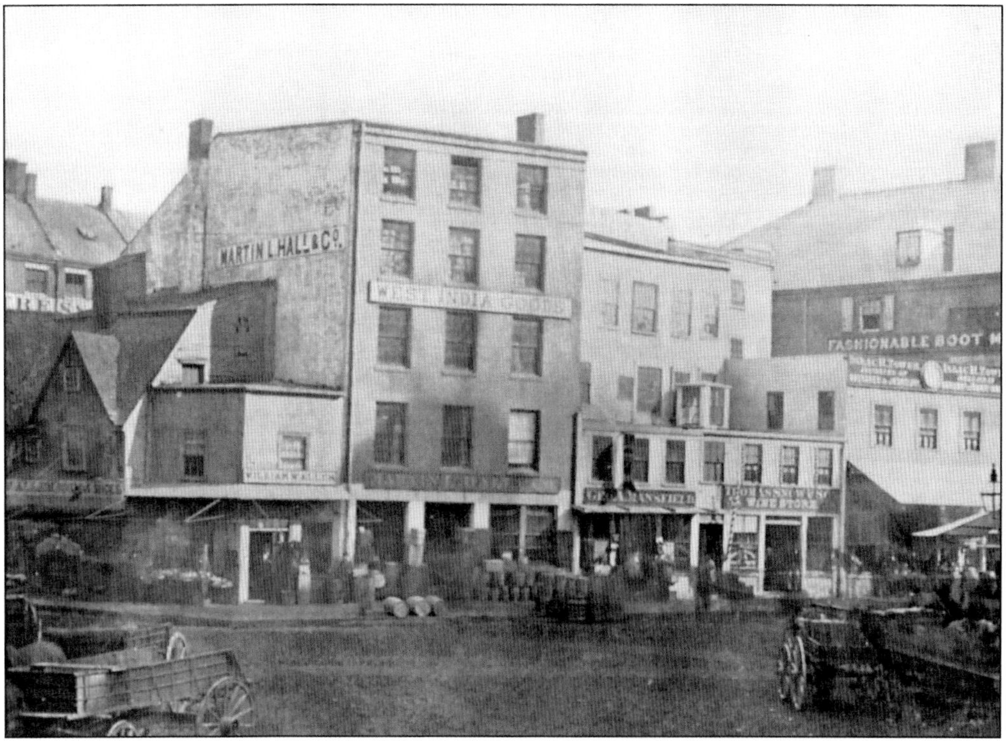

Faneuil Hall Square had stores fronting toward Faneuil Hall. From left to right are the Old Feather Store, Martin L. Hall & Company's West India Goods, George A. Mansfield and Company, Thomas Snow & Son's Wine Store, and Isaac H. Tower's Watch and Jewelry Store. (Courtesy of the BPL)

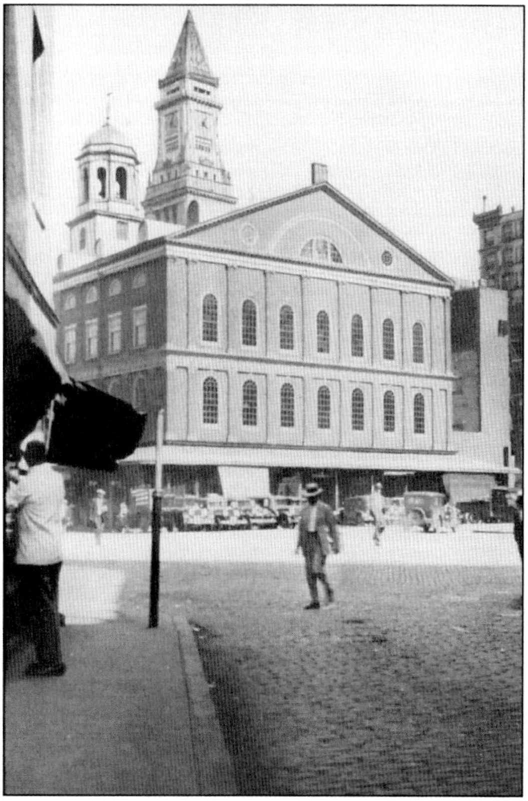

Faneuil Hall in the 1930s was the site of the produce market that supplied Boston with fresh fruit and vegetables. Delivery trucks had replaced the horse-drawn wagons of just two decades earlier. The tower of the Boston Custom House, designed by Peabody and Stearns and built in 1915 above the original structure of 1847, rises above Faneuil Hall.

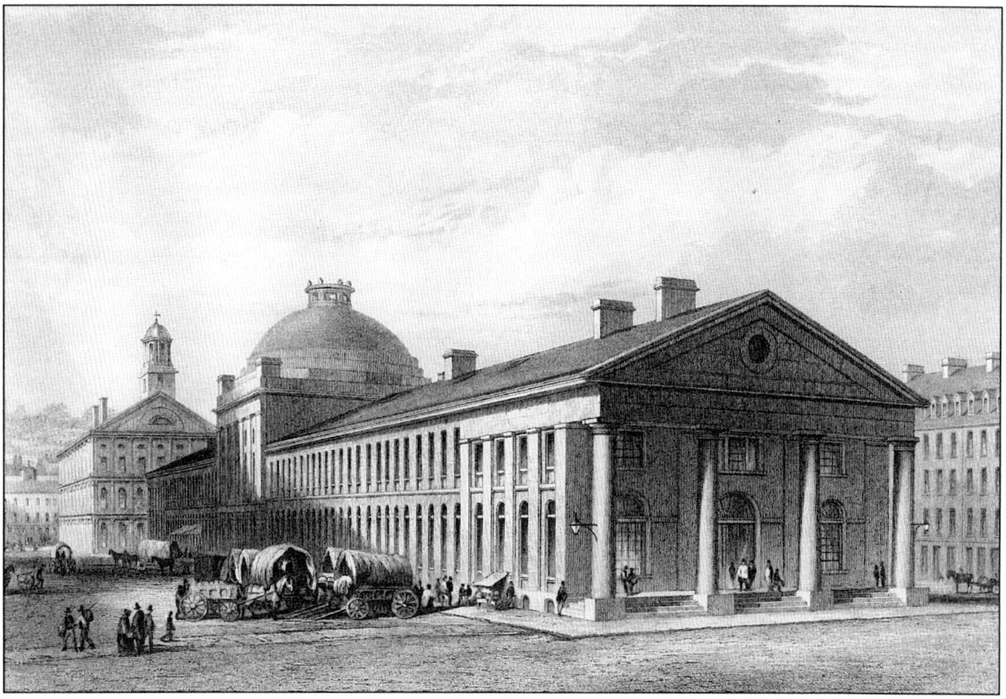

Quincy Market was built on filled land to the east of Faneuil Hall between 1824 and 1826. Designed by Alexander Parris, its use of granite in the popular Greek Revival style of architecture made for an impressive market.

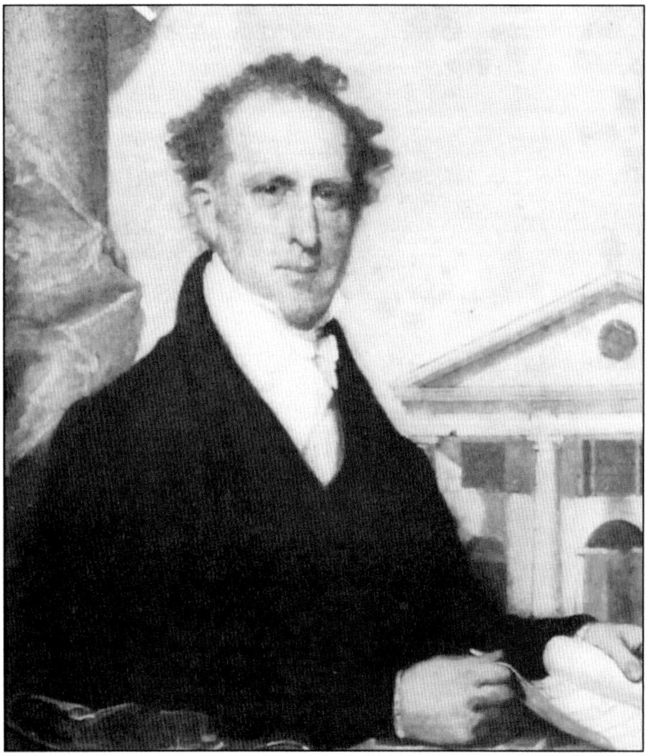

Josiah Quincy (1772–1864), for whom Quincy Market was named, was the second mayor of Boston, serving from 1823 to 1828. Considered Boston's most progressive mayor, he not only built Quincy Market, but reorganized the fire department and built the House of Industry and House of Correction in South Boston. Following his term as mayor, he served as president of Harvard and was the author of the *History of Harvard University*, *A History of the Boston Athenaeum*, and the *Municipal History of the Town and City of Boston*.

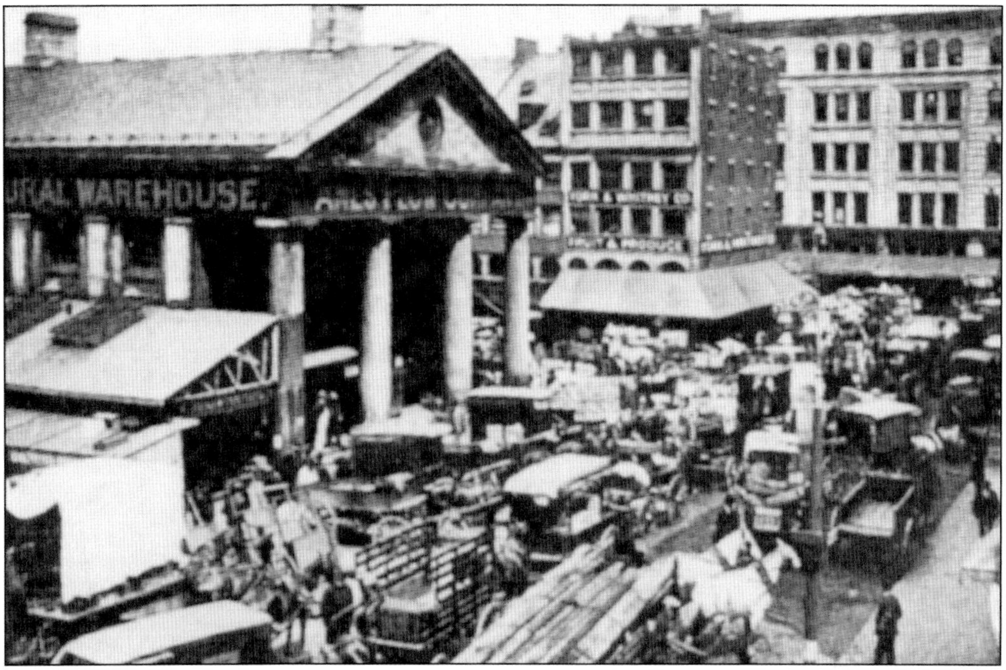

Quincy Market was a bustling produce center in the nineteenth century. Horse-drawn wagons carrying farm-fresh produce arrived at dawn, creating traffic jams outside the market. On the left is Quincy Market with the South Market beyond.

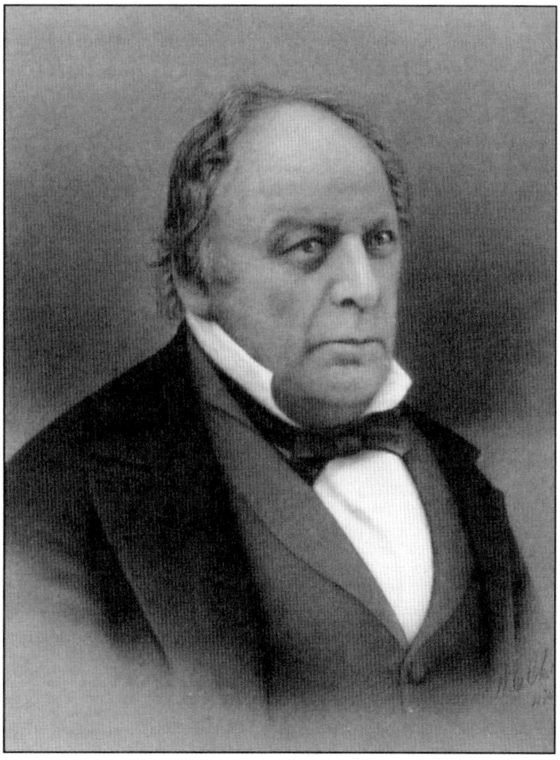

Alexander Parris (1780–1852) was a well-known architect who designed Quincy Market and the flanking North and South Markets. Parris also designed Saint Paul's Cathedral (1820) on Tremont Street and David Sears' mansion (1819, now the Somerset Club) on Beacon Street. (Courtesy of the BPL)

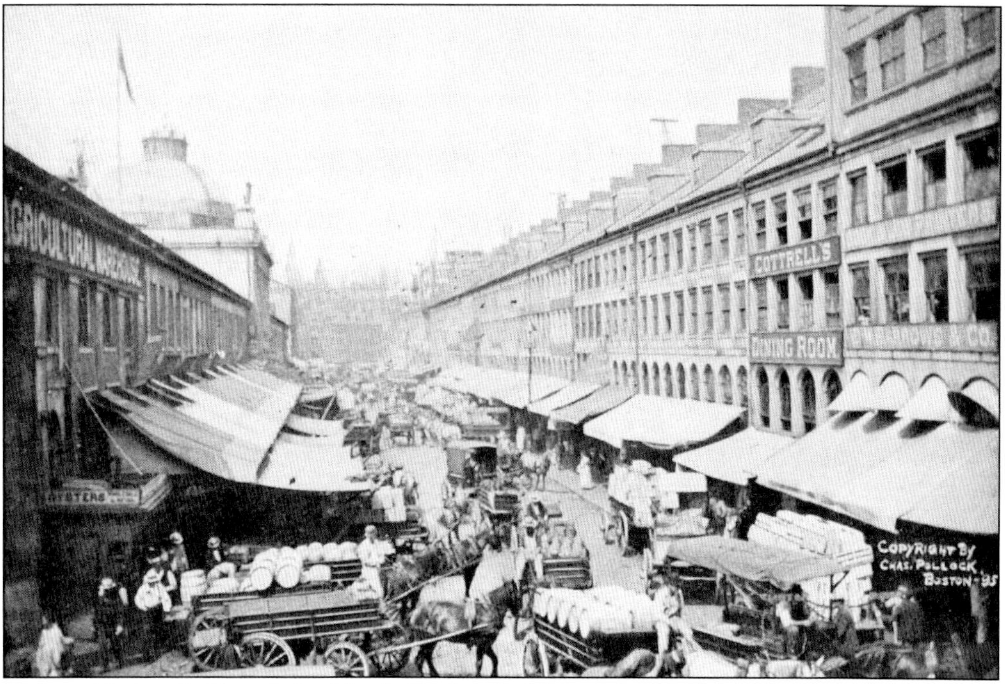

Quincy Market (left) and the North Market had horse and wagons delivering provisions to stalls at various times throughout the day. The North Market had Cottrell's Dining Room and the world famous Durgin Park Restaurant, where merchants and farmers sat side by side at long tables during dinner.

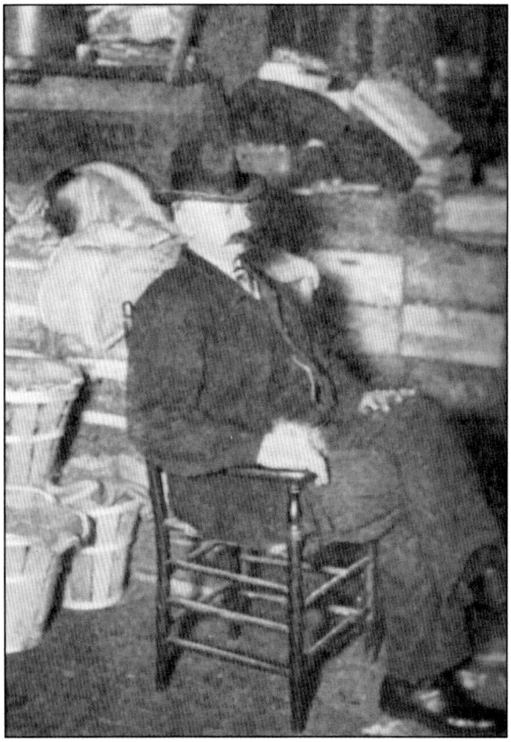

Mr. Symmes was the night watchman at Quincy Market at the turn of the century. It was said of him that "asleep or awake he has eyes all over him, like a traditional schoolma'am. He knows by instinct who has business down here at night, and who has not."

Merchants would bargain at dawn with farmers who brought farm-fresh fruits and vegetables to Quincy Market.

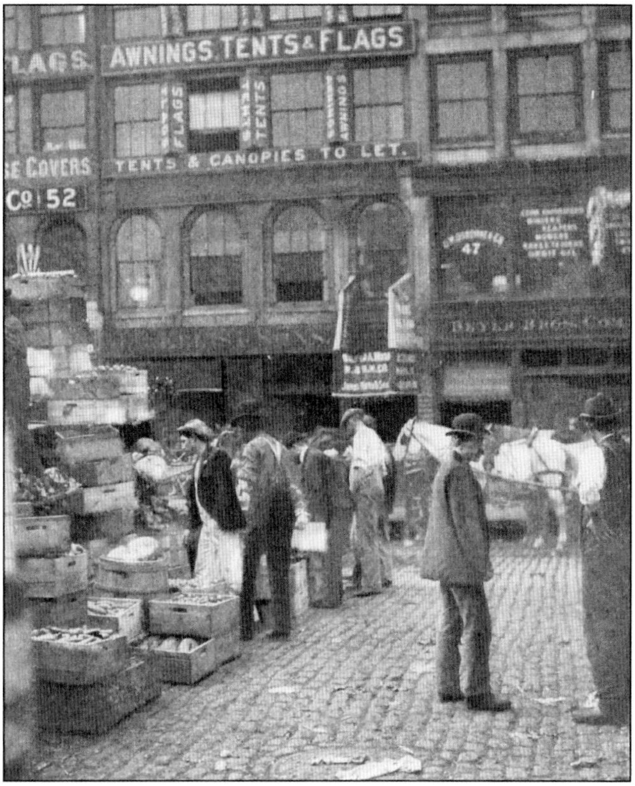

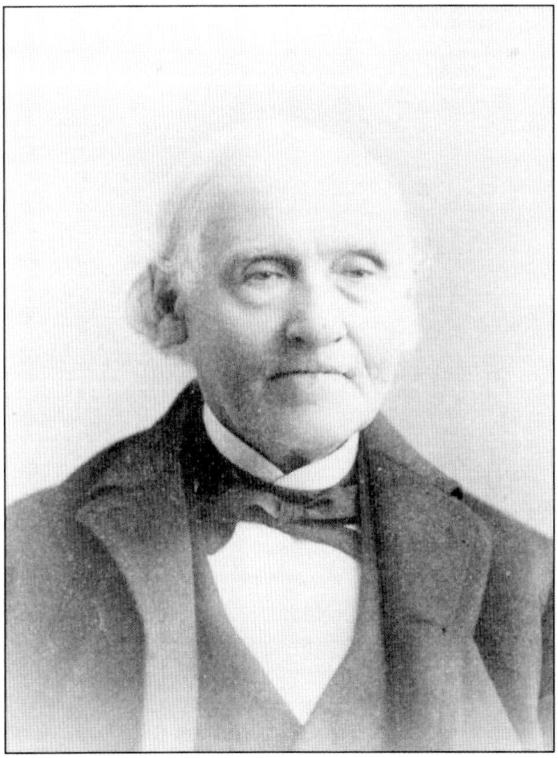

John P. Squires began his career in 1838 as a clerk in the stall of Nathan Robbins in Faneuil Hall. By the late nineteenth century his own business, John P. Squire & Company, was "the third largest pork-packing establishment in the United States," and employed one thousand men who slaughtered over eight hundred thousand hogs annually.

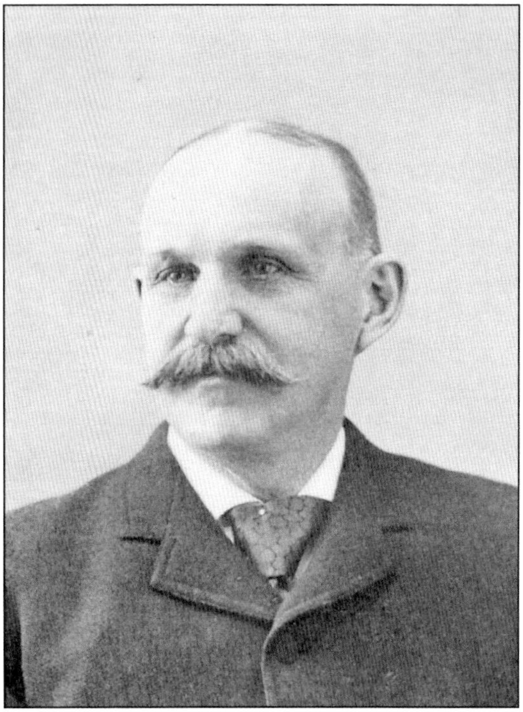

Andrew Woodbury Preston was the general manager of the Boston Fruit Company. Founded in 1888, the Boston Fruit Company initially began buying fruit in the West Indies for shipment to Boston, thereby creating an extended fruit season, and later by cultivating their own fruit on plantations in Jamaica.

H.A. Hovey & Company was one of eighty independent firms at Faneuil Hall Market. Considered the oldest butterhouse in Boston, Hovey's was founded in 1826 and delivered their product by truck, rather than horse and wagon, a century after being founded.

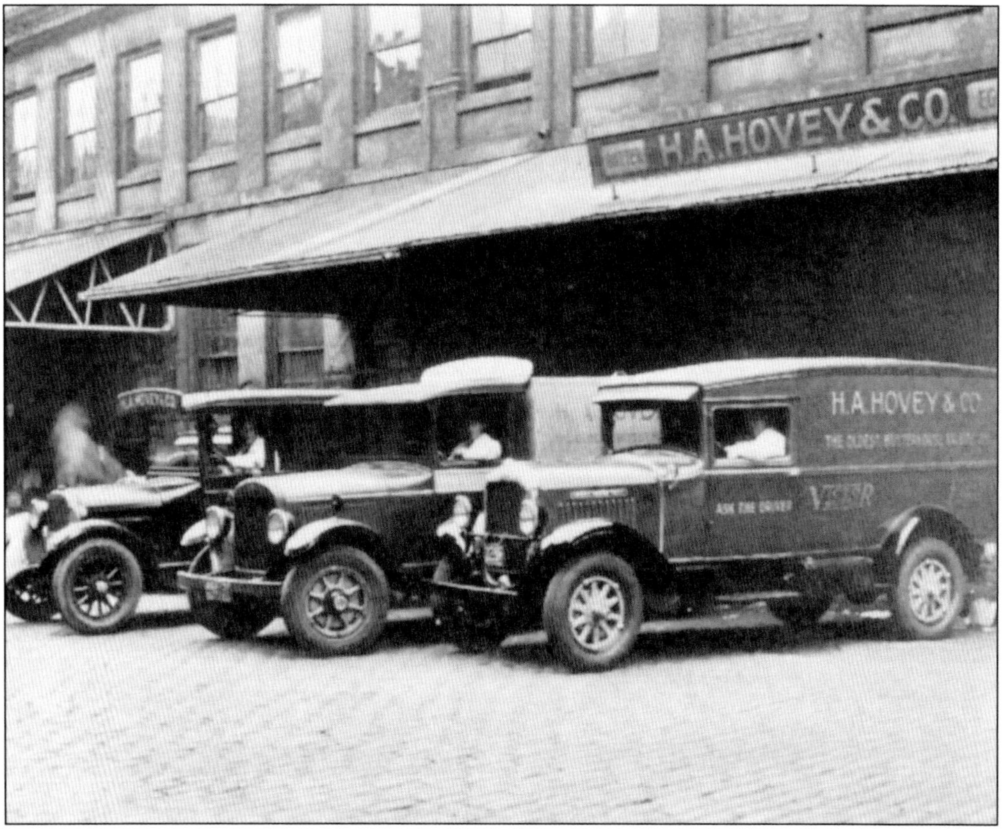

Three

Houses of Worship

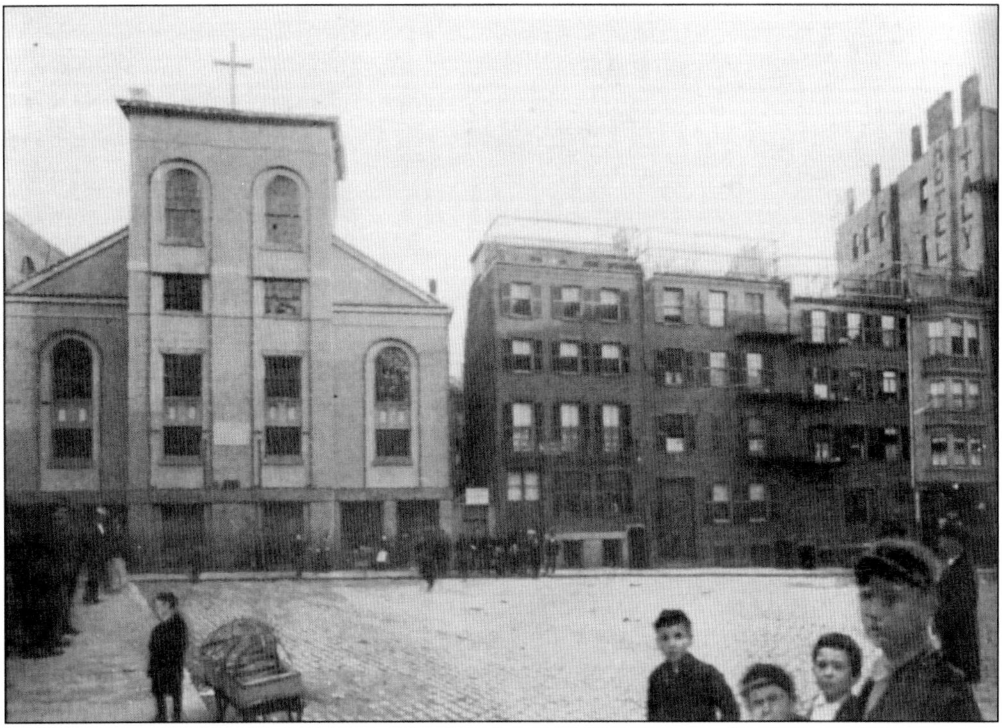

The former Seamen's Bethel was remodeled as the Sacred Heart Church in 1888. Children stand at the corner of Prince and Garden Court Streets in North Square at the turn of the century.

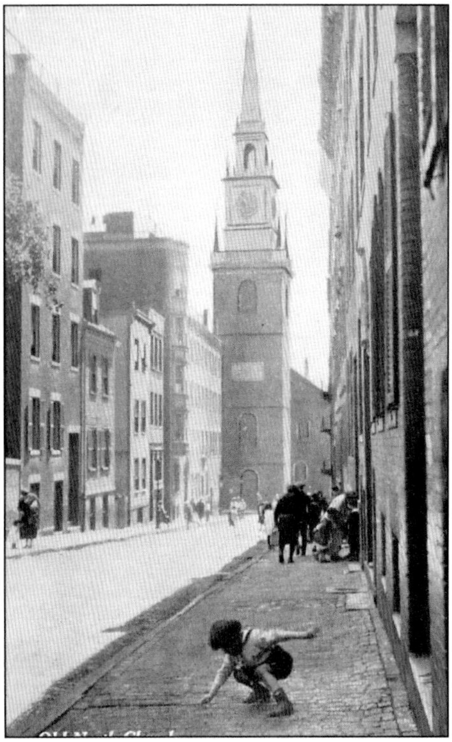

A child plays on Hull Street in the 1930s. The densely built tenements and apartment buildings opposite the Old North Church made for an ever-busy neighborhood.

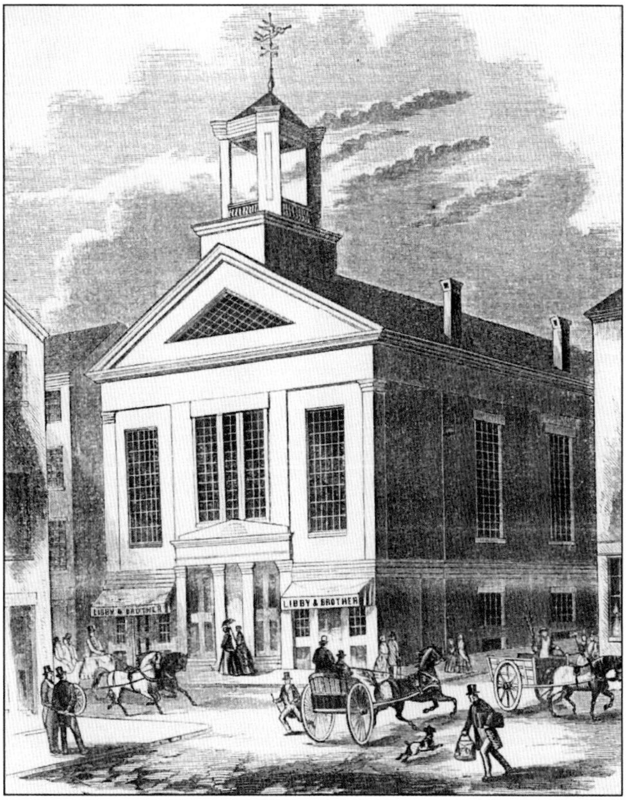

The First Universalist Church was built on Hanover Street in 1839. This was the church of Reverend John Murray, the founder of Universalism. The upper floor was used as the church; the first floor was rented to Libby & Brother to provide additional church income.

The "Old Cockrel" Church on Hanover Street suffered roof and spire damage in the Great Gale of September 1869. The weather vane was made in 1721 by Deacon Shem Drowne and placed on the spire of the New Brick Church. When the church shown here was built in 1844, the cock was regilded and mounted high above Hanover Street, where it remained until the gale. (Courtesy of the BPL)

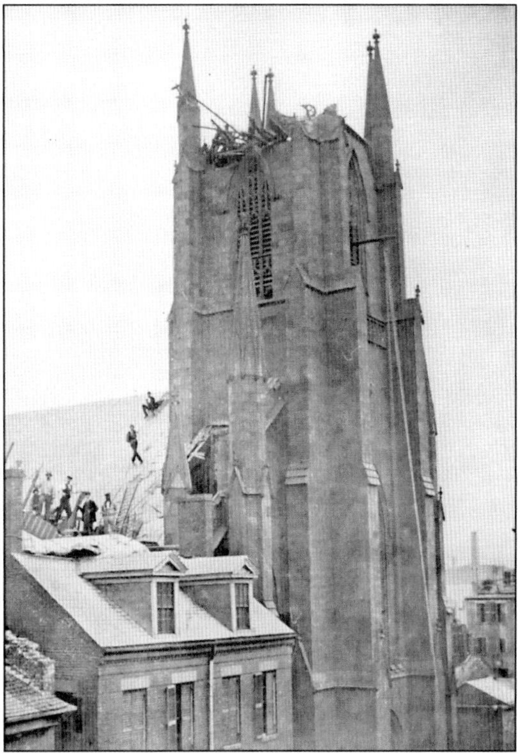

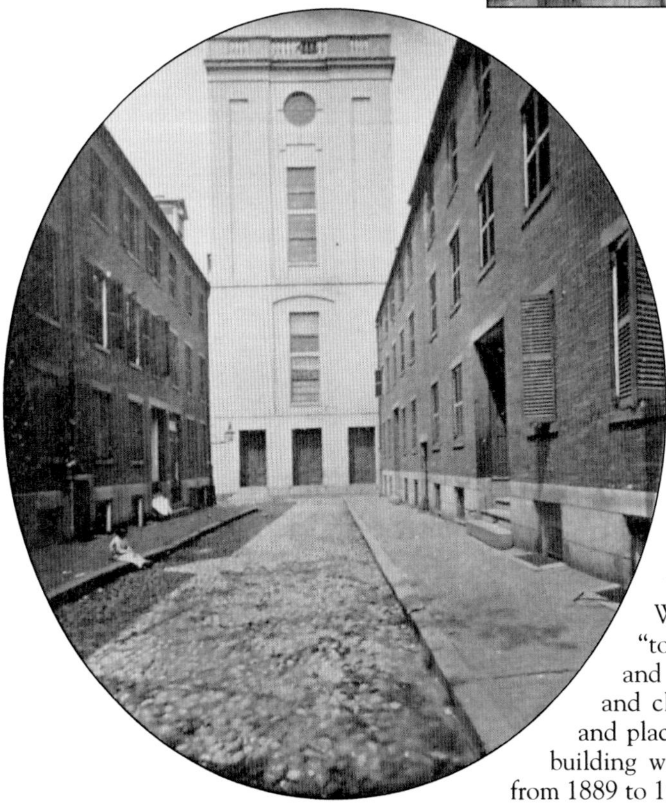

The Baldwin Place Baptist Church was built in 1810 on an alley off Salem Street. The building was sold in 1865 to the Home for Little Wanderers, whose object was "to rescue children from want and shame, provide them with food and clothing, give them instruction, and place them in proper homes." The building was used as Temple Beth Israel from 1889 to 1920 by the Jews of North End.

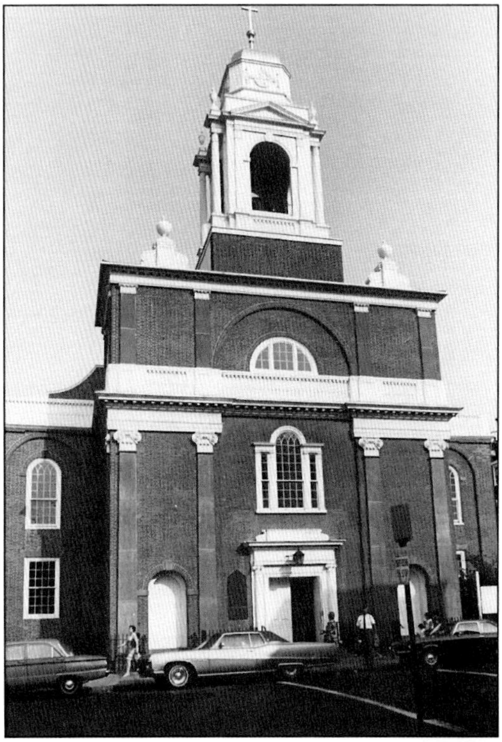

Saint Stephen's Church was built in 1804 on Hanover Street as the New North Religious Society. Sold to the Roman Catholics in 1862, it is the only surviving church designed by Charles Bulfinch in Boston. (Courtesy of the BPL)

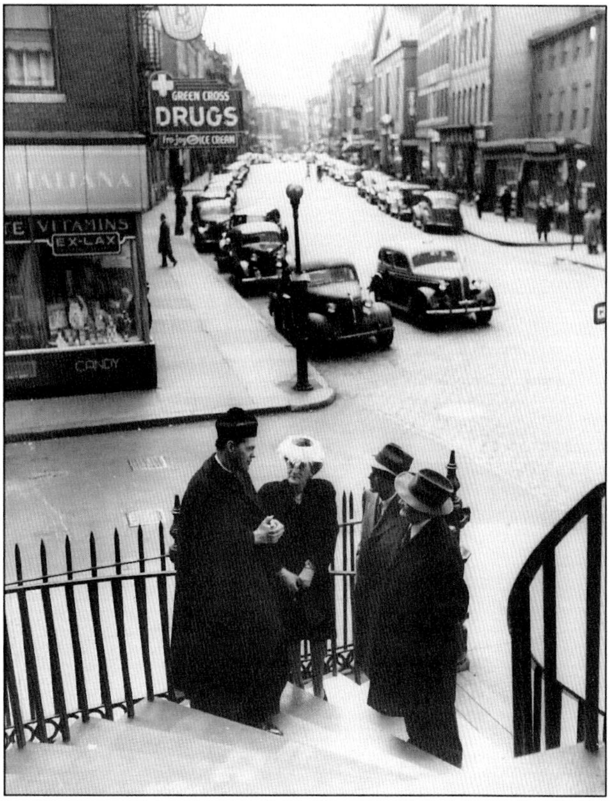

Parishioners speak with a priest on the steps of Saint Stephen's Church. These stairs were removed during the restoration of the church, which was undertaken by Richard Cardinal Cushing in 1964–65. (Courtesy of the BPL)

Saint Mary's of the Sacred Heart Church, consecrated in 1836, was a simple stone structure at the corner of Endicott and Thacher Streets. In 1877, a twin-towered church, soaring to a height of 170 feet, was designed by Patrick C. Keeley and built on the site of the old church. The 1877 building serving the neighborhood until its unfortunate demolition in 1979.

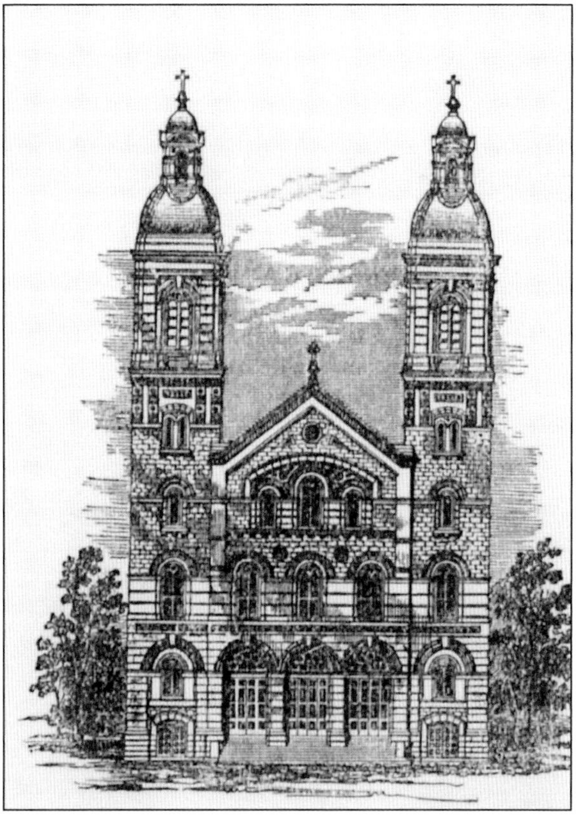

The nave of Saint Mary's Church was an impressive space that led to a marble altar. Supported by Corinthian columns, the barrel-vaulted ceiling and the rich stained-glass windows spoke volumes about the goals and aspirations of the immigrants who worshiped here. (Courtesy of Vito Aluia)

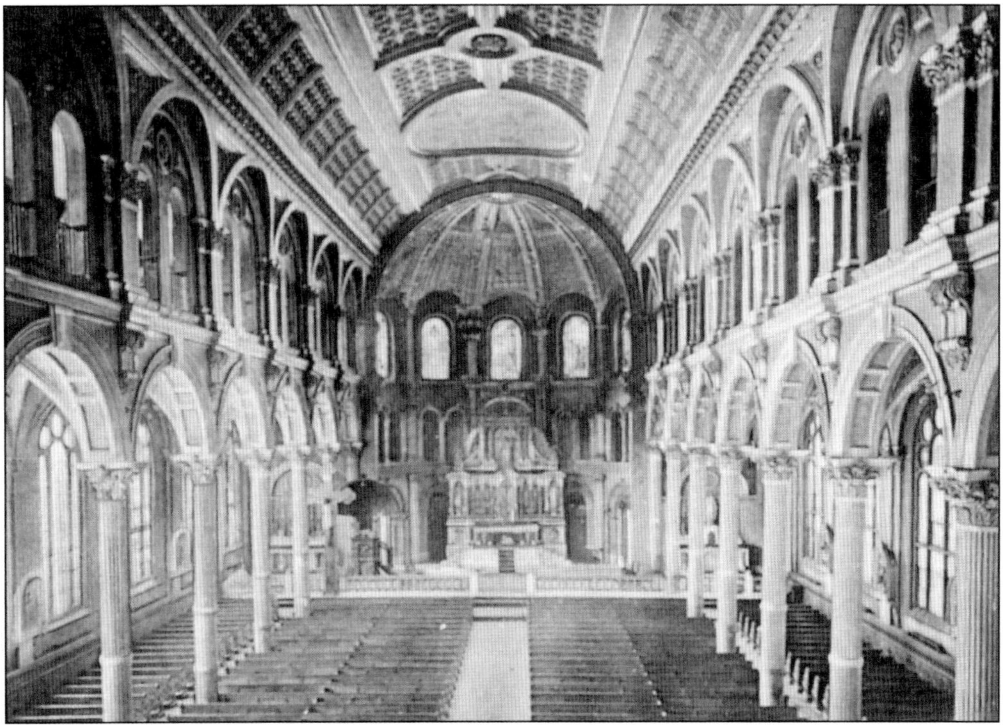

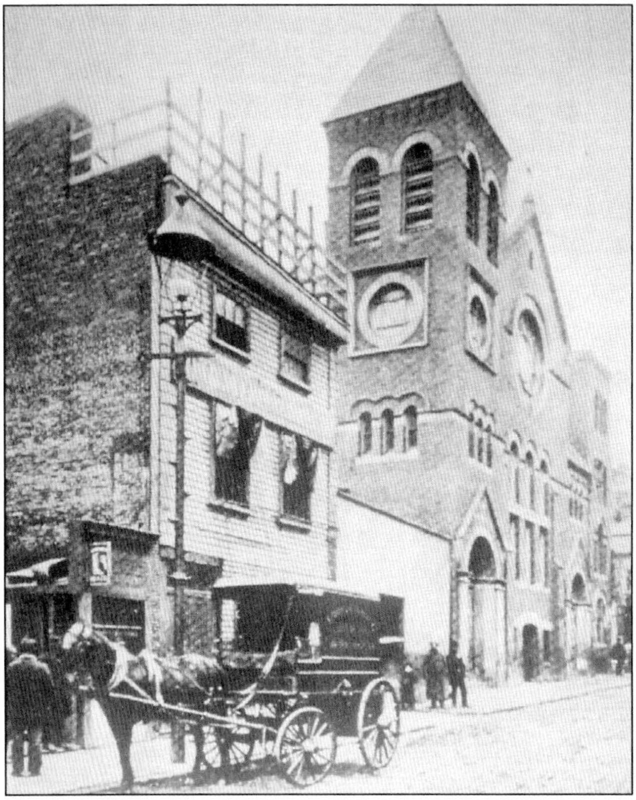

Saint Leonard's Church was founded in 1873 on Prince Street by Italian immigrants; it is the oldest Italian church in Boston and the second oldest in the United States. The first pastor was Reverend Father Guerrini, O.S.F. (Courtesy of the Sammarco Family)

Children participated in a May procession outside Sacred Heart Church on North Square in 1963. A statue of the Blessed Virgin was carried through the streets and was followed by children who had recently received their first Holy Communion. Note the Paul Revere House on the right. (Courtesy of Vito Aluia)

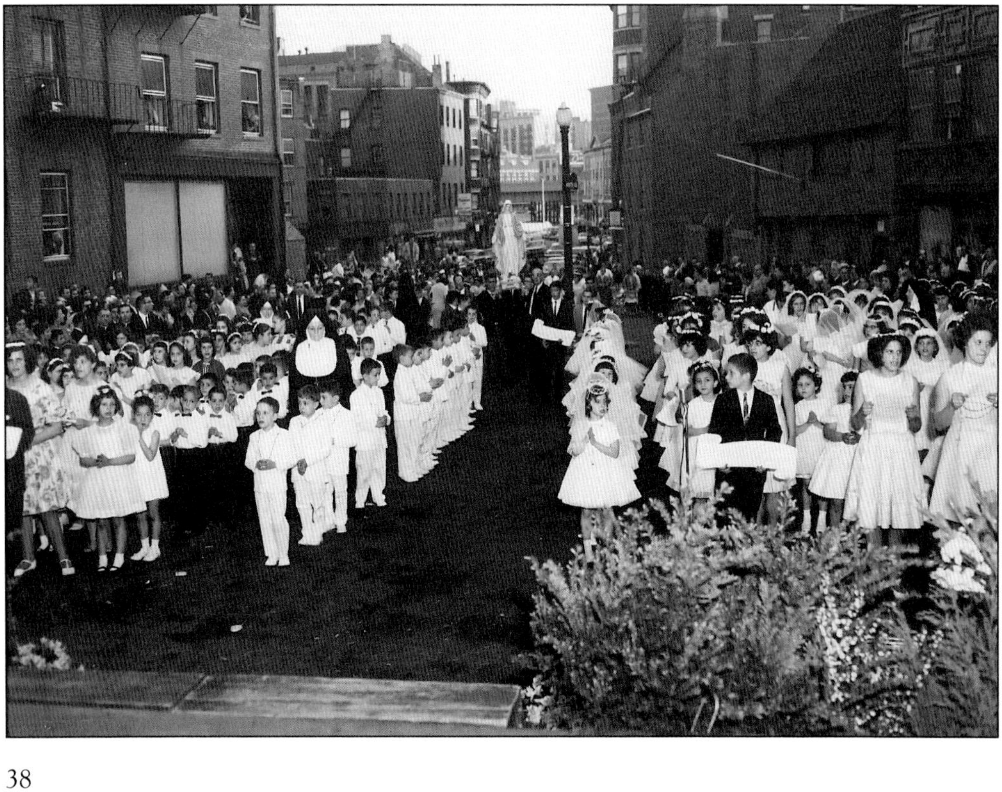

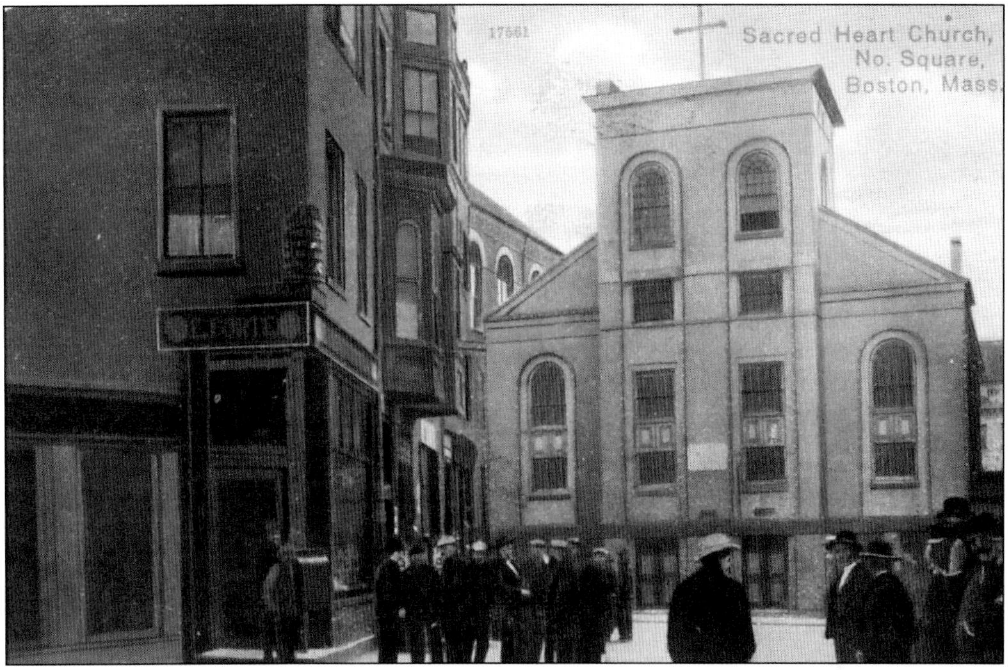

Sacred Heart Church was only slightly changed in its exterior facade after being sold by the Seamen's Bethel. Founded in 1888, the new parish was staffed by the Missionary Fathers of Saint Charles Boromeo and the masses were sung in Italian. (Courtesy of Vito Aluia)

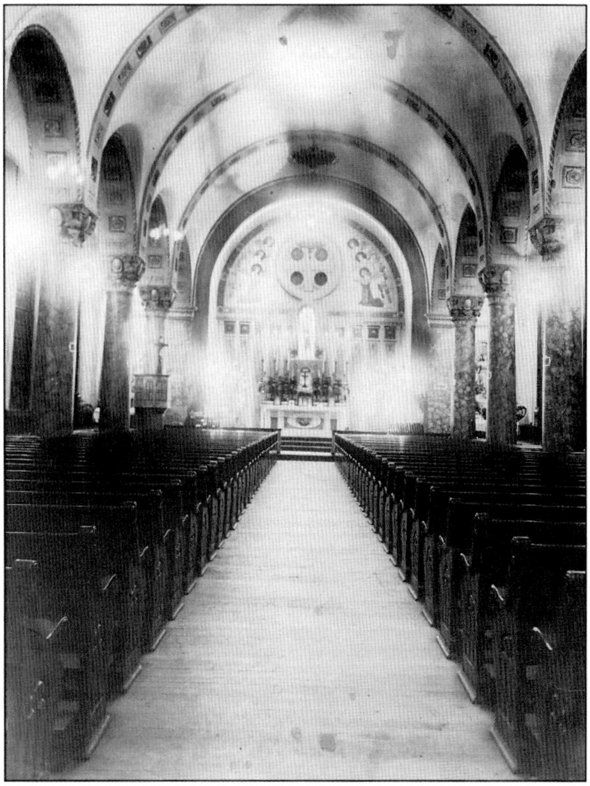

The nave of Sacred Heart Church is a simple but impressive space. Marble columns support the arched ceiling and lead to an altar, on which is inscribed "Jesus, Meek and Humble of Heart." (Courtesy of Vito Aluia)

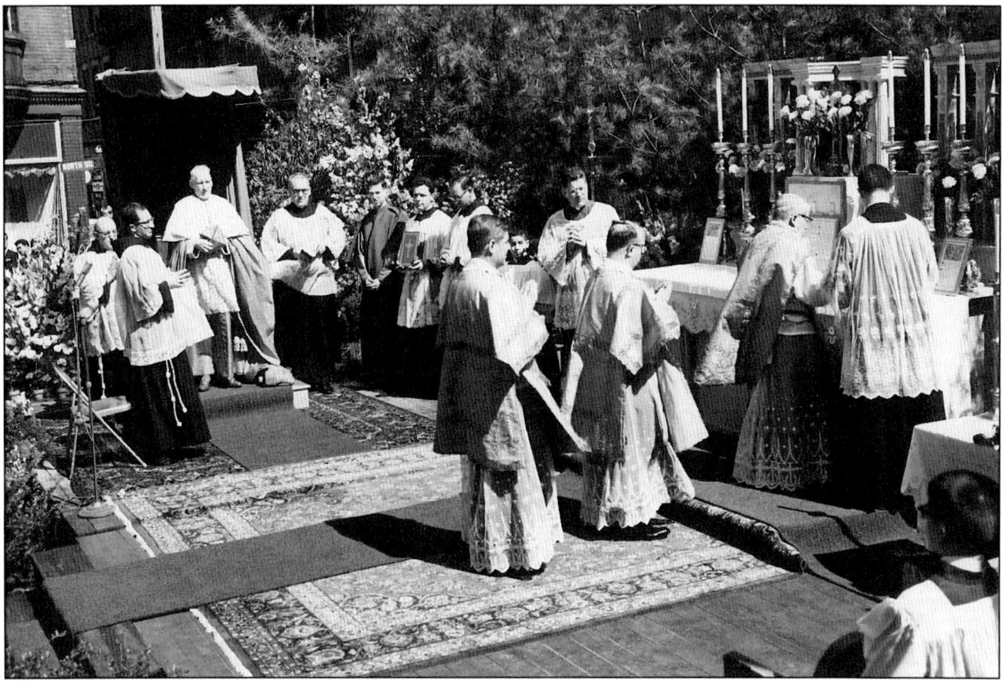

The 75th anniversary of Sacred Heart Church was celebrated in 1963 by an al fresco mass which was said on North Square by Richard Cardinal Cushing. With evergreen trees behind the portable altar and oriental rugs covering the makeshift floor, the mass proved both impressive and memorable. (Courtesy of Vito Aluia)

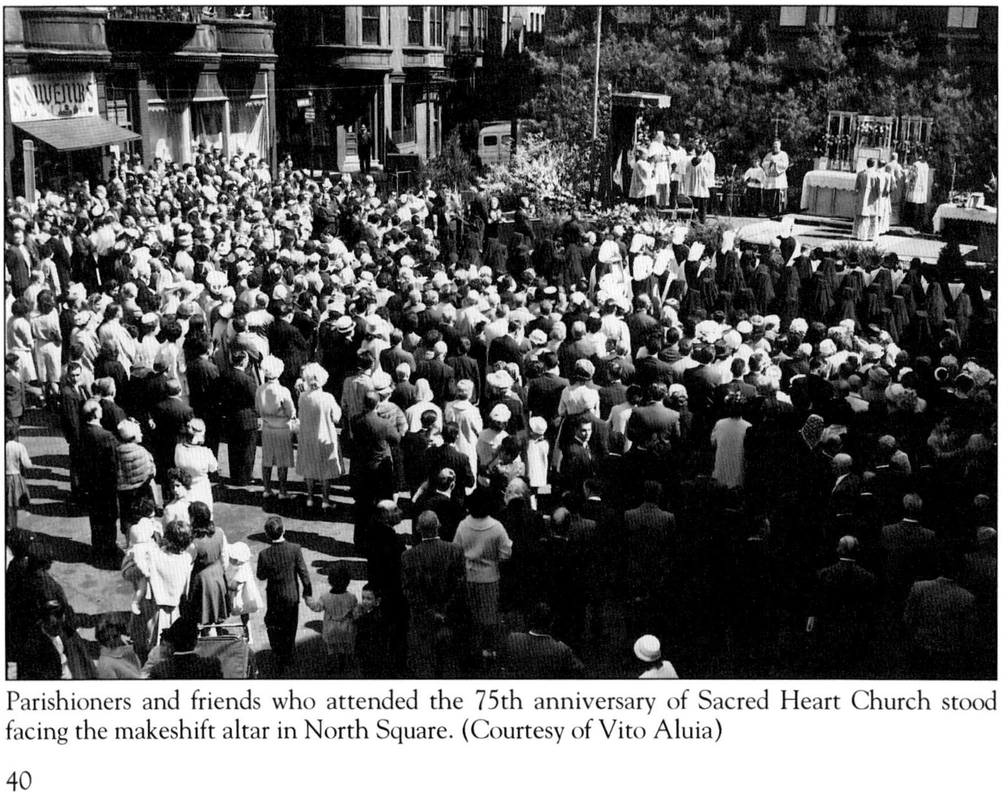

Parishioners and friends who attended the 75th anniversary of Sacred Heart Church stood facing the makeshift altar in North Square. (Courtesy of Vito Aluia)

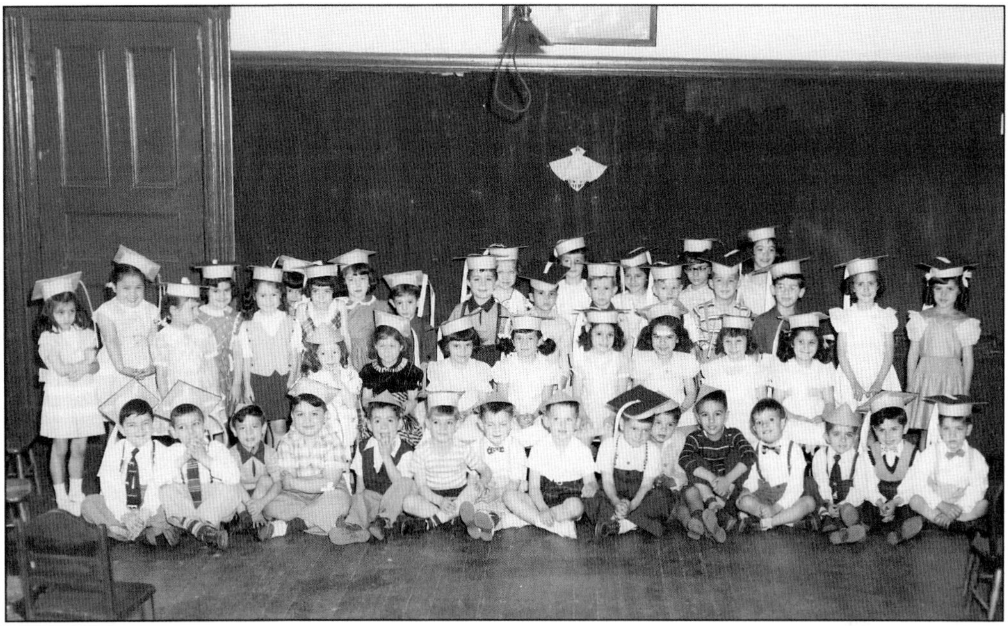

The kindergarten class of the Saint John School of Sacred Heart Church graduated in 1952 with proper style. (Courtesy of Vito Aluia)

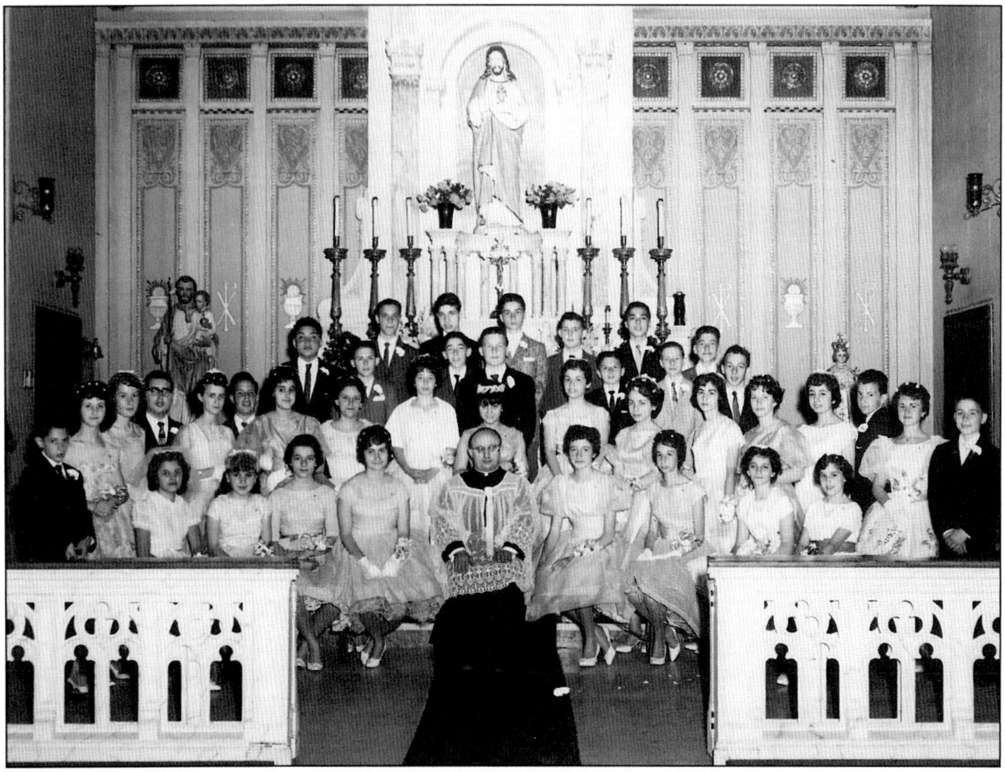

This eighth grade class graduated from the Saint John School of Sacred Heart Church in 1960. Father Louis, pastor of Sacred Heart Church, poses with the proud, and remarkably well-dressed, graduates on the altar of the church. (Courtesy of Vito Aluia)

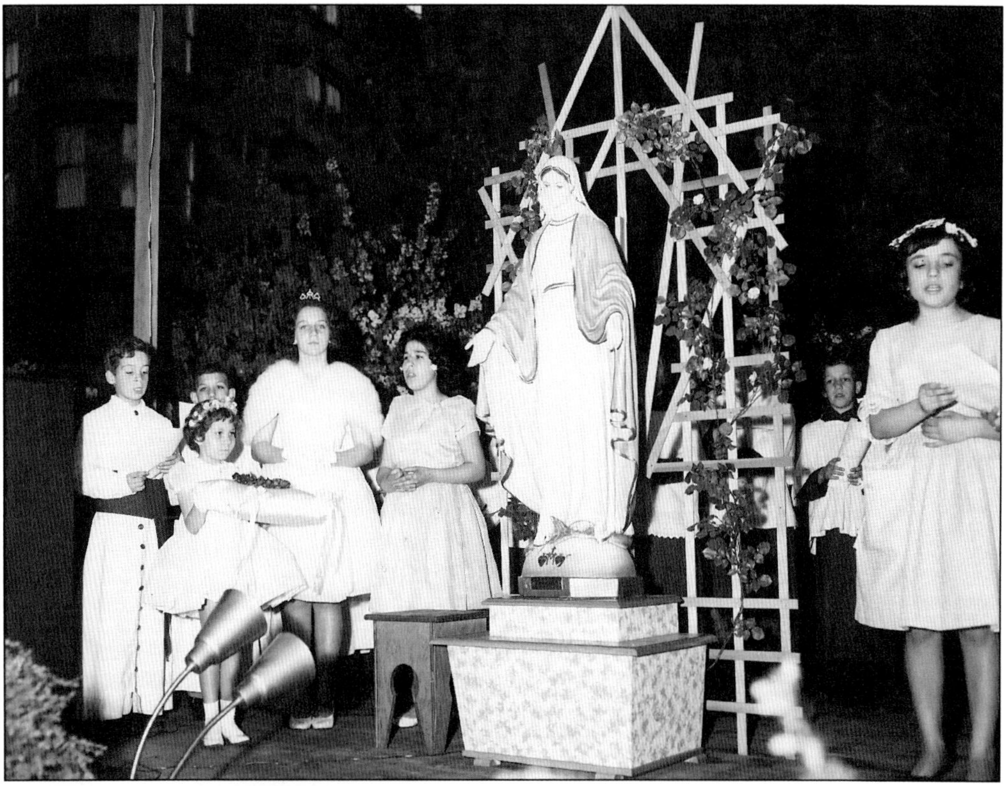

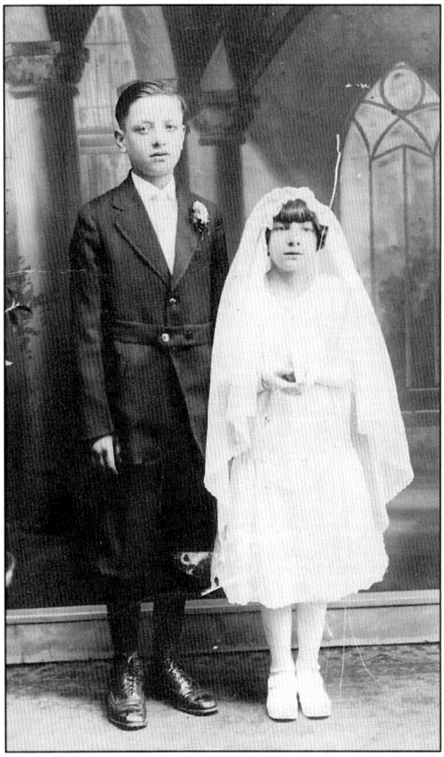

The crowning of the statue of the Blessed Virgin was part of a Marian Day celebration by parishioners of Sacred Heart Church during the 75th anniversary celebration in 1963. A young girl, on the left, holds a crown of roses on a pillow as participants sing "Hail Holy Queen." (Courtesy of Vito Aluia)

Two children pose for their photograph after having made their first Holy Communion at Saint Leonard's Church in 1924. (Courtesy of the Sammarco Family)

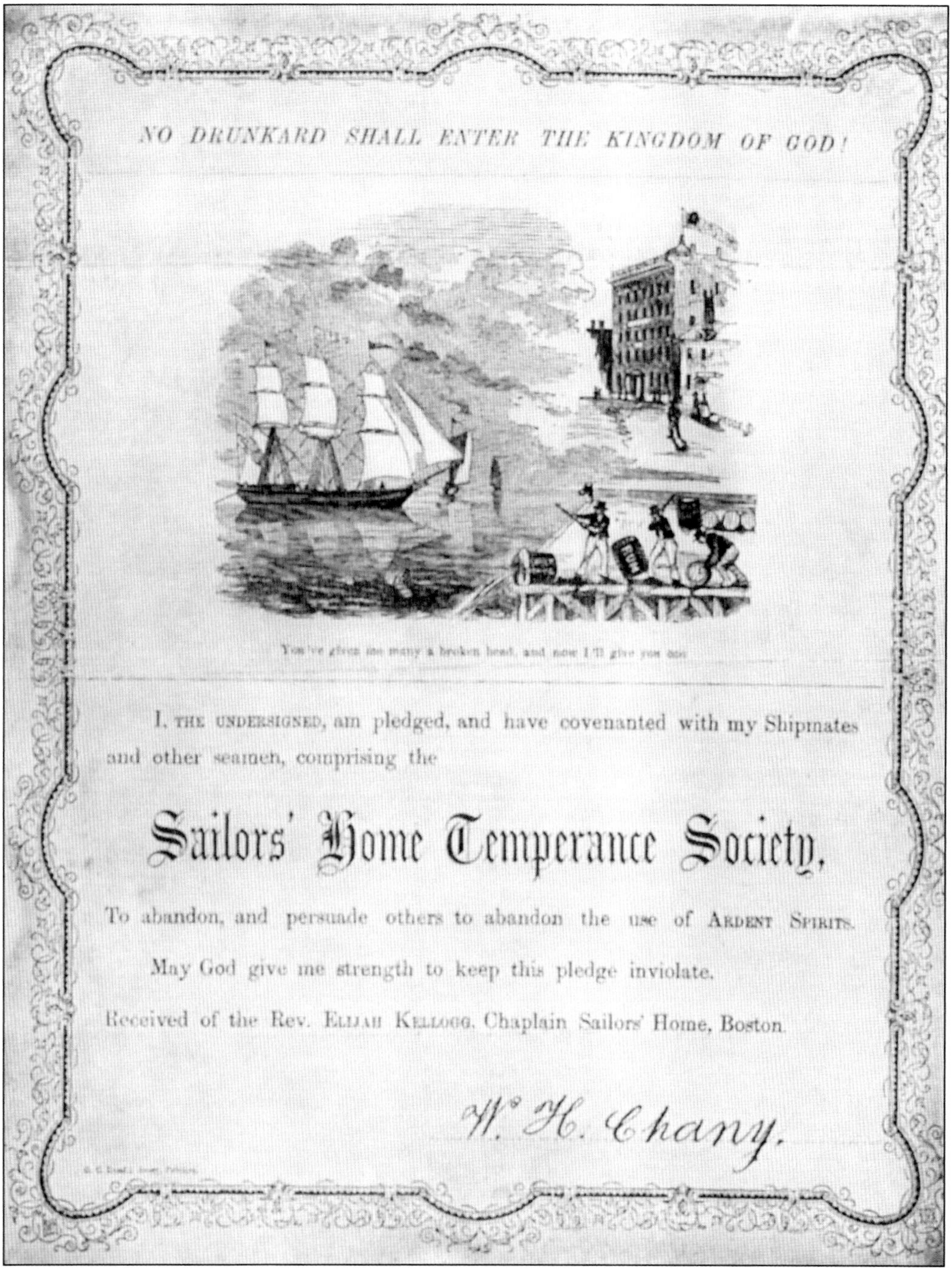

NO DRUNKARD SHALL ENTER THE KINGDOM OF GOD!

You've given me many a broken head, and now I'll give you one

I, THE UNDERSIGNED, am pledged, and have covenanted with my Shipmates and other seamen, comprising the

Sailors' Home Temperance Society,

To abandon, and persuade others to abandon the use of ARDENT SPIRITS.

May God give me strength to keep this pledge inviolate.

Received of the Rev. ELIJAH KELLOGG, Chaplain Sailors' Home, Boston.

Wm. H. Chany.

The Sailors' Home had a Temperance Society that encouraged members to "abandon, and persuade others to abandon the use of Ardent Spirits" as "NO DRUNKARD SHALL ENTER THE KINGDOM OF GOD!"

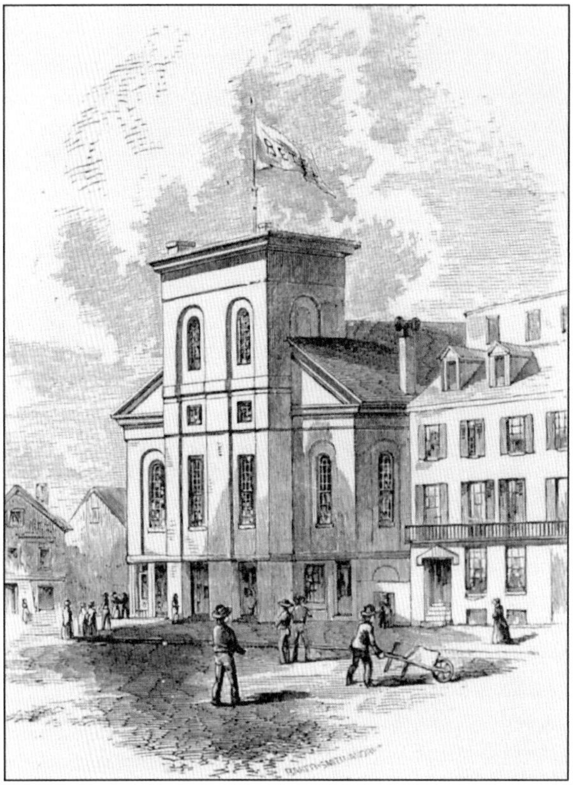

The Bethel in North Square was founded in 1828 by the Port Society for the City of Boston for the "moral and religious instruction of seamen."

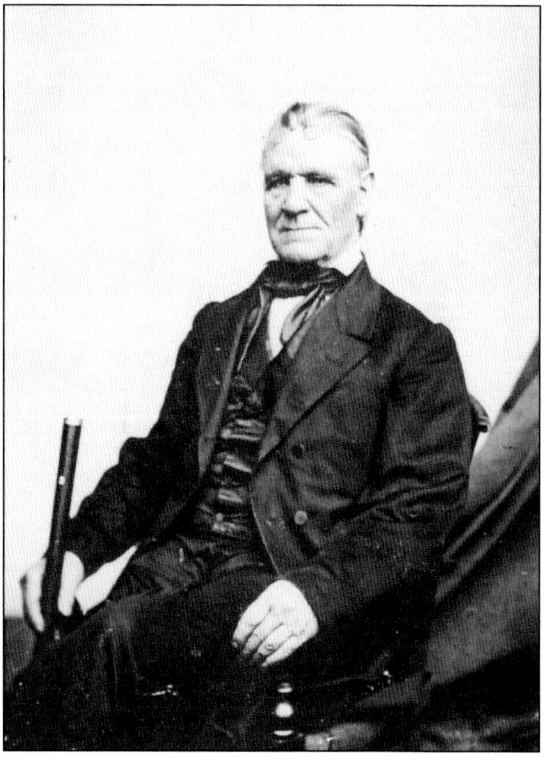

Reverend Edward T. Taylor (1793–1871), or Father Taylor as he was more popularly known, was pastor of the Seamen's Bethel in North Square for forty years. Born in Richmond, Virginia, he went to sea early in life and later was called to the ministry, and subsequently the Seamen's Bethel.

Mother Taylor, or Deborah D. Millett Taylor (1795–1869), was a devoted wife, mother, and ardent Methodist who assisted her husband in his church and in its outreach to sailors whose ships were docked in Boston. Their home was erected on the former site of the Clarke-Frankland House on Garden Court Street.

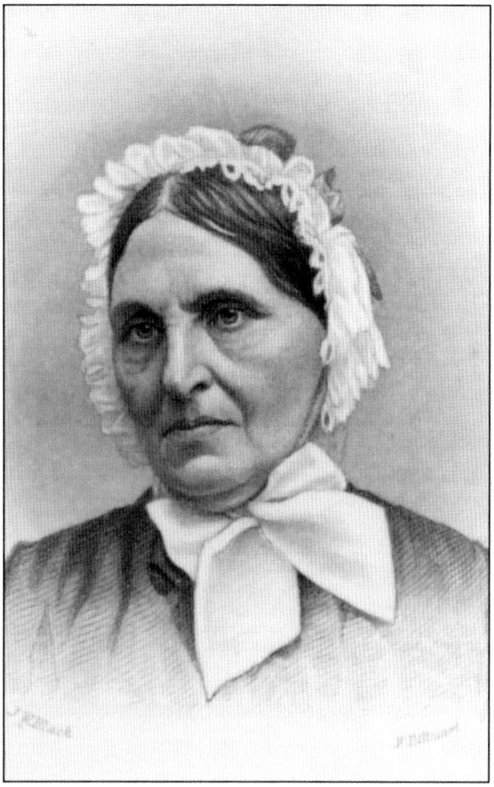

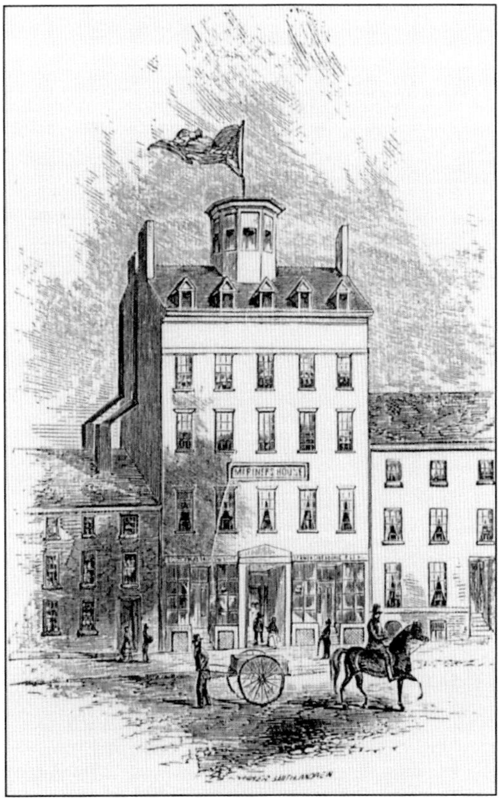

The Mariners' House was built in 1847 at 11 North Square by the Boston Port Society. It still serves the sailors who call at the port of Boston, and offers them rooms, meals, and activities.

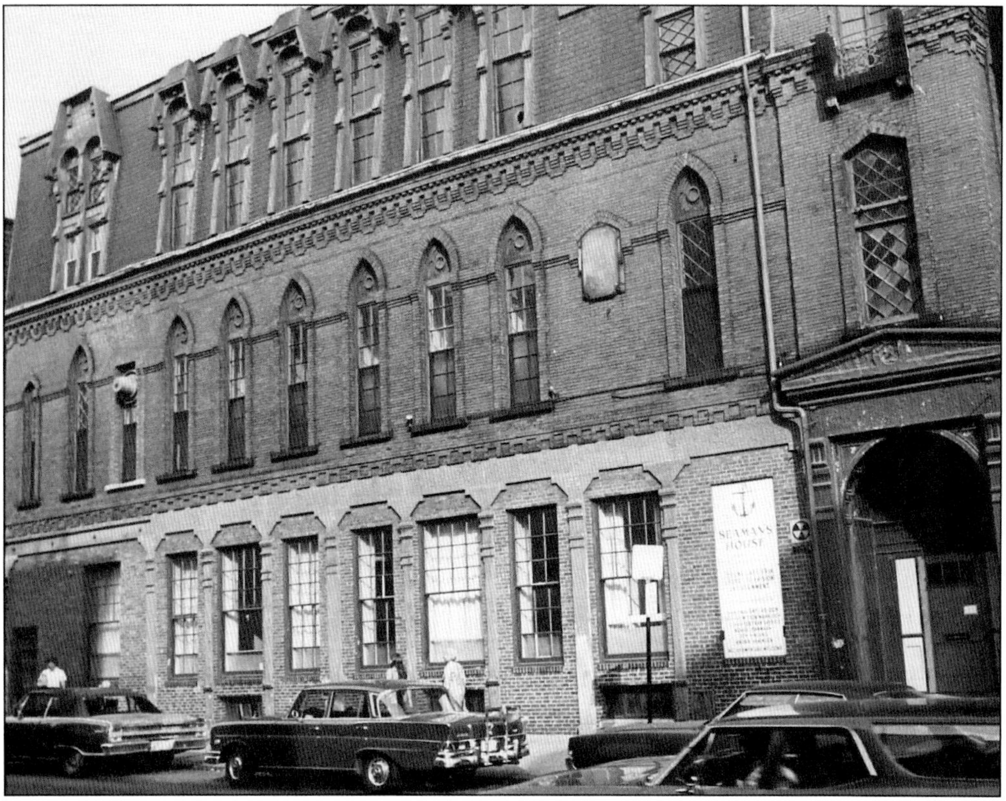

The Seaman's House was on Hanover Street, near Richmond Street. Originally known as Cockerel Hall, in honor of the Cockerel Church, the building housed congregation Shomre Beth Abraham from 1886 to 1893 and congregation Chevra Thilim from 1893 to 1899. Today it has been converted to residences. (Courtesy of the BPL)

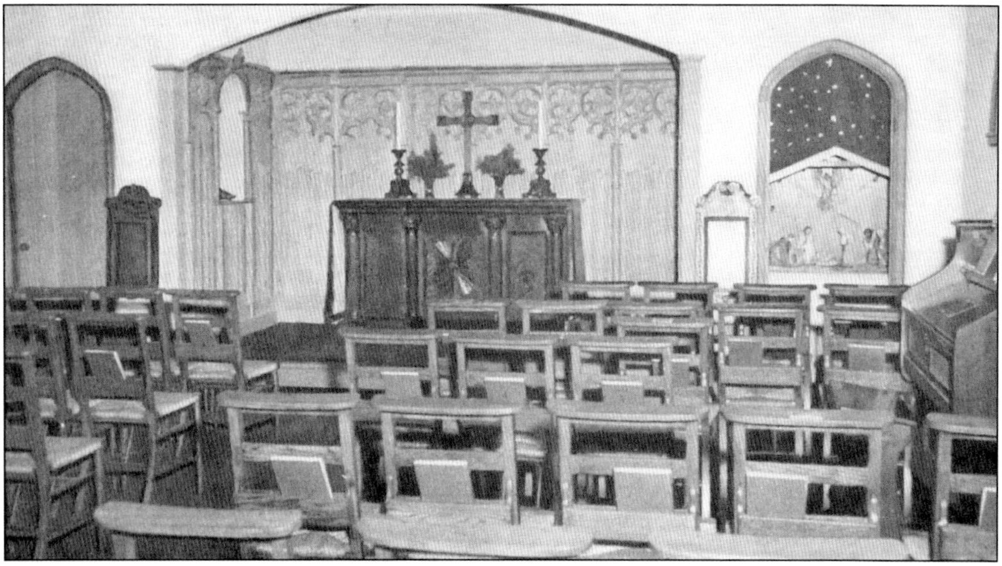

The Chapel of Saint Mary for Sailors was on the fifth floor of the Seaman's House. (Courtesy of Vito Aluia)

Four

Ciao North End

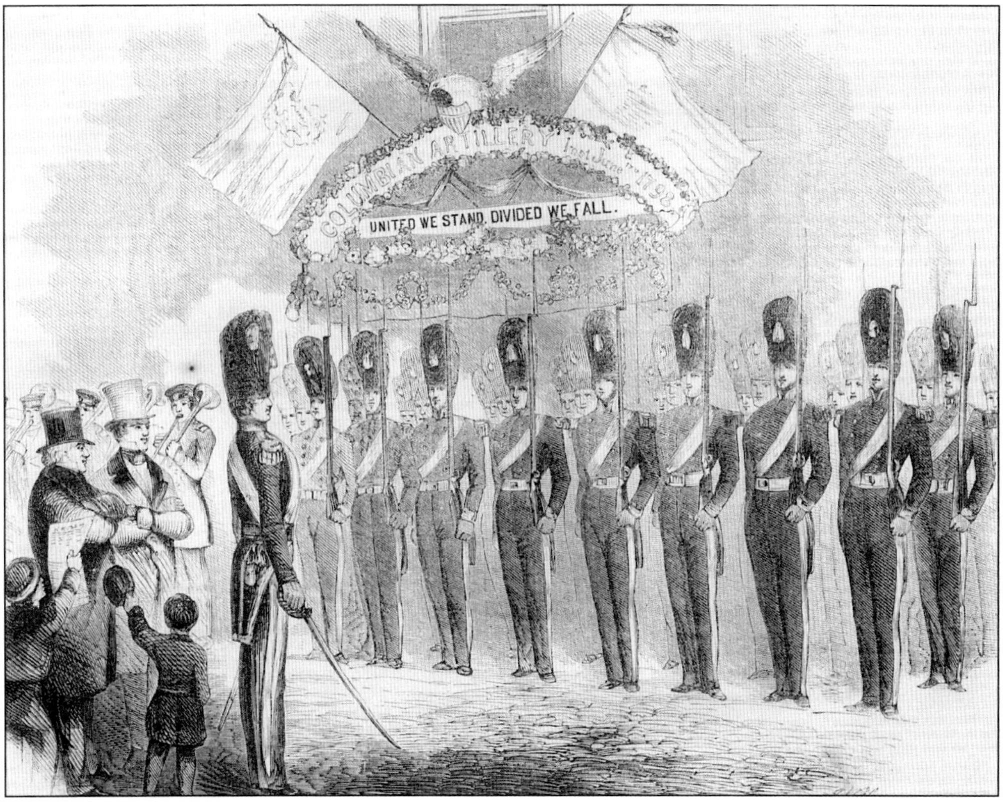

The Columbian Artillery was founded on June 17, 1798, and had as its motto "United We Stand, Divided We Fall." Their armory was in the Gun House on Cooper Street and the "good fellowship and brotherly feeling that has so long characterized this company, is worthy of all praise and emulation, and should serve to promote this excellent and most desirable state of things in other city associations of this character."

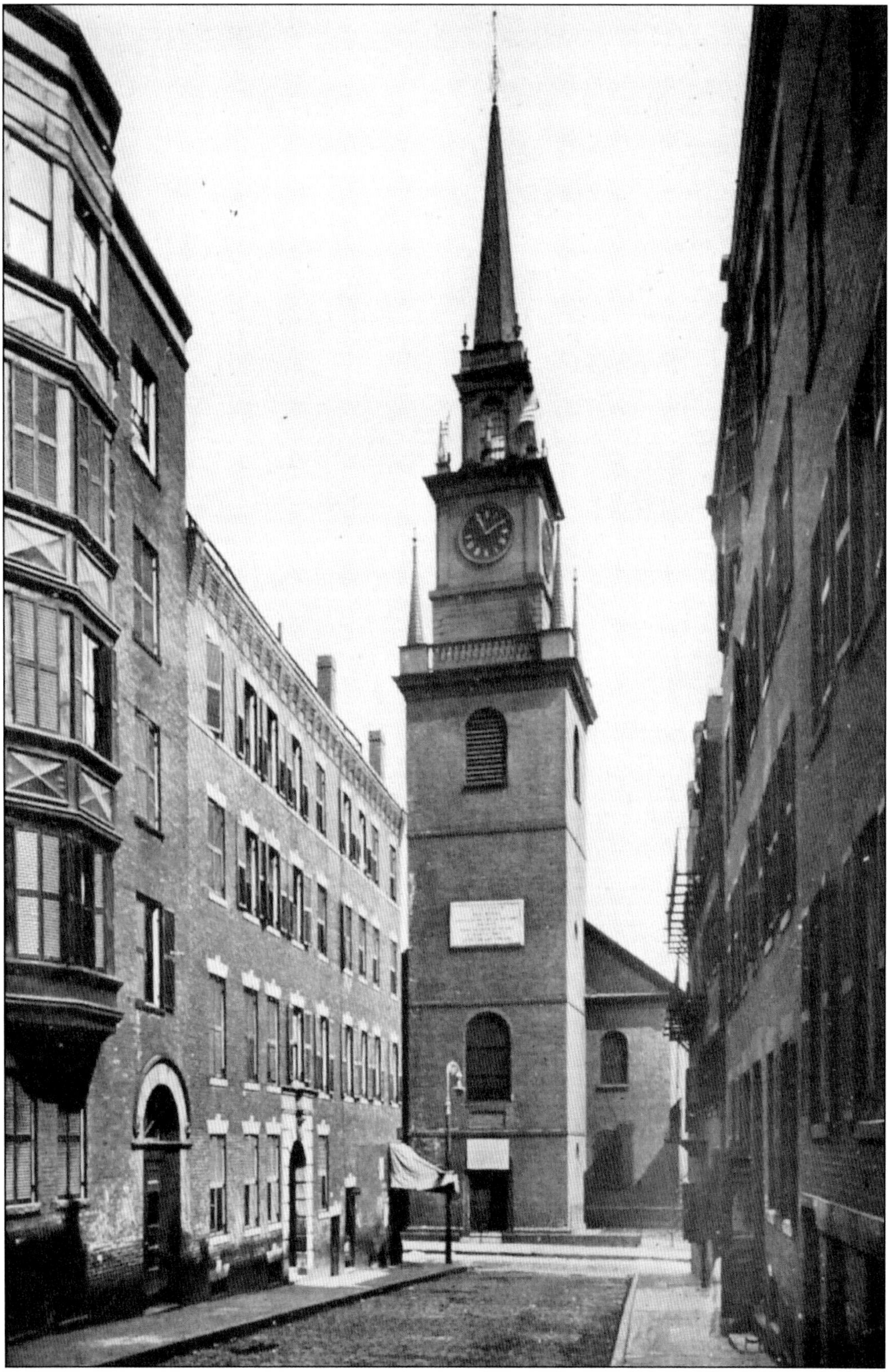

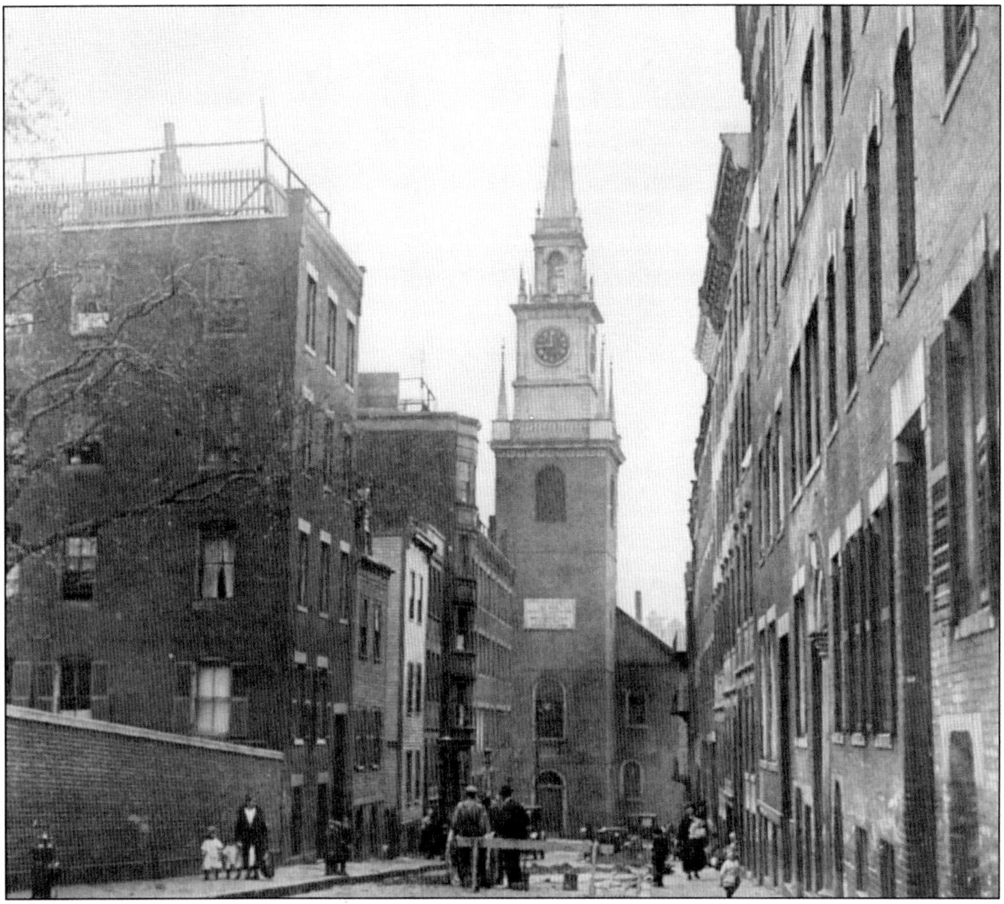

Hull Street, in the first decade of the twentieth century, was the center of the "great immigrant section of the city." Street workers are repairing the cobblestone street as neighborhood residents go about their business.

OPPOSITE PAGE: The Old North Church, designed by William Price and built in 1723, is the oldest church building in the city of Boston. It was from its spire that the lanterns were hung by Robert Newman to alert the patriots of the march of the British troops to Lexington and Concord, prompting Paul Revere to ride through Middlesex County shouting "The British are coming!"

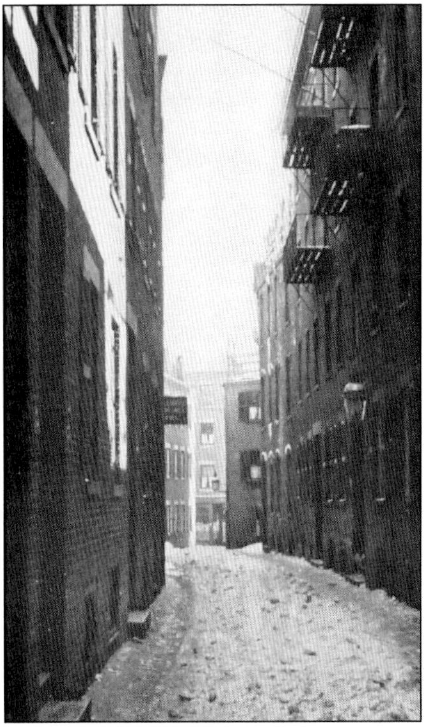

Methodist Alley, named for the Methodist church built here in 1796, was one of dozens of alleyways that connected streets in the North End, creating a maze of ways, alleys, streets, and paths. Today, it is known as Hanover Avenue.

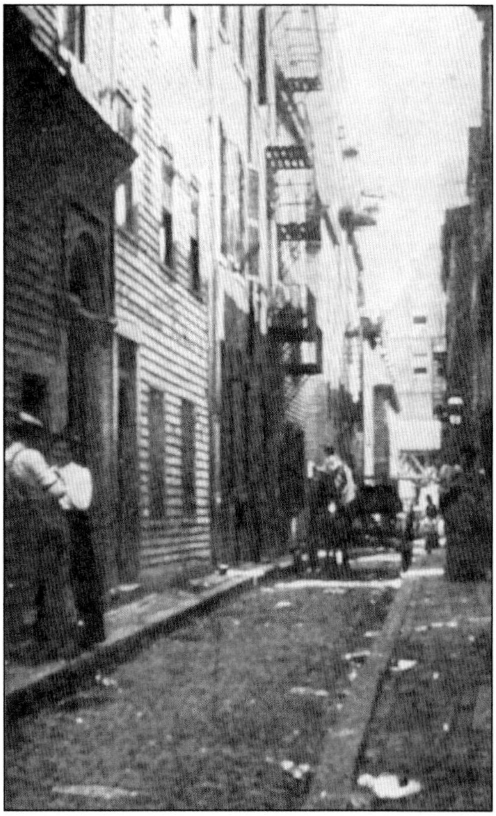

Salutation Alley, which runs from Hanover Street to Commercial Street, was a narrow alleyway that was named for the Salutation Tavern, a popular inn of "North End mechanics and others for political discussions." In the nineteenth century there were numerous children playing in the center of the way and overcrowded tenements on both sides of the street.

Paul Revere lived in this house, considered the oldest house in Boston proper (built 1680), from 1770 to 1800. By the late nineteenth century the house, which faces North Square, was hemmed in on both sides by apartment buildings, including "The Angelo" on the left.

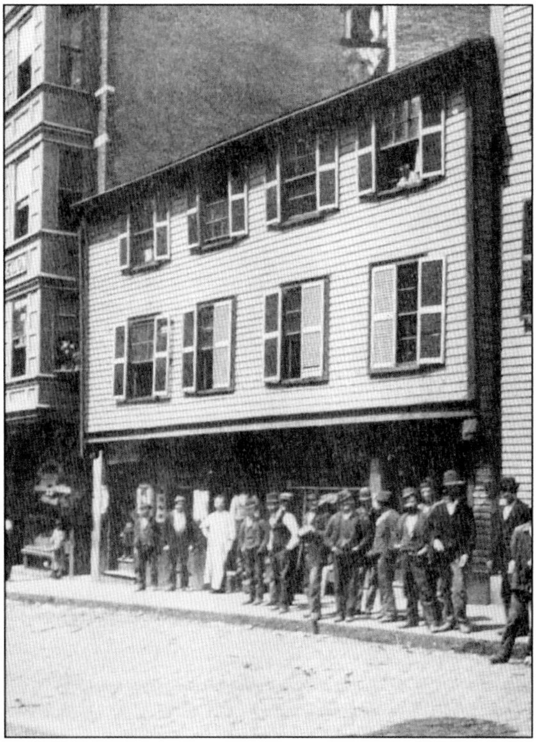

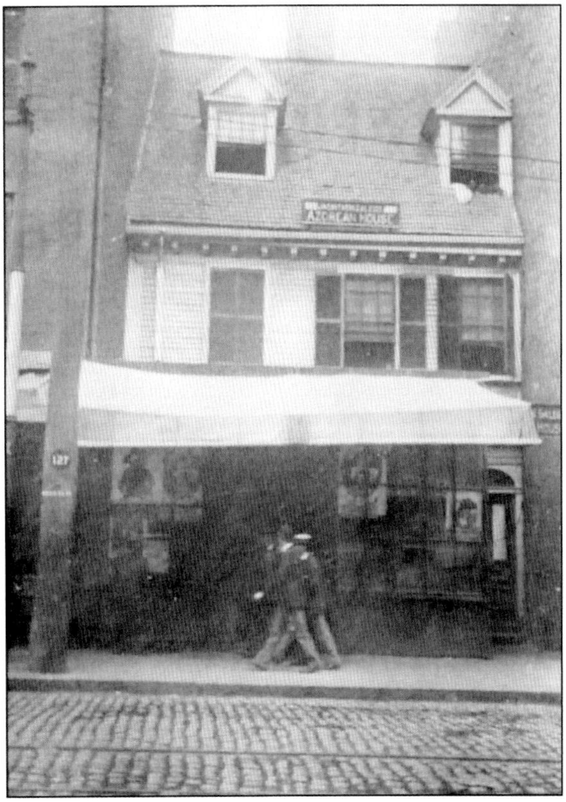

The Mather-Eliot House was built by Increase Mather in 1677 on Hanover Street, near Tileston Street. It later served as the home of Andrew and John Eliot, father and son ministers of the New North Church. By 1890, it had become the Azorean House, a rooming house for sailors visiting Boston from the Azore Islands. (Courtesy of the BPL)

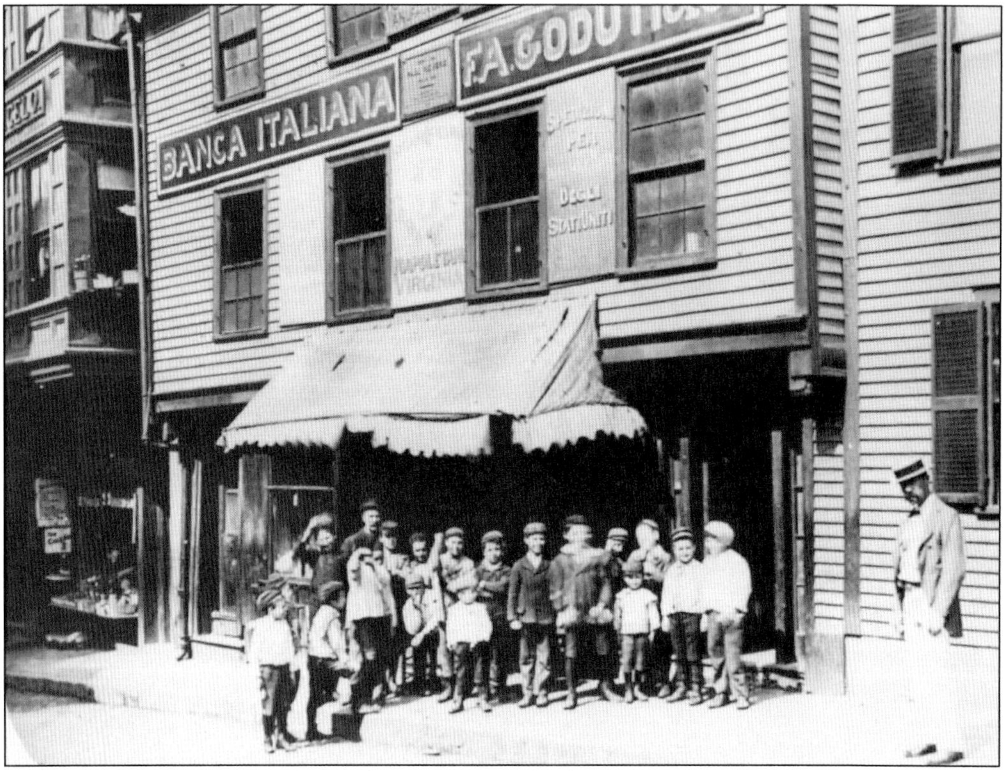

By the turn of the century, the Paul Revere House had become the Banca Italiana and the cigar factory of F.A. Goduti & Company. A group of boys stand in front of the bank's entrance in this photograph of 1905. (Courtesy of the BPL)

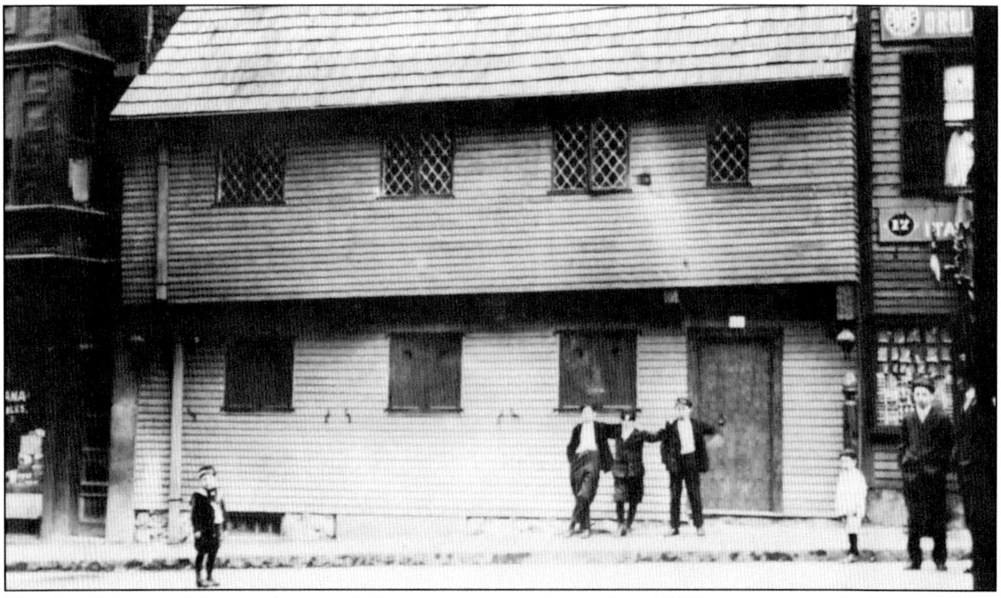

The Paul Revere House Memorial Association was formed in 1907 to preserve the home of the patriot and silversmith. Restored by architect Joseph Everett Chandler, according to how he perceived it originally appeared, it was photographed in 1909. (Courtesy of the BPL)

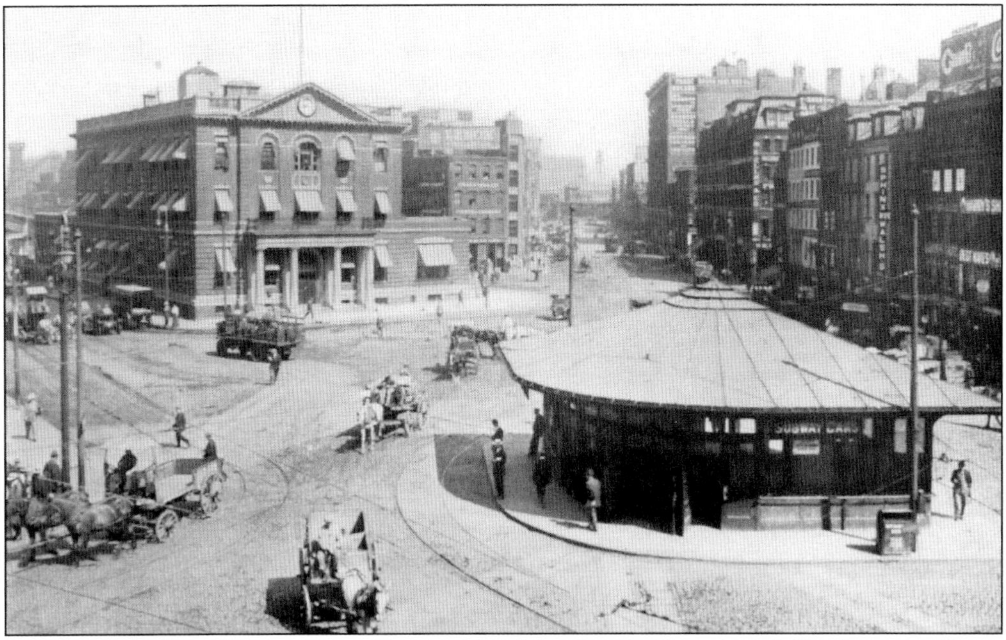

Haymarket Square is the junction of New Chardon, New Sudbury, North Washington, Cross, and Blackstone Streets. The kiosk of the Haymarket Square station rises on the right and the city of Boston Relief Station is on the left.

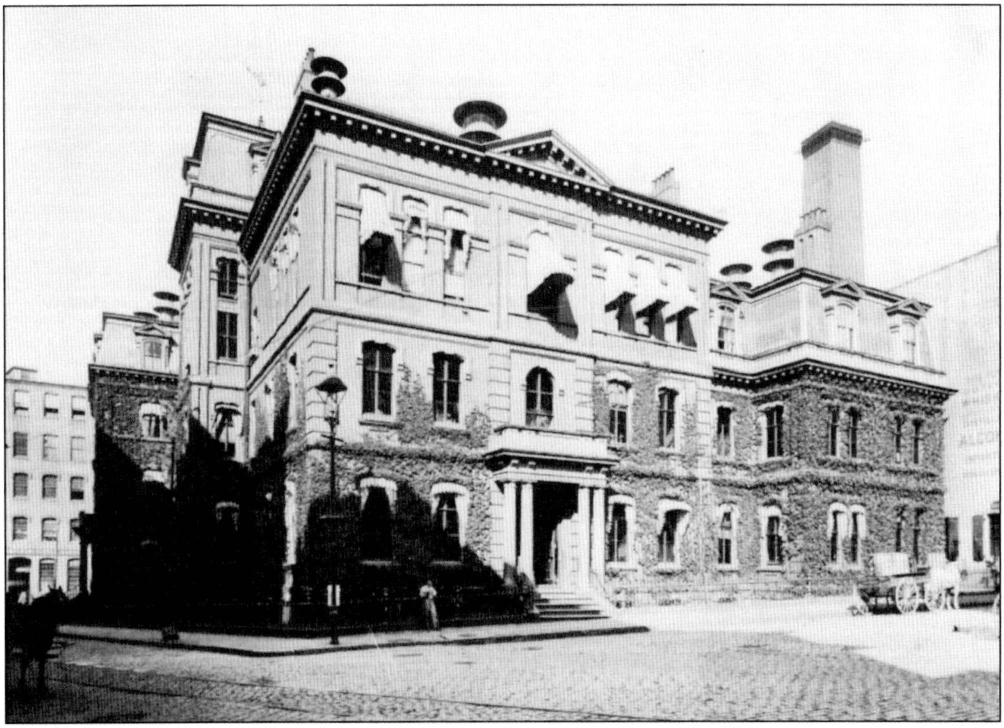

Designed by the architectural firm Sturgis and Brigham, the relief station offered medical care for the burgeoning immigrant population of Boston with nurses and doctors who spoke their language. (Courtesy of the BPL)

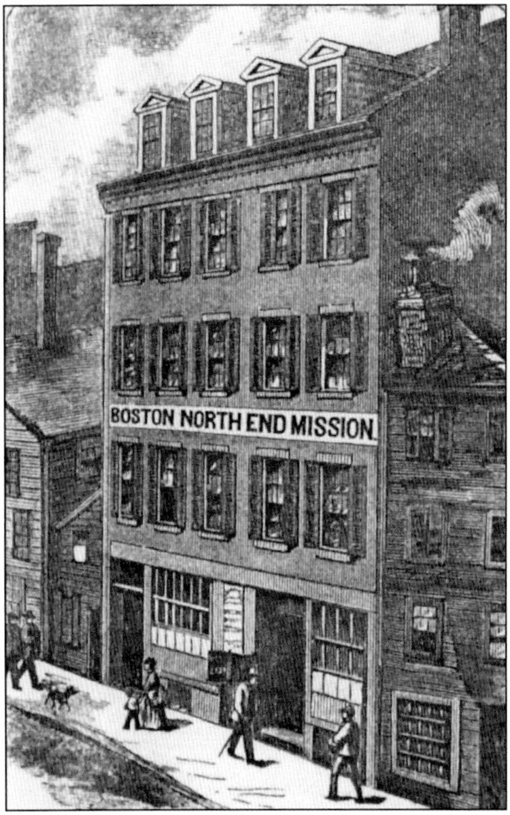

The North End Mission was at 201 North Street near North Square "where many poor people have been furnished with food and clothing and sent on their way to rejoicing."

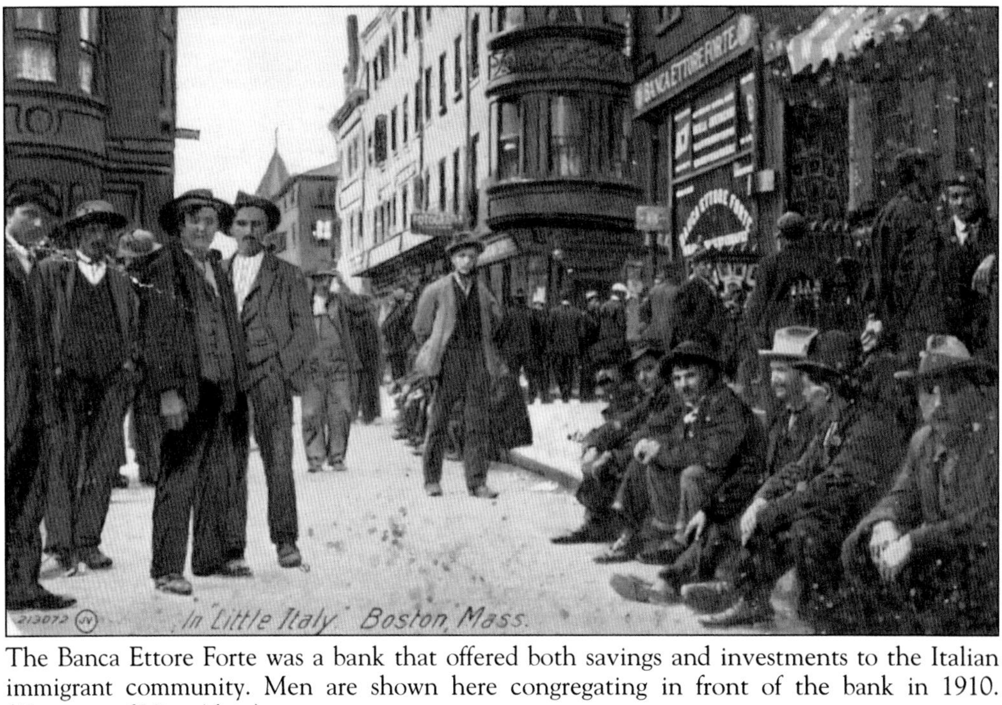

The Banca Ettore Forte was a bank that offered both savings and investments to the Italian immigrant community. Men are shown here congregating in front of the bank in 1910. (Courtesy of Vito Aluia)

John F. Fitzgerald was a North End *Dearo* (Dear Old North Enders). Born on Moon Street to parents who immigrated from Ireland, he later served as mayor of Boston (1906–1907 and 1910–1913) and was the grandfather of President John Fitzgerald Kennedy and Senator Edward M. Kennedy.

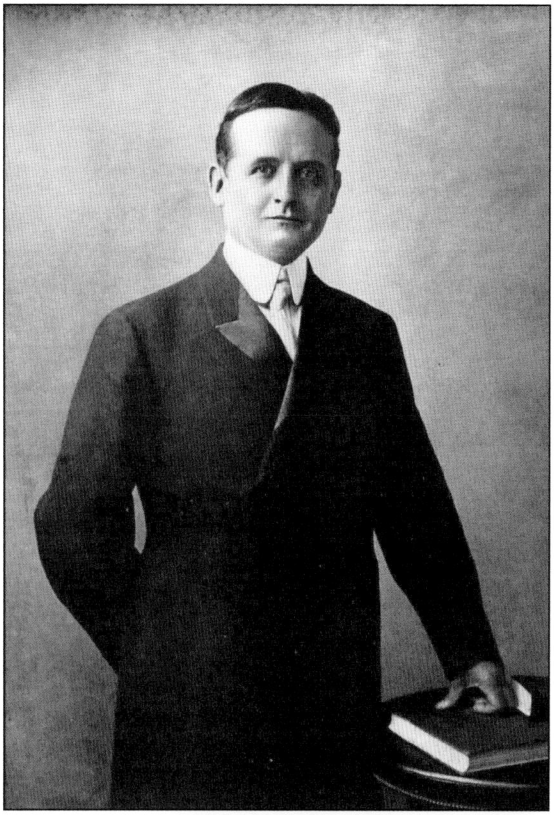

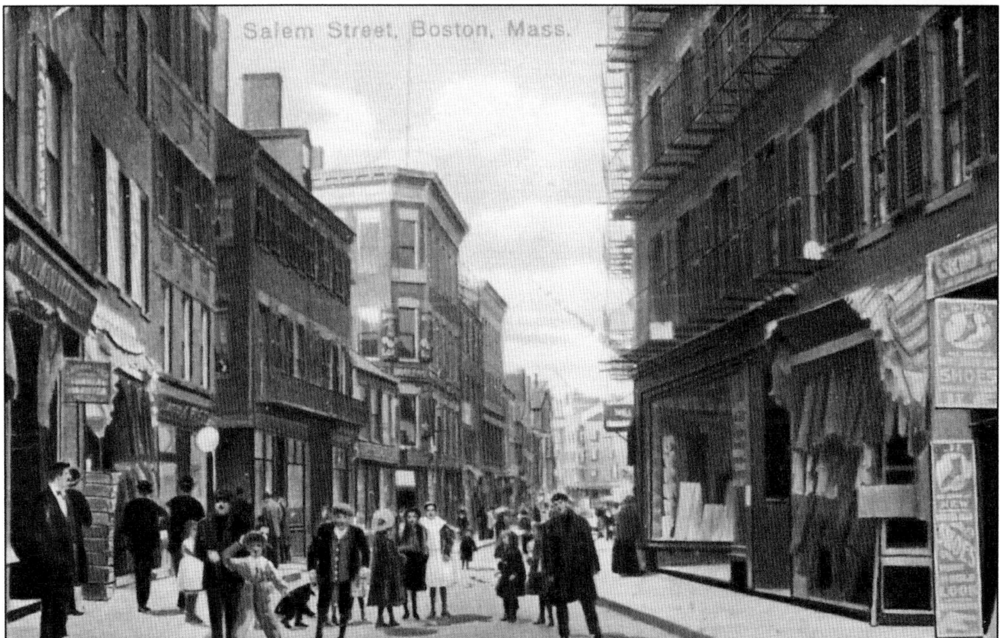

Salem Street at the turn of the century had numerous specialty shops and ethnic food stores on the first floor of the tenements. (Courtesy of Vito Aluia)

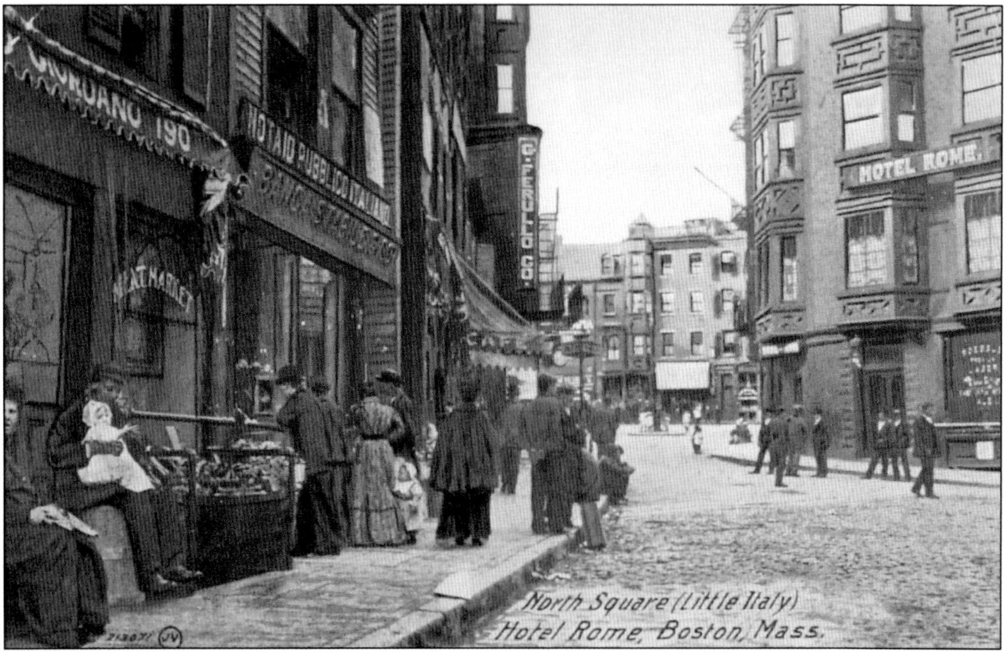

Once the site of the Old North Meetinghouse, which was pulled down by the British, North Square was often referred to as "Little Italy" at the turn of the century. On the left is Giordano's store, the Notaio Publico Italiano, Banca Stabile & Company, and the G. Ferullo Company. On the right is the Hotel Rome, a large apartment building facing North Square. (Courtesy of Vito Aluia)

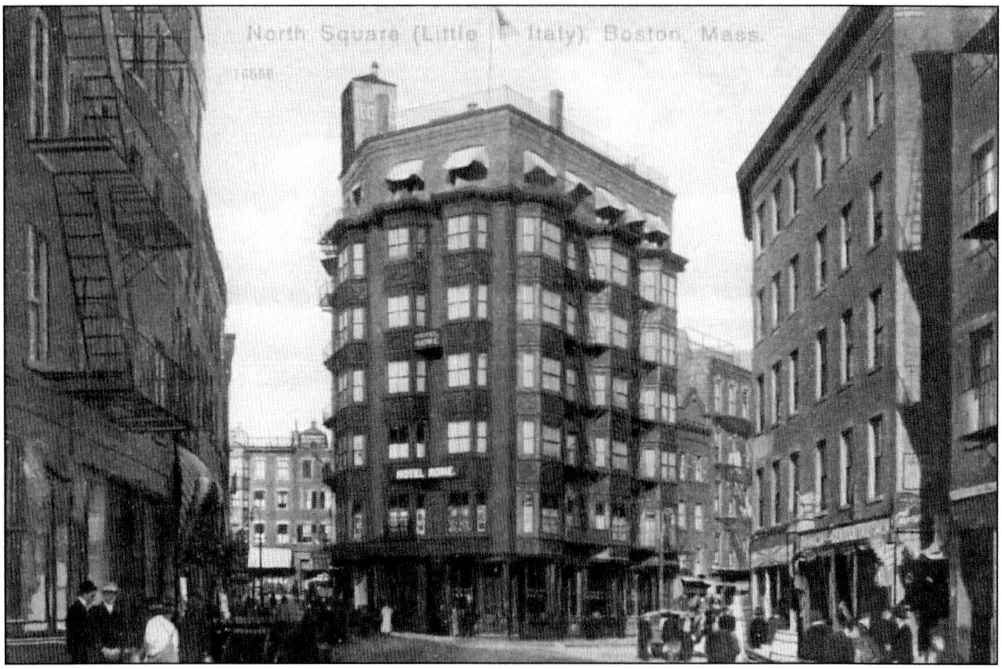

The Hotel Rome dominated North Square at the turn of the century. (Courtesy of Vito Aluia)

Giuseppe and Lucia Pironti Giannelli immigrated to Boston from Avellino in the paesa of Montefalceone, Italy. This formal portrait shows the family in 1908. In the first row are Lucia Pironti Giannelli, Joseph Giannelli, and Giuseppe Giannelli; Domenicio, Concetta and Antonio Giannelli are in the second row. (Courtesy of the Sammarco Family)

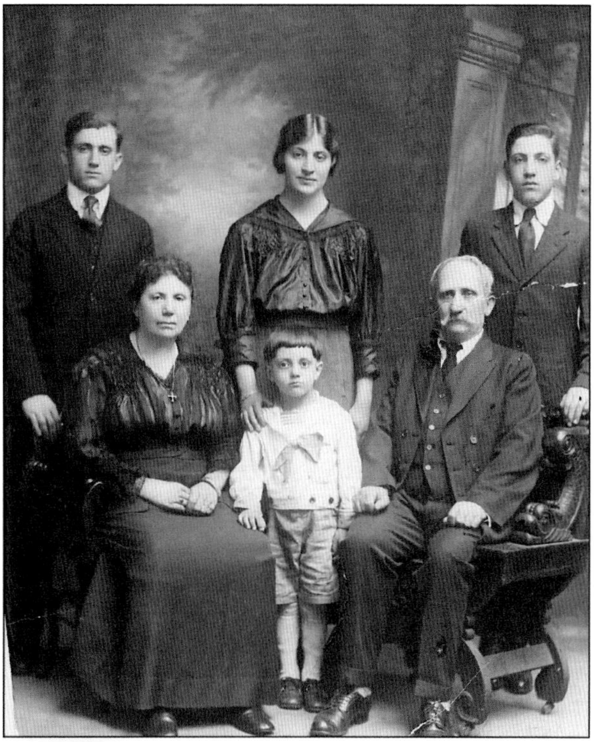

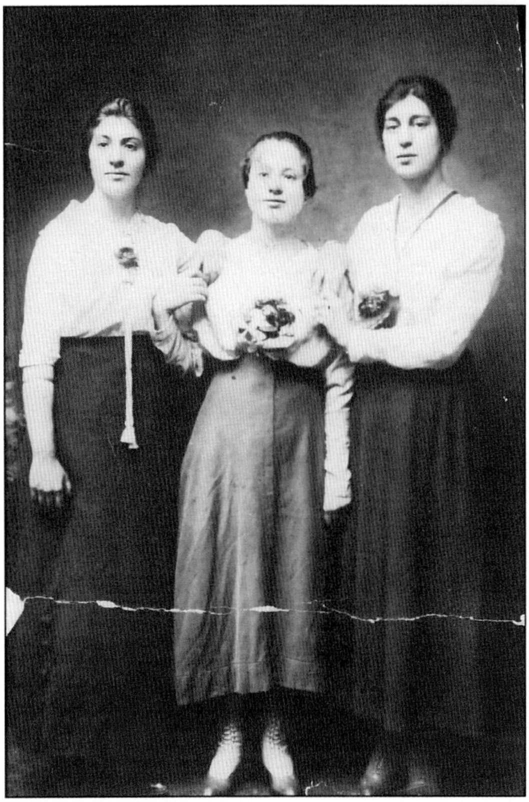

The three daughters of Giuseppe and Lucia Pironti Giannelli strike a pose as the "Three Graces." From the left are Mary, Rose, and Concetta Giannelli. (Courtesy of the Sammarco Family)

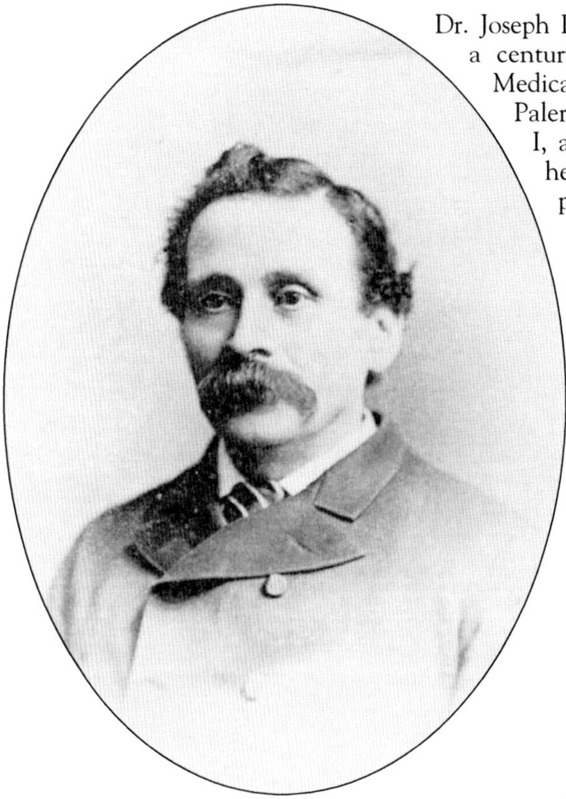

Dr. Joseph Pagani was a noted physician in Boston a century ago. A graduate of the Emulazione Medicale Societa of Rome, the University of Palermo, the Instituto Academico Umberto I, and the Sodalizio Margherita at Naples, he immigrated to Boston in 1868, and practiced medicine at 356 Hanover Street in the North End. (Courtesy of the Sammarco Family)

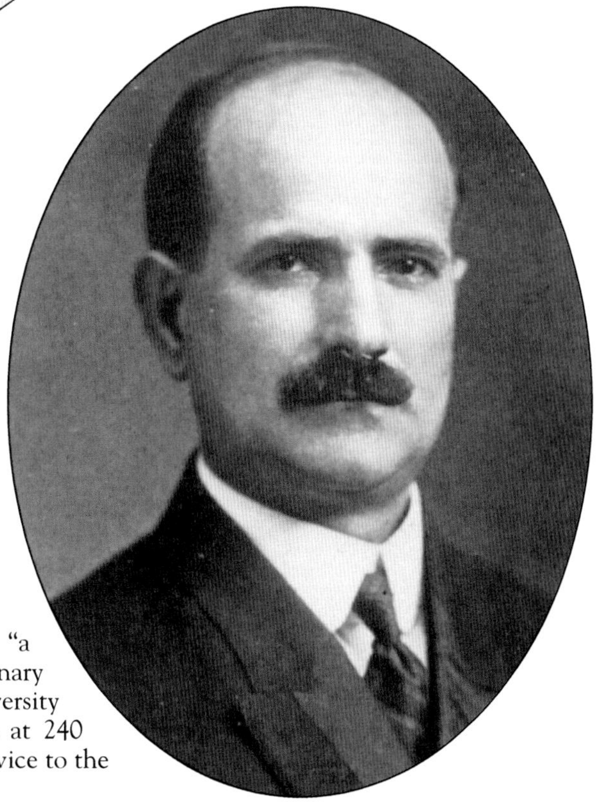

Frank M. Zottoli was described as "a criminal lawyer of more than ordinary ability." A graduate of the Boston University Law School, he kept his law offices at 240 Hanover Street and provided legal service to the community for half a century.

Marciano Di Pesa and his son Alfred ran the exclusive Hotel Napoli, a restaurant "patronized by Boston's most fastidious diners." A popular Italian restaurant, the cuisine and service was considered perfect. In addition, an orchestra rendered classical selections during the afternoon and evening.

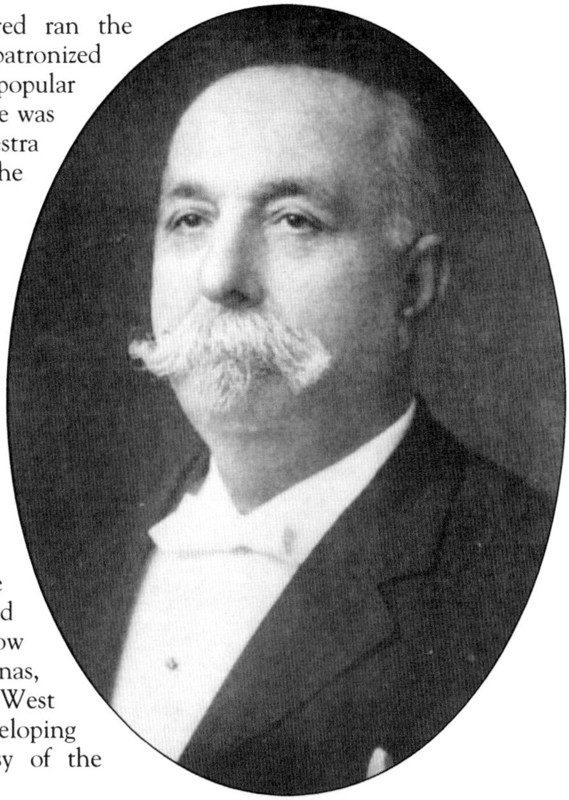

Luigi Sammarco (on the left) and workers of the United Fruit Company stand in front of a pickup truck. Since 1888, the United Fruit Company had offered Bostonians not only hands of yellow bananas but red and plantain bananas, tangerines, and oranges grown in the West Indies. United Fruit led the way in developing a market for tropical fruits. (Courtesy of the Sammarco Family)

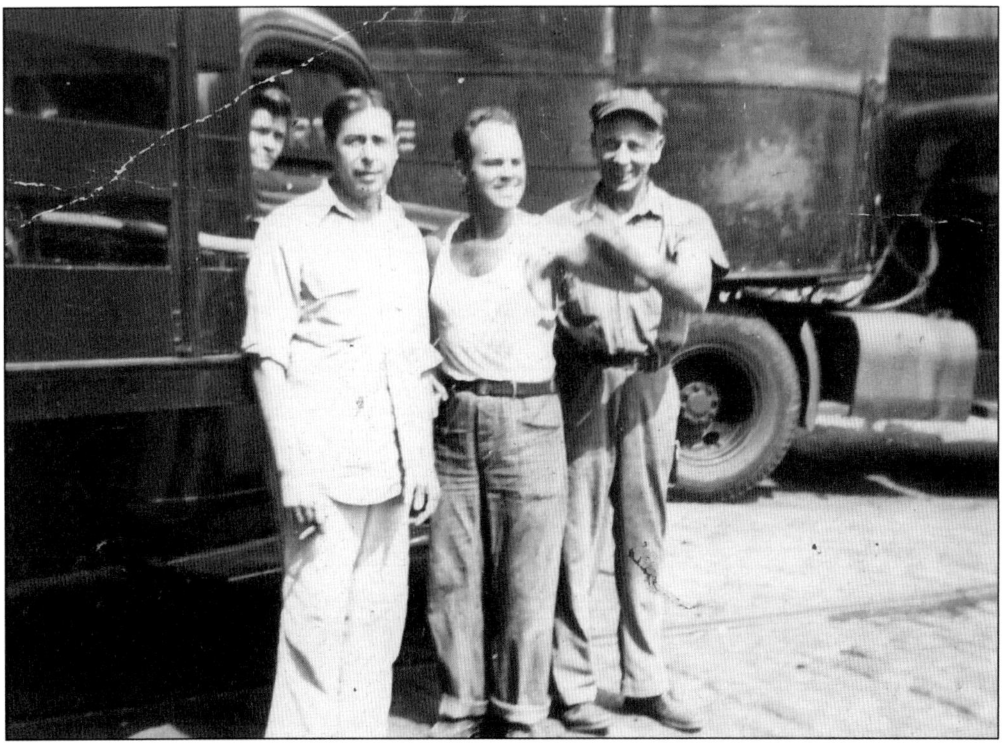

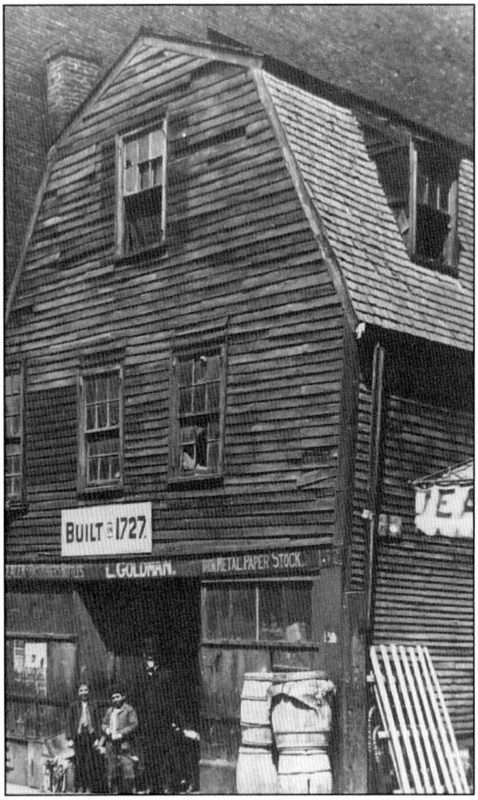

The Thoreau House was built in 1727 by an ancestor of the illustrious literary family of that name from Concord, Massachusetts. By 1910, the house had become the shop of Levi Goldman, a Jewish merchant who dealt in iron, metal, and paper stock. (Courtesy of Vito Aluia)

During the late nineteenth century, the North End was the home of immigrants from numerous European countries. Two women sit in front of 67 Salem Street, which is D. Deutsch's shop. Next door is a Jewish "Ladies & Gents Restaurant." (Courtesy of the BPL)

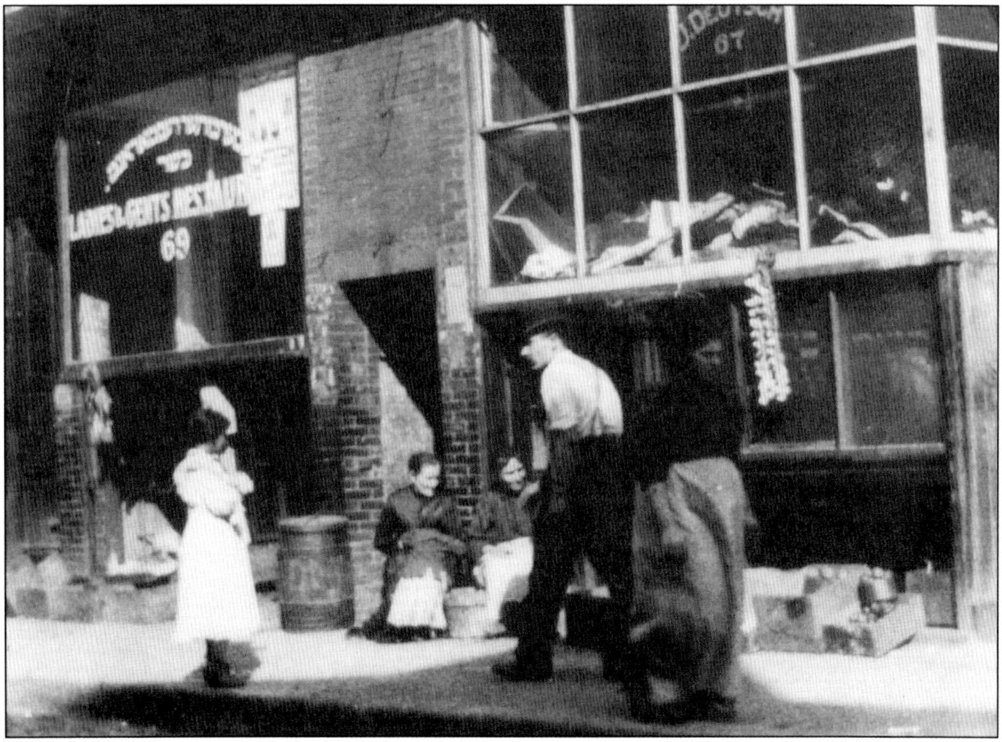

Five

Businesses and Industry History

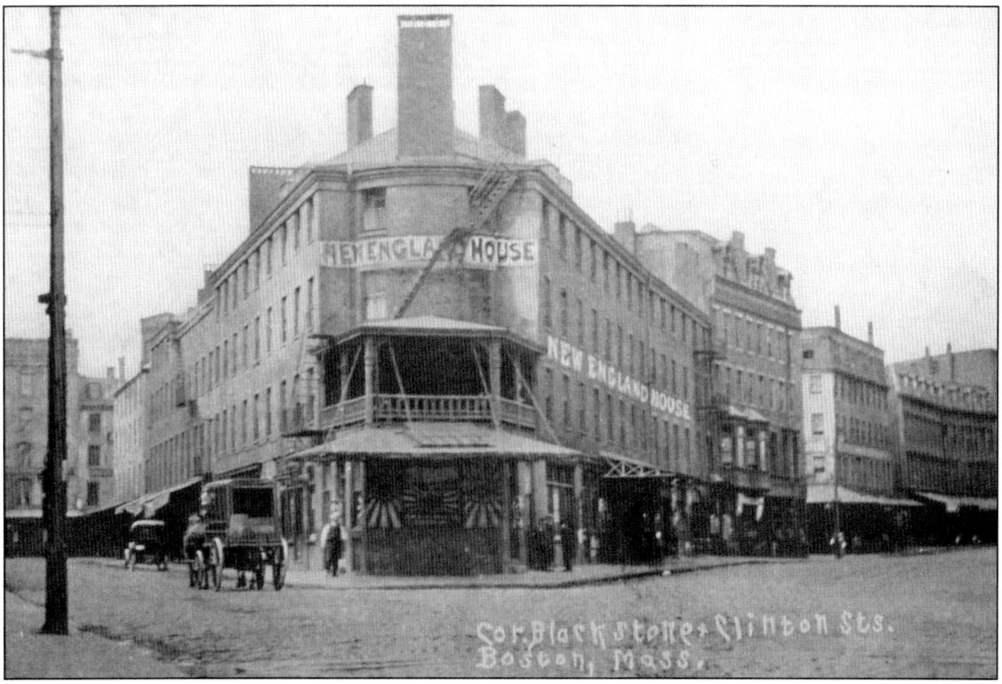

The New England House was at the corner of Blackstone and Clinton Streets. A popular hotel in the mid-nineteenth century, the New England House was one of many such establishments in Boston. (Courtesy of Vito Aluia)

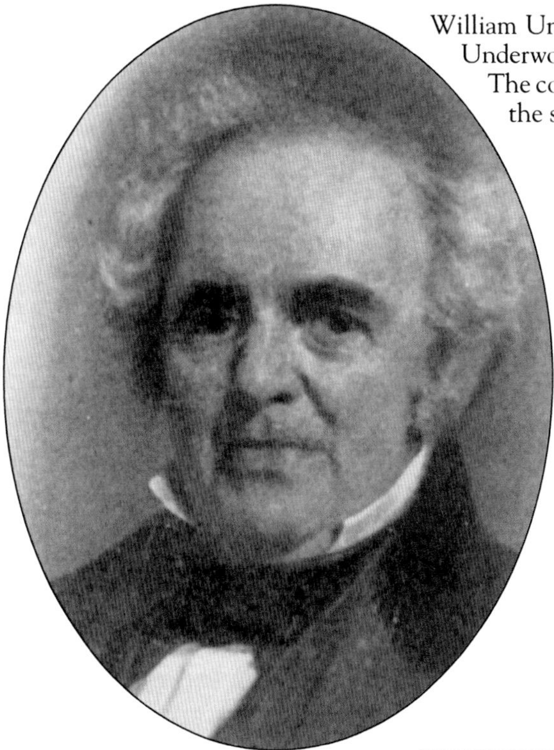

William Underwood was the founder of the William Underwood Company, located at 52 Fulton Street. The company dealt in canned foods, among them the still popular Underwood's Deviled Ham.

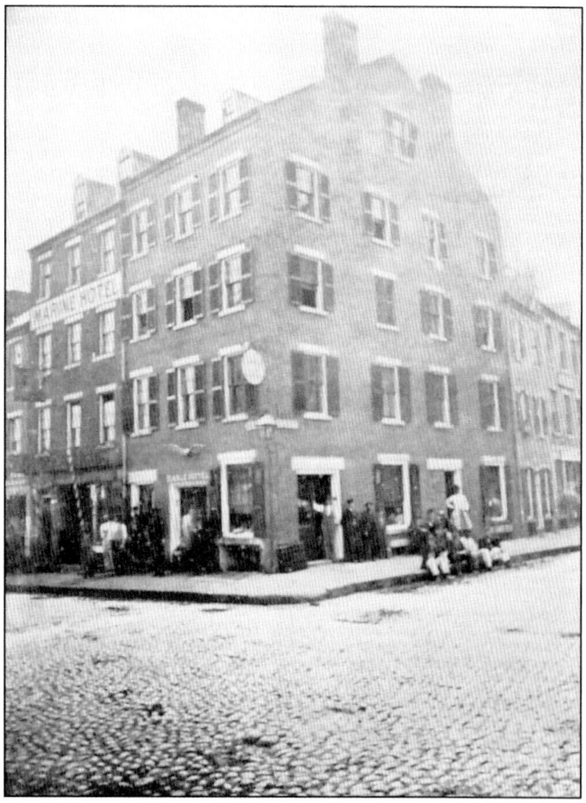

The Eagle Hotel was at the corner of Fulton and Lewis Streets, and is shown here in 1855. The Marine Hotel is on the left. (Courtesy of the BPL)

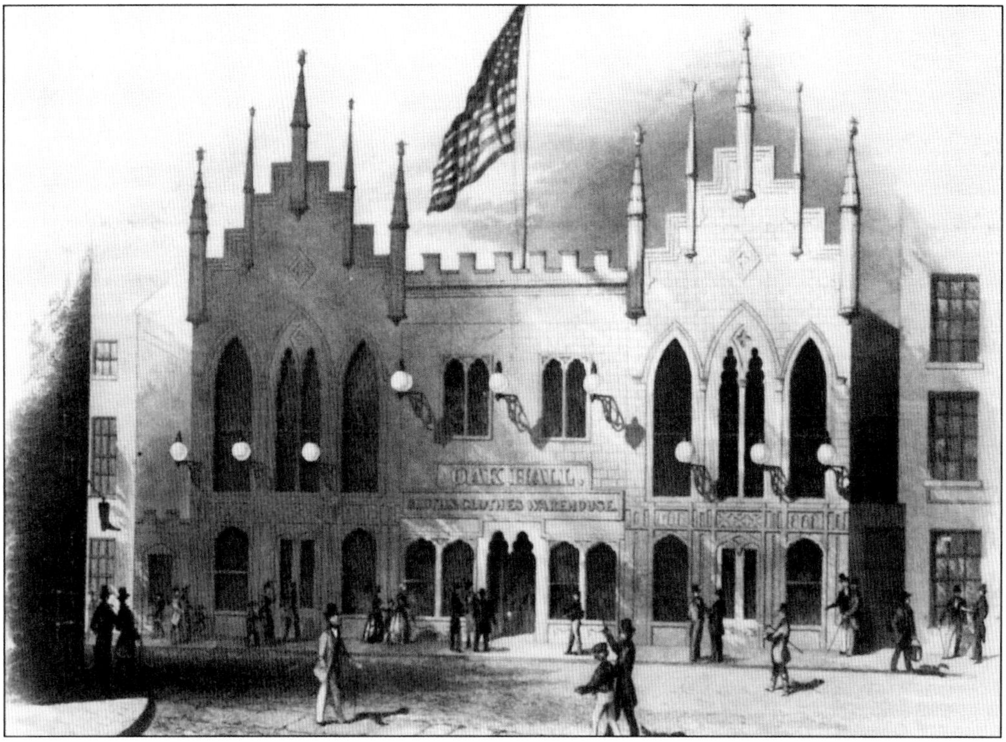

Oak Hall was a popular clothing warehouse where ready-made clothing was readily available. Its exterior facade was a crenelated and pinnacled folly with lancet windows that looked out onto Hanover Street.

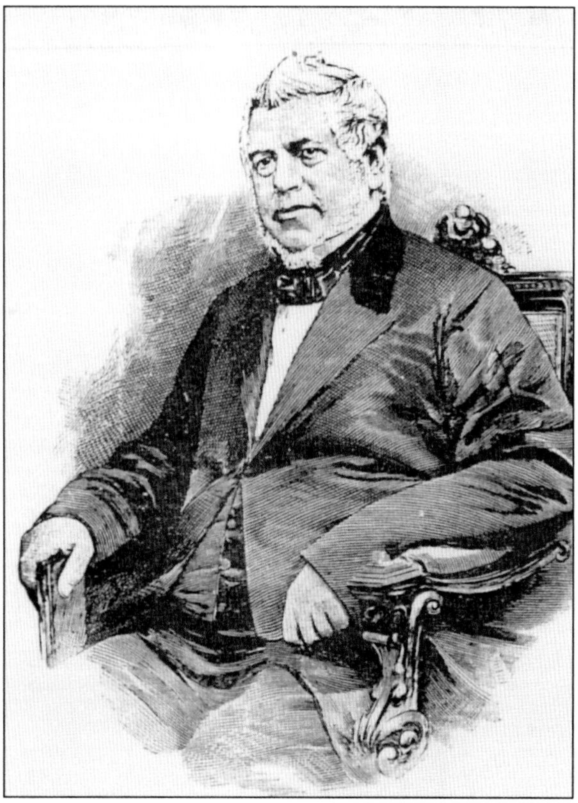

Andrew Carney (1794–1864) was an immigrant from Ireland who, along with Jacob Sleeper, opened a clothing business that was known as Carney & Sleeper. Considered "one of Boston's great Irishmen," he was the founder of Carney Hospital in 1863, whose mission was "to afford relief to the sick poor; and though it is in charge of the Sisters of Charity, it receives patients of all religious denominations. Chronic, acute, and other cases are received, contagious diseases alone excepted."

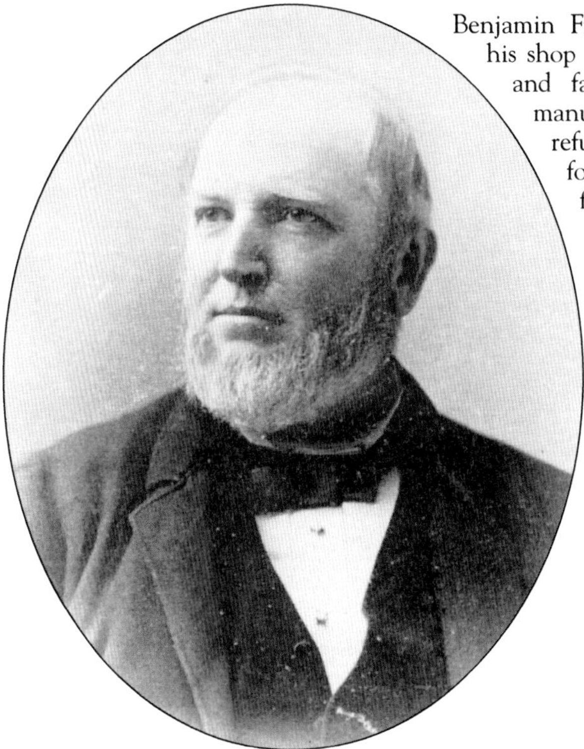

Benjamin Franklin Sturtevant revolutionized, in his shop on Sudbury Street, the mechanic arts and facilitated industrial progress in the manufacture of fans "for the removal of light refuse material from all classes of machines, for the ventilation of apartments, and for the blowing of boiler, forge and cupola fires."

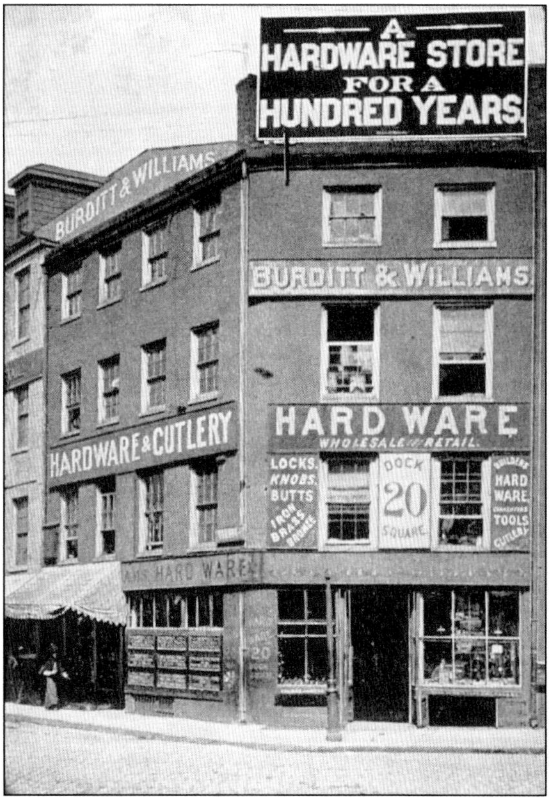

Burditt & Williams was a hardware store at 20 Dock Square that was founded in 1860. Charles A. Burditt and Joseph Williams began the store, which provided locks, knobs, butts, hardware, and tools in a building that had housed a hardware store since 1795.

James Martin & Son, founded in 1838, manufactured awnings, flags, tents, sails, and horse goods at their factory at 87–97 Richmond Street.

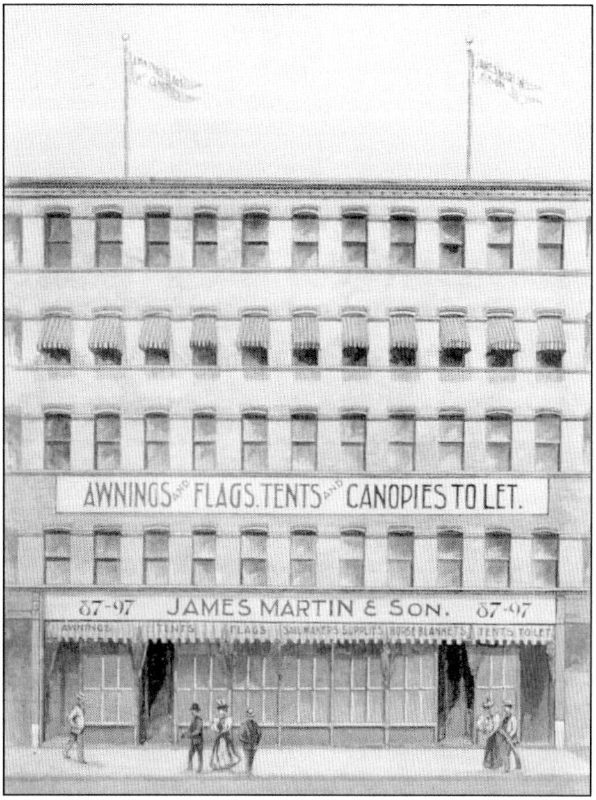

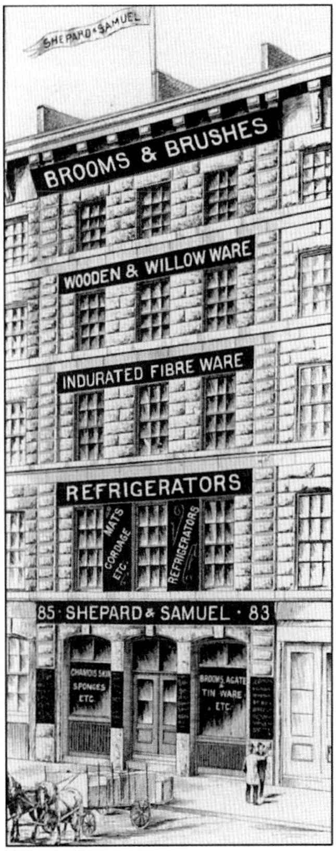

Shepard & Samuel were jobbers of brooms and brushes, wooden and willowware, indurated fibre ware and refrigerators at 83 and 85 Commercial Street.

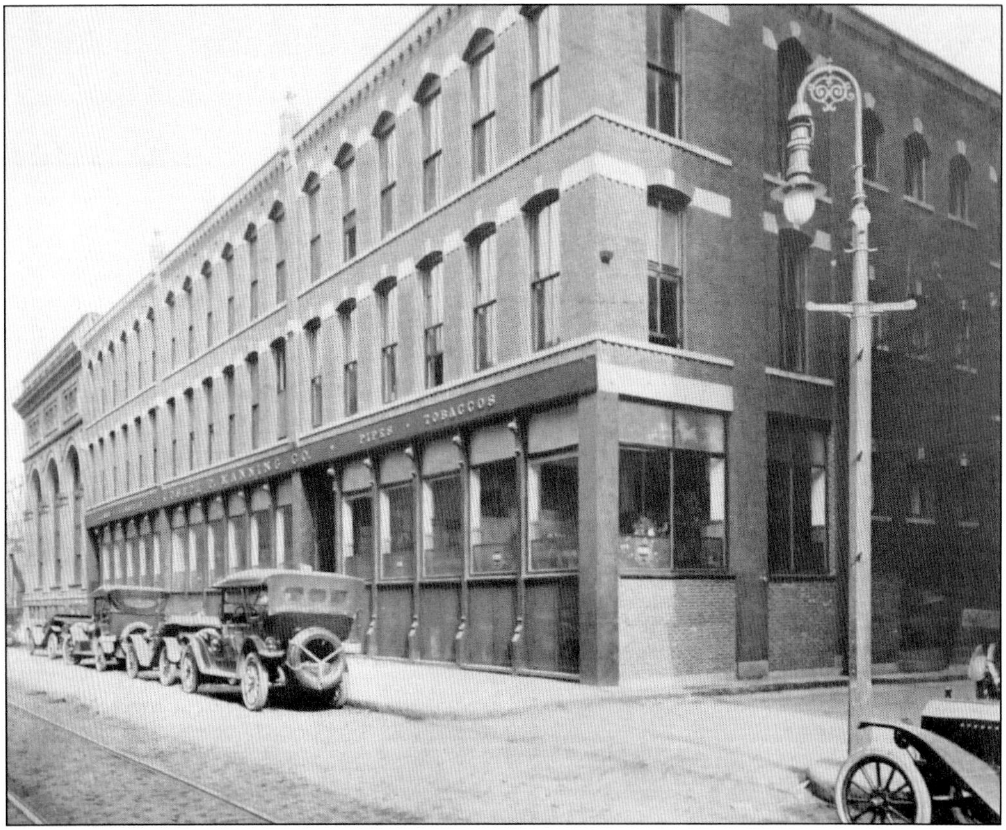

The Joseph P. Manning Company was located on Atlantic Avenue near Hanover Street. Selling pipes and tobaccos, the store was the first commercial concern in Boston to adopt automobiles for delivery service.

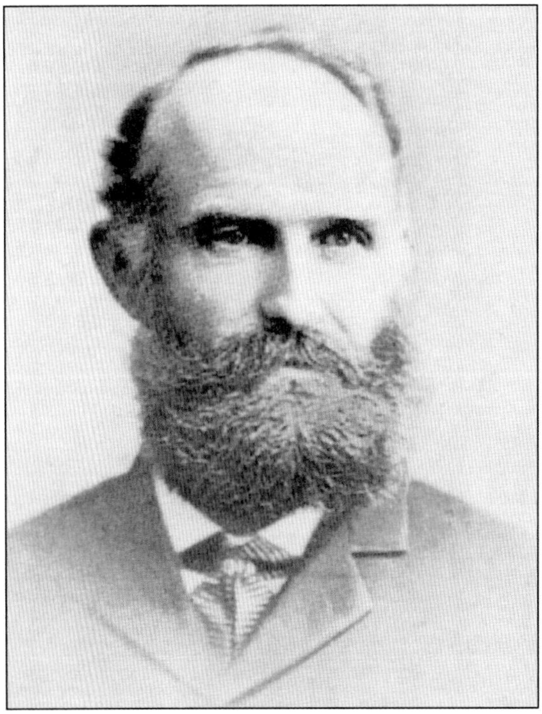

George E. Knight offered coffee and tea at his store at 87 and 89 Blackstone Street. Knight was the successor to H.P. Webster and specialized in Chase & Sanborn coffee.

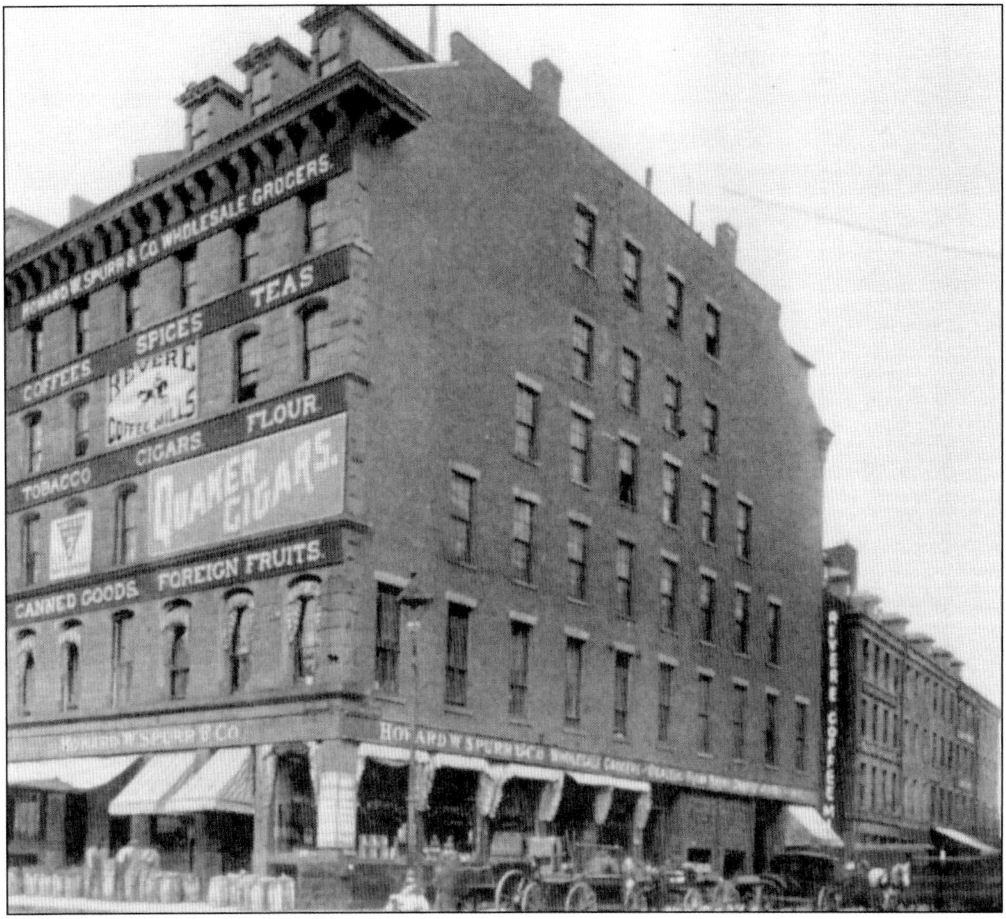

Howard W. Spurr & Company was a wholesale grocery company that was established in 1875 at 19 and 21 Commercial Street. It offered coffees, spices, and teas, as well as choice foreign fruits, canned goods, tobacco, cigars, and flour.

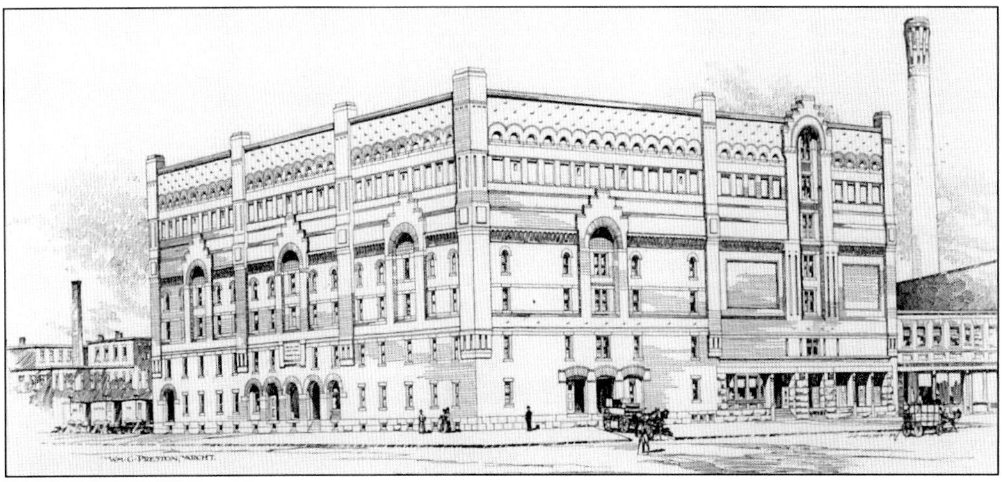

Quincy Market Cold Storage was a massive refrigerated warehouse that was built on Commercial Street in the North End.

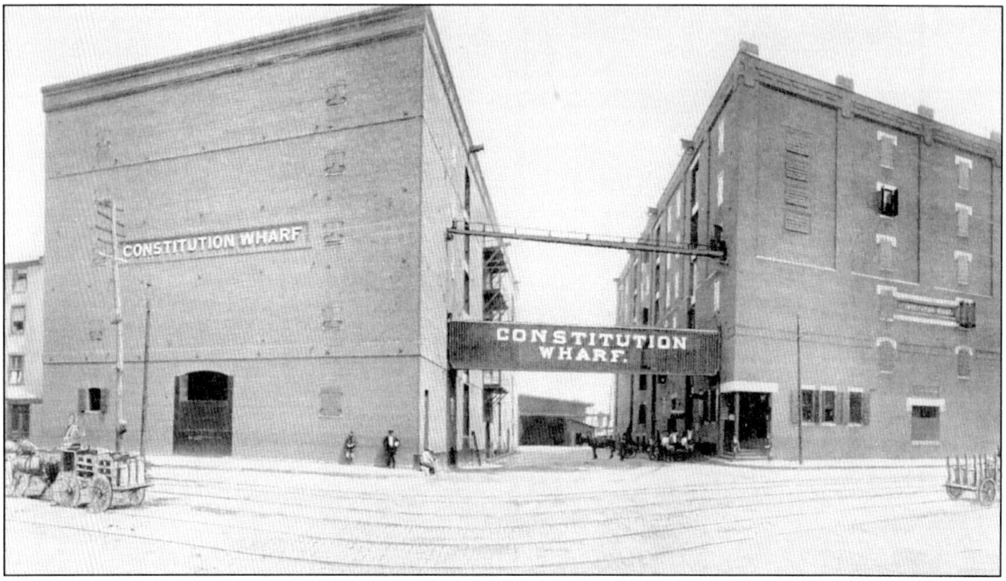

The Constitution Wharf Company was a warehouse for both bonded and free merchandise. Built on the site of the shipyard where the USS *Constitution* was built in 1797, the wharf had deep water for steamers and track connections with all railroads running from Boston.

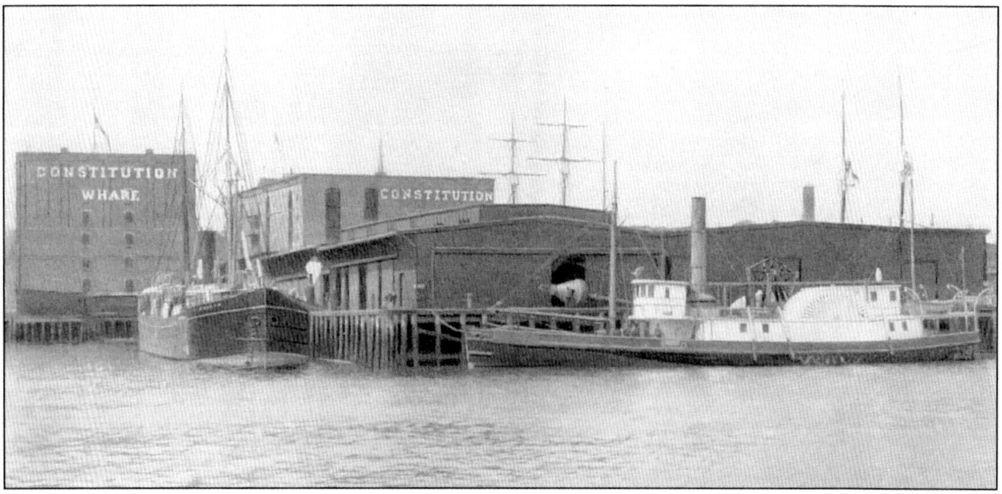

From Boston Harbor, Constitution Wharf was 460 feet long and had a covered shed for the unloading of freight. The steamer *North Gwalia* is shown on the left discharging sugar from Egypt and the steamship *Verbena*, a lighthouse tender, is on the right.

The Prince Macaroni Company, founded by Michael La Marca, Joseph Scaminara, and Michael Cantella, manufactured "Italian style" macaroni in the North End. Macaroni had been produced as early as 1874 in the North End. Among the companies shown here are the Boston Macaroni Company and the Maravigna Macaroni Company on North Street.

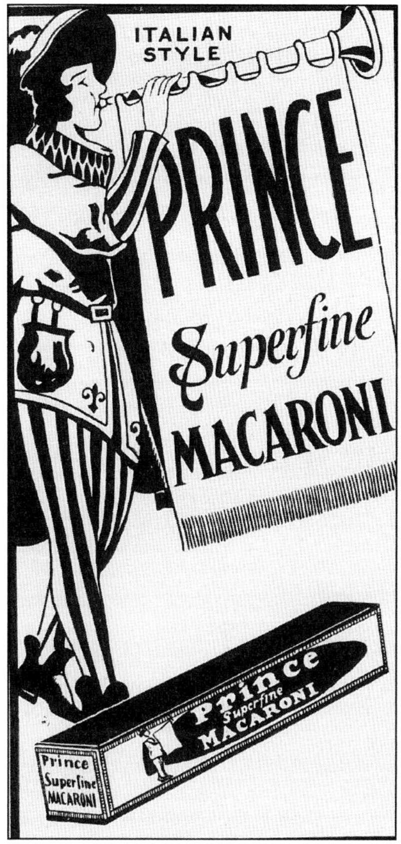

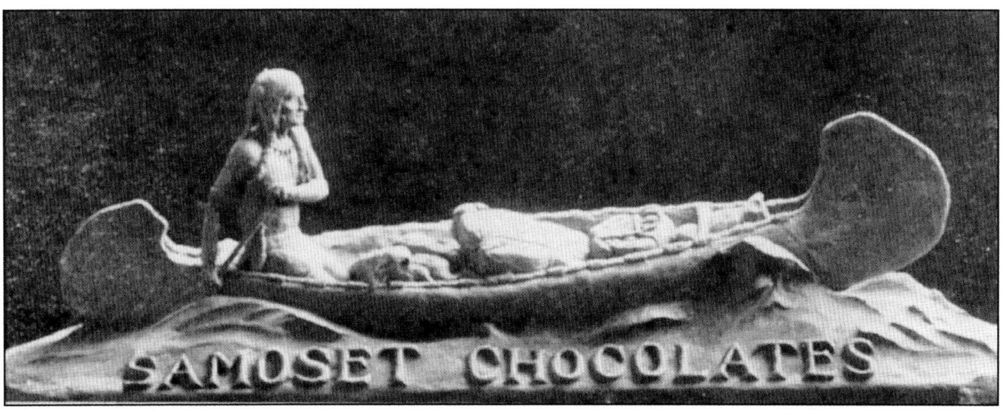

Samoset Chocolates were both pure and delicious and were considered the "chief" of all the chocolates produced in Boston. At their factory on Hanover Street, master candy makers hand-dipped creams, caramels, and fruits for a great variety and assortment of bonbons.

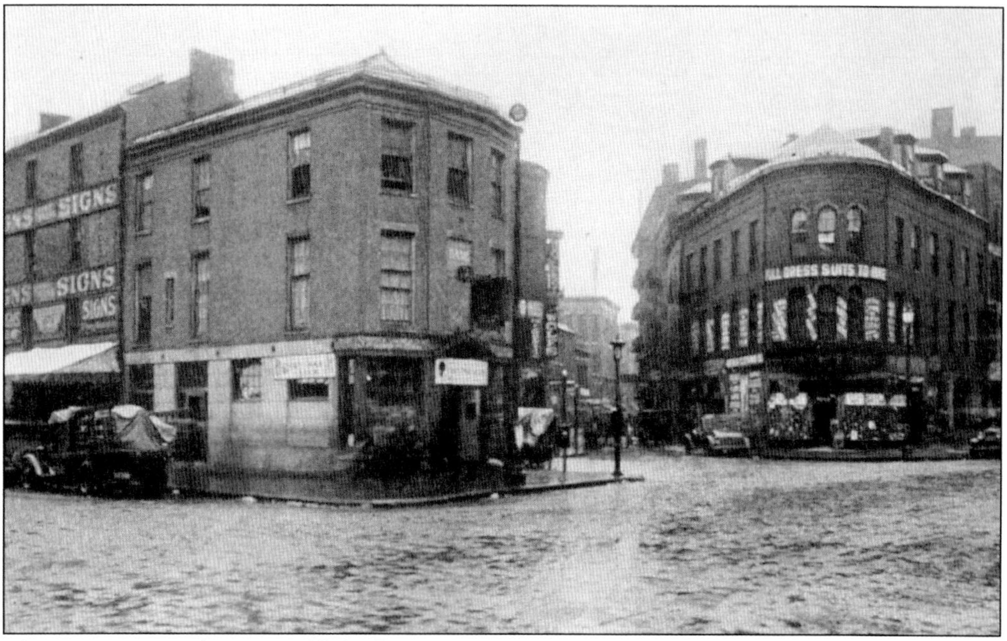

The Seamens Bank was established to encourage sailors to save the hard-earned wages they made on ocean-going voyages. The North End branch of the bank was at 158 Hanover Street.

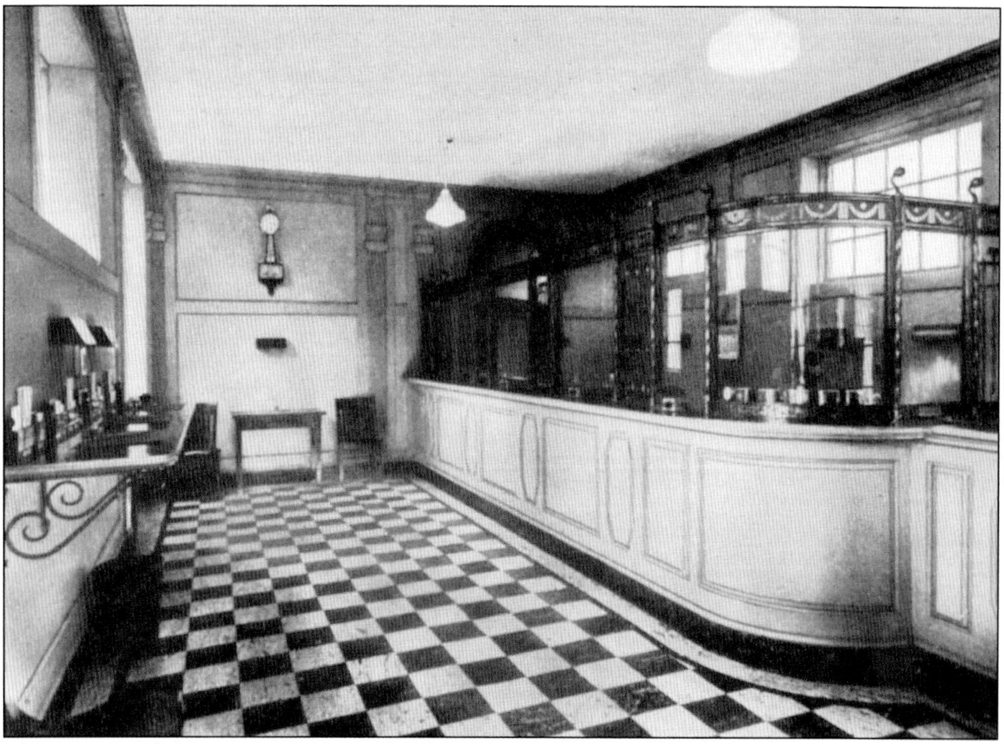

The interior of the North End branch of the Seamens Bank had teller cages on the right and a counter for the seamen account holders on the left.

Six

The Neighborhood

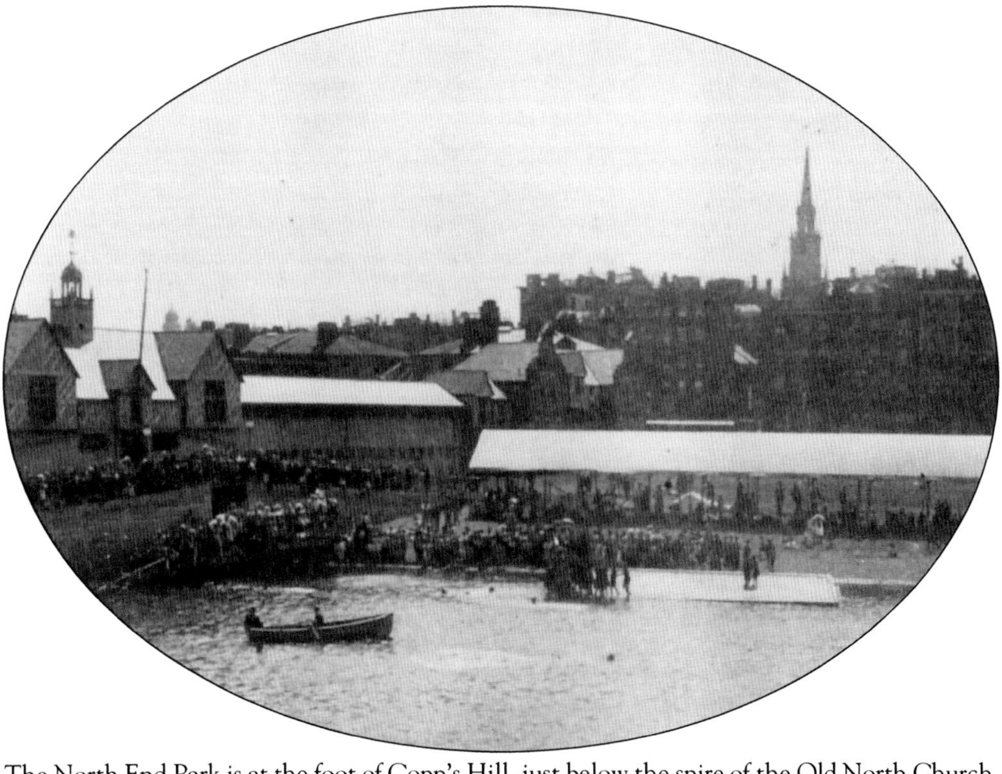

The North End Park is at the foot of Copp's Hill, just below the spire of the Old North Church. The park had a beach, laundry, women's building, and a children's tent for residents of the North End.

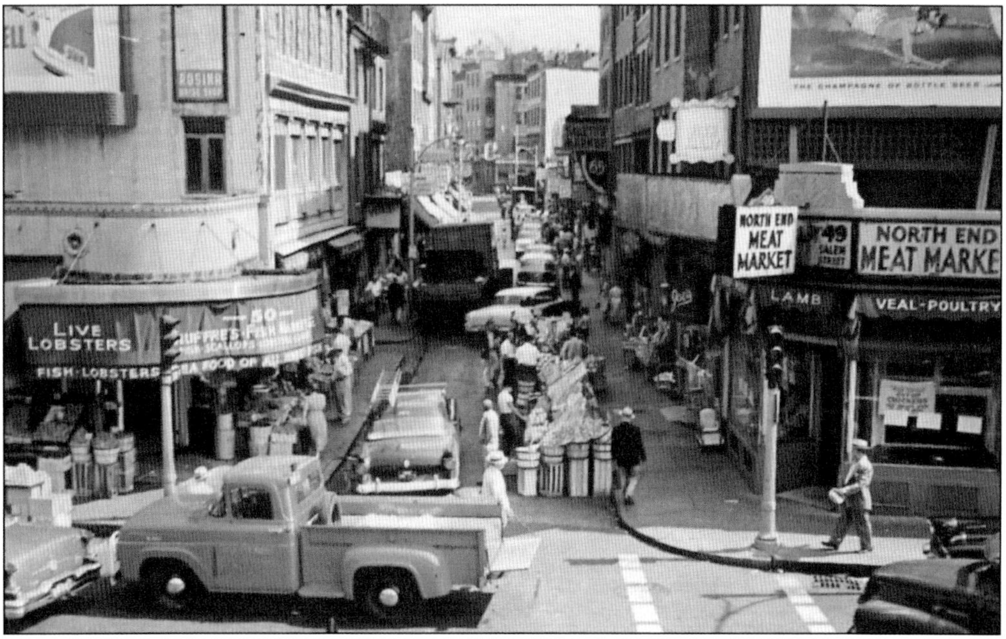

Salem Street at Cross Street has been a bustling intersection since the nineteenth century. In this *c.* 1950 photograph, street vendors display fresh fruits and vegetables while shops offer live lobsters, fish, lamb, veal, and poultry. (Courtesy of Vito Aluia)

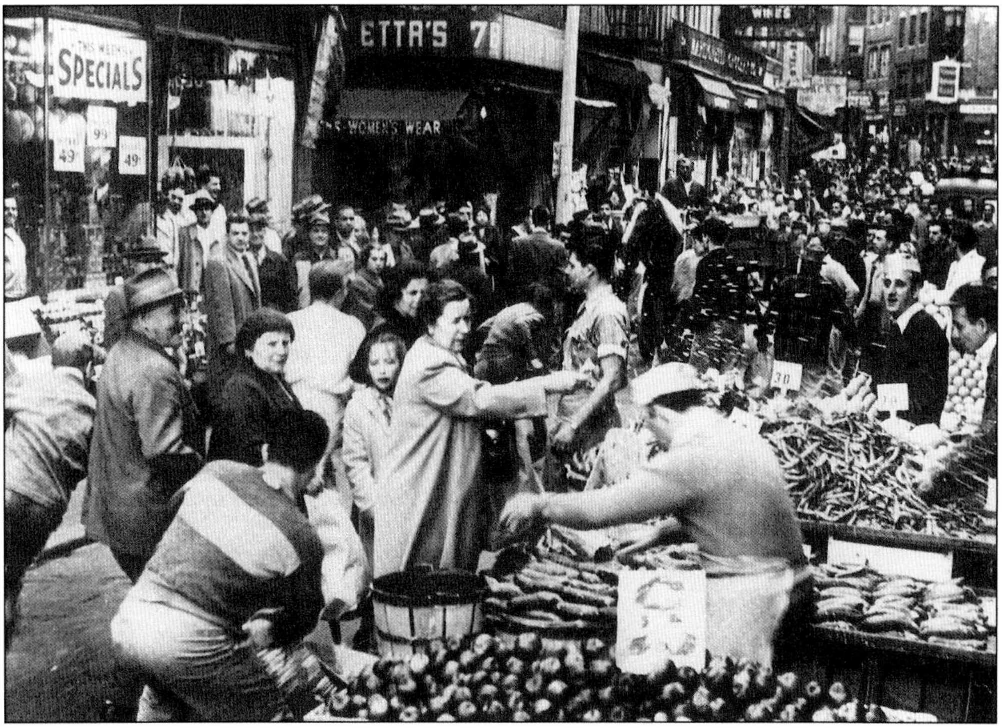

Street vendors on Salem Street offered their produce in wood baskets heaped full of fresh fruits and vegetables. On weekends, the crowds shopping in the North End were so large that there was little, if any, room to move, let alone shop.

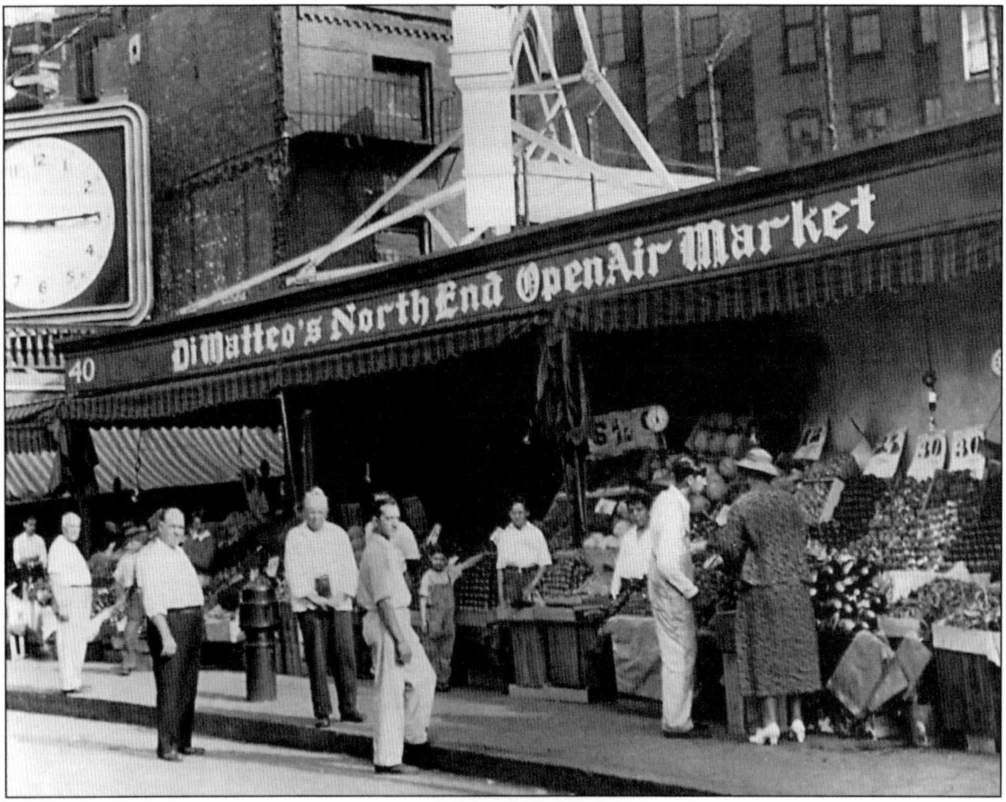

Di Matteo's North End open-air market was on Cross Street, near Salem Street. (Courtesy of Pizzeria Regina North End)

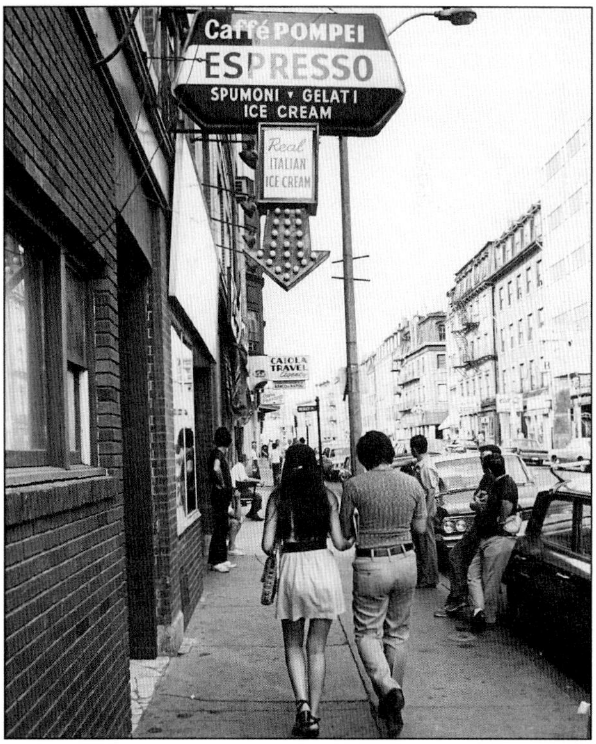

A young couple strolls down Hanover Street in the early 1970s. Caffe Pompei, a tradition in the North End, offers not only coffee and espresso but spumoni, gelati, and ice cream. (Courtesy of the BPL)

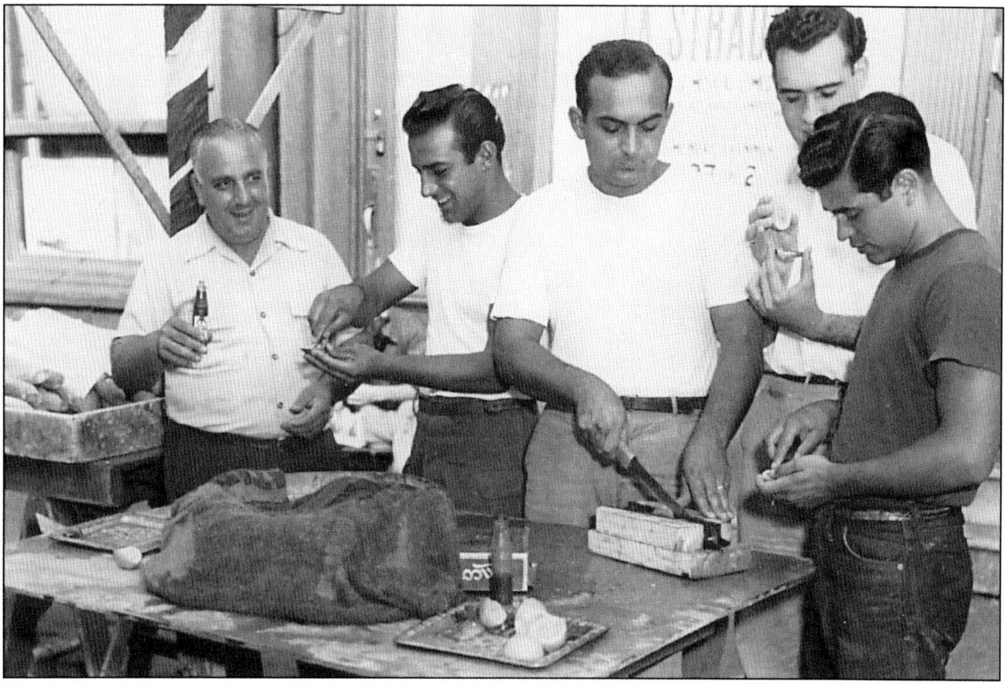

A street vendor is opening fresh clams at a street corner in the North End in the early 1950s. Fresh oysters and cherrystone clams have been sold *al fresco* for centuries; with a squirt of lemon juice or a dash of tabasco, what could be better? (Courtesy of Pizzeria Regina)

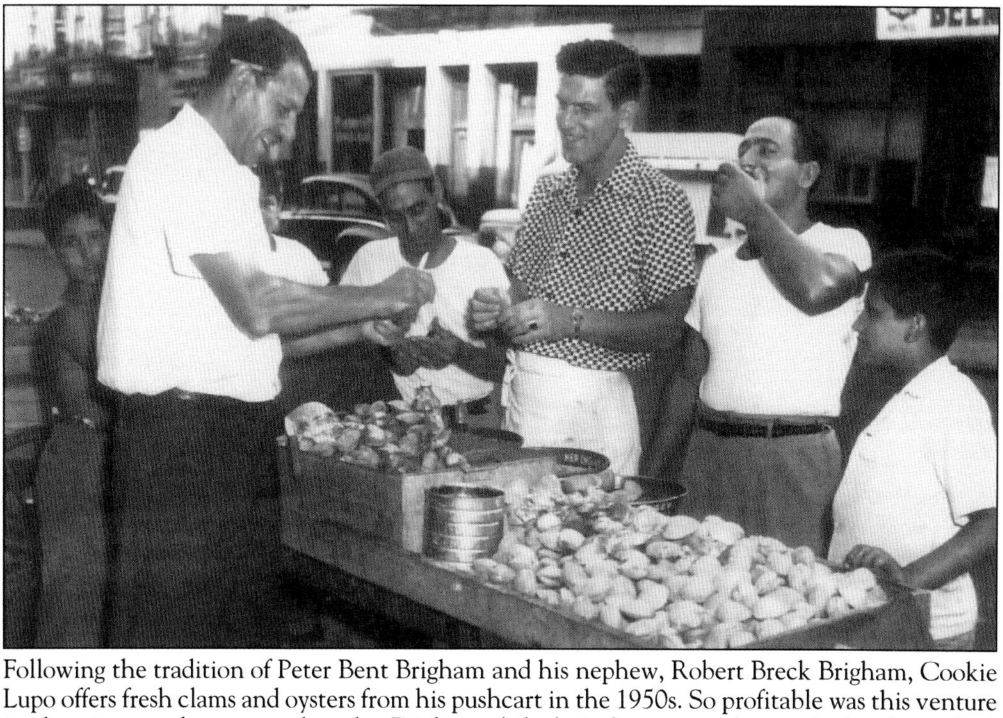

Following the tradition of Peter Bent Brigham and his nephew, Robert Breck Brigham, Cookie Lupo offers fresh clams and oysters from his pushcart in the 1950s. So profitable was this venture in the nineteenth century that the Brighams left their fortunes to hospitals that bore their names in everlasting gratitude. (Courtesy of Pizzaria Regina)

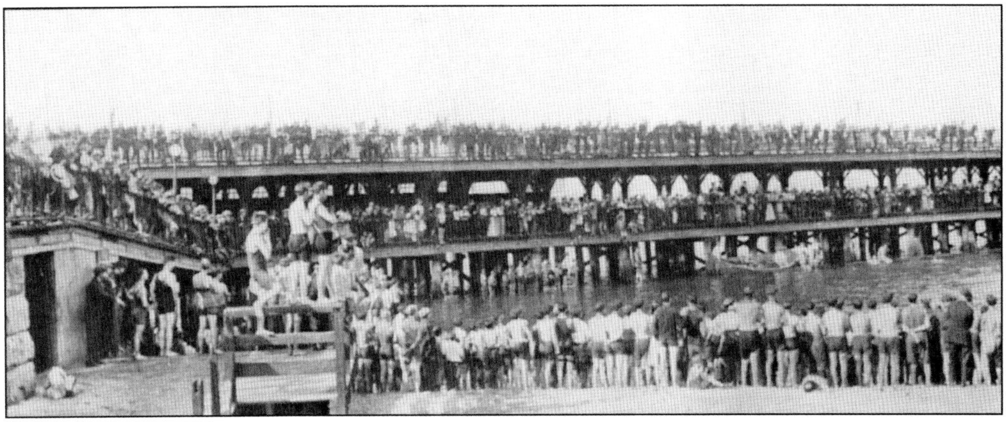

A city swimming meet at the North End Park in 1912 brought spectators from near and far. Many of the spectators line the bridge crossing the Charles River that connects the North End and Charlestown.

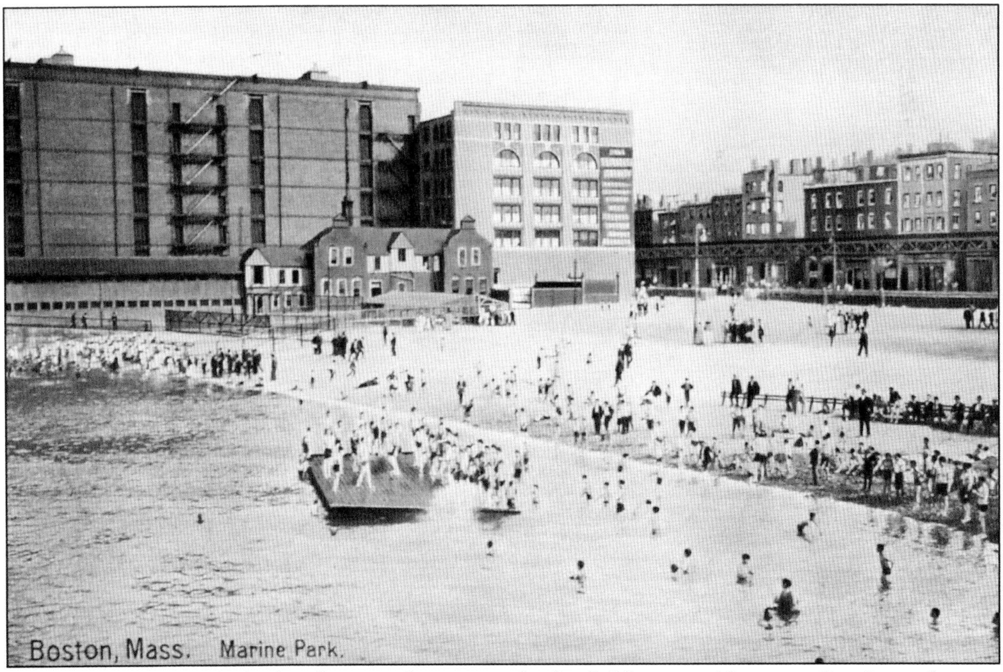

The North End Park had a floating barge to which children could swim. On the right can be seen the tracks of the Elevated Railway that connected South and North Stations along Atlantic Avenue and Commercial Street. (Courtesy of Vito Aluia)

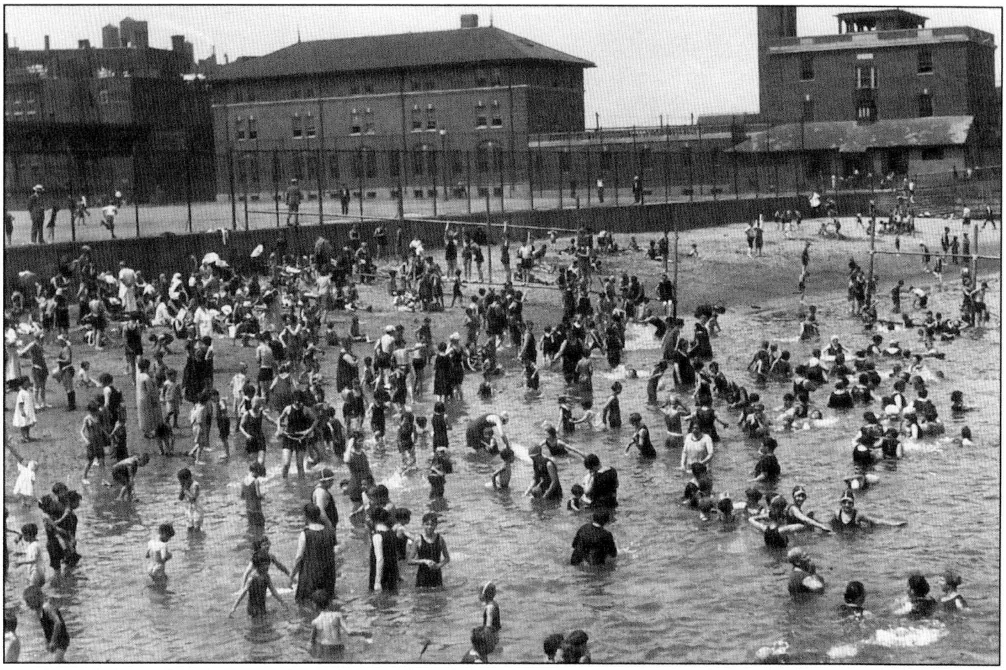

In the 1930s, children and adults cool off during a hot summer day at the North End Park. (Courtesy of the BPL)

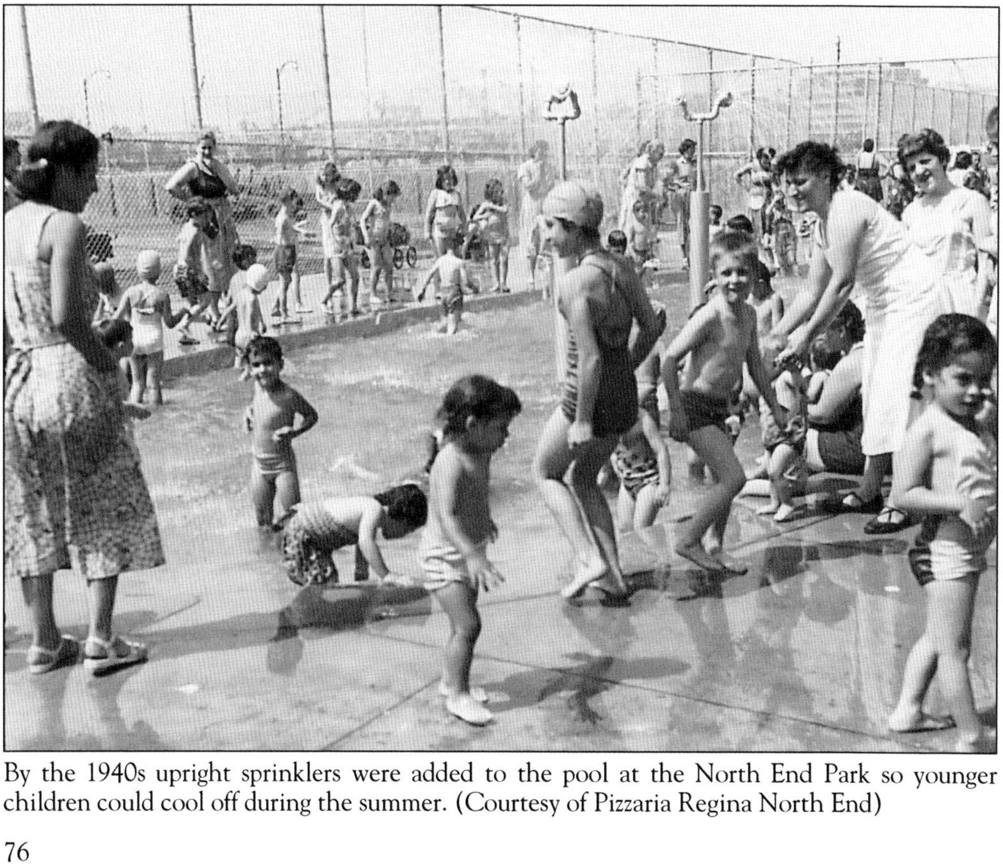

By the 1940s upright sprinklers were added to the pool at the North End Park so younger children could cool off during the summer. (Courtesy of Pizzaria Regina North End)

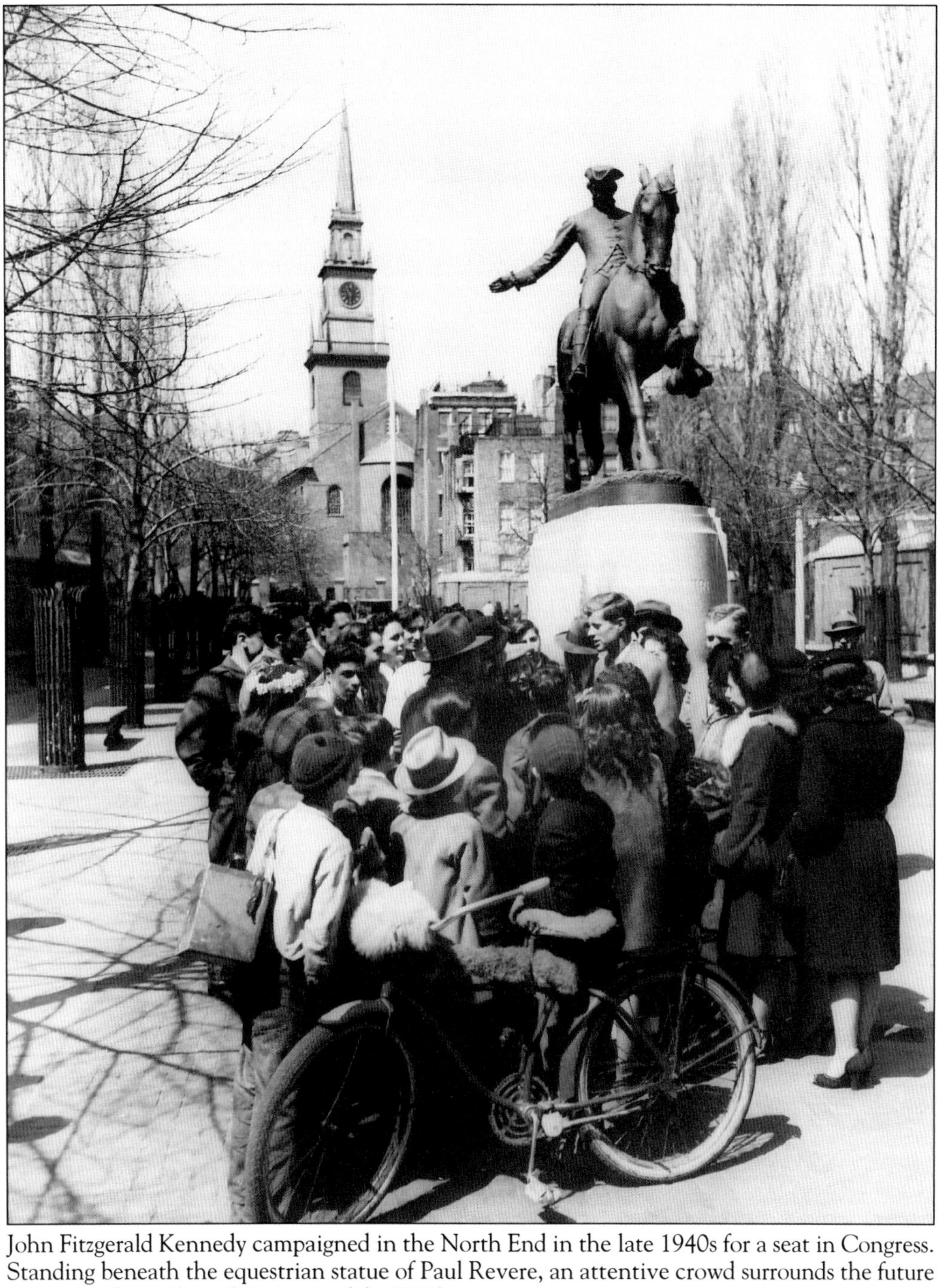

John Fitzgerald Kennedy campaigned in the North End in the late 1940s for a seat in Congress. Standing beneath the equestrian statue of Paul Revere, an attentive crowd surrounds the future senator and president. (Courtesy of the BPL)

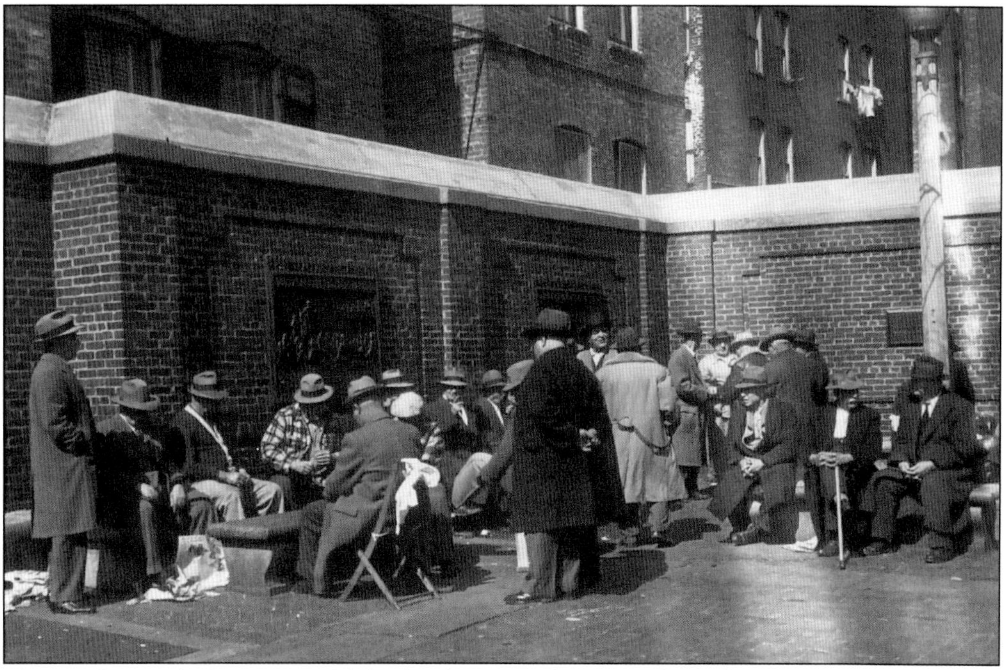

The Prado was laid out in 1933 by landscape architect Arthur Shurcliff as an open space connecting Hanover and Unity Streets. Known as Webster Avenue, it was one of the narrowest lanes in Boston. On the brick walls surrounding the prado were mounted plaques designed by Robert Savage Chase that recount the history of the North End. A group of men play cards and chat while enjoying the early spring sunshine in the early 1940s. (Courtesy of the BPL)

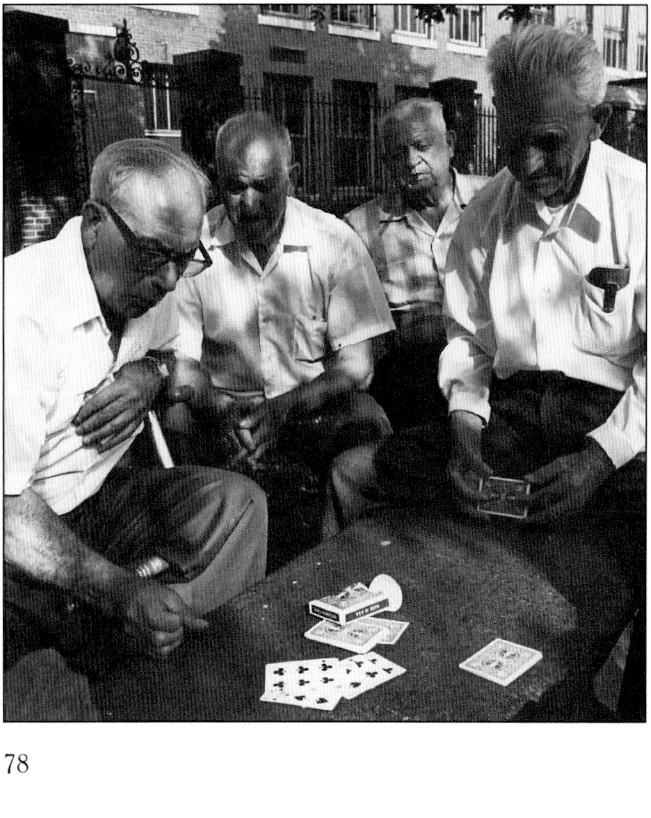

A group of men play cards in a corner of the Prado in 1970. (Courtesy of the BPL)

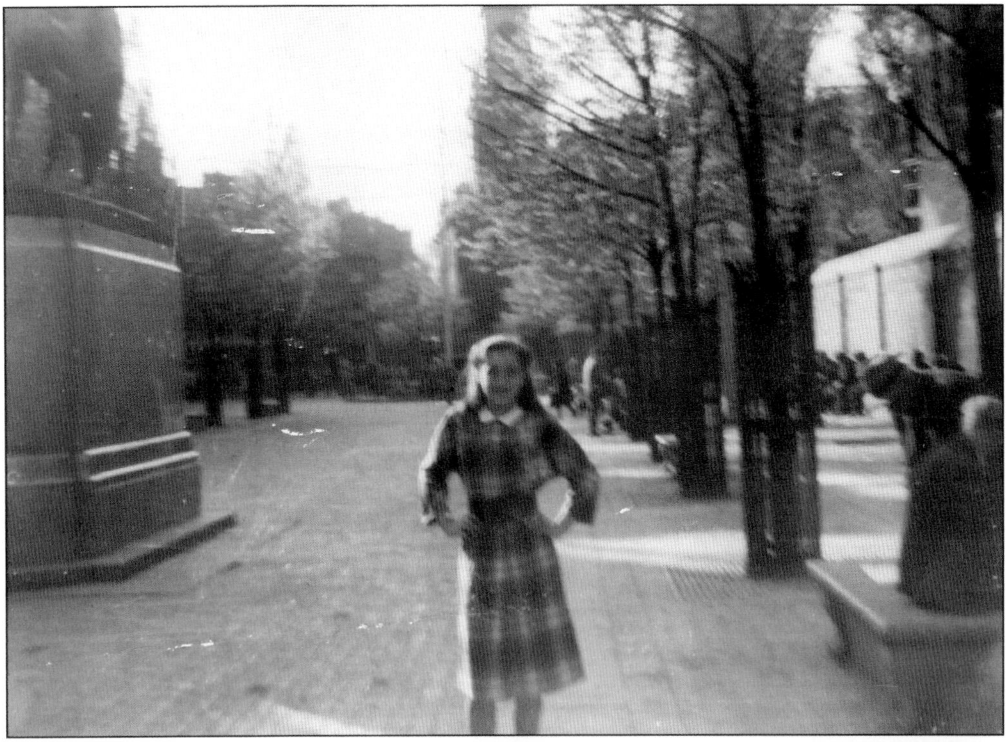

A neighborhood girl models a new frock in the Prado beside the statue of Paul Revere in the mid-1950s. The statue had been modeled by Cyrus E. Dallin in 1885 and was cast in bronze in 1940 through the generosity of the George Robert White Fund. (Courtesy of the BPL)

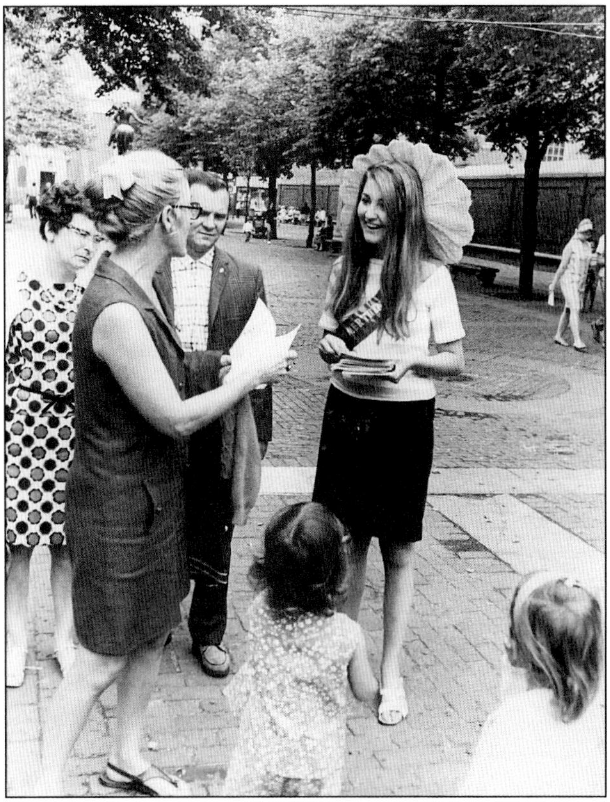

Summerthing was a popular neighborhood arts festival instituted by Mayor Kevin H. White. A young member of the Summerthing staff has a knitted sunray, the logo of Summerthing, on her head as she distributes leaflets on the annual summer activities. Since 1968, over fifteen hundred performances and events have been held. (Courtesy of the BPL)

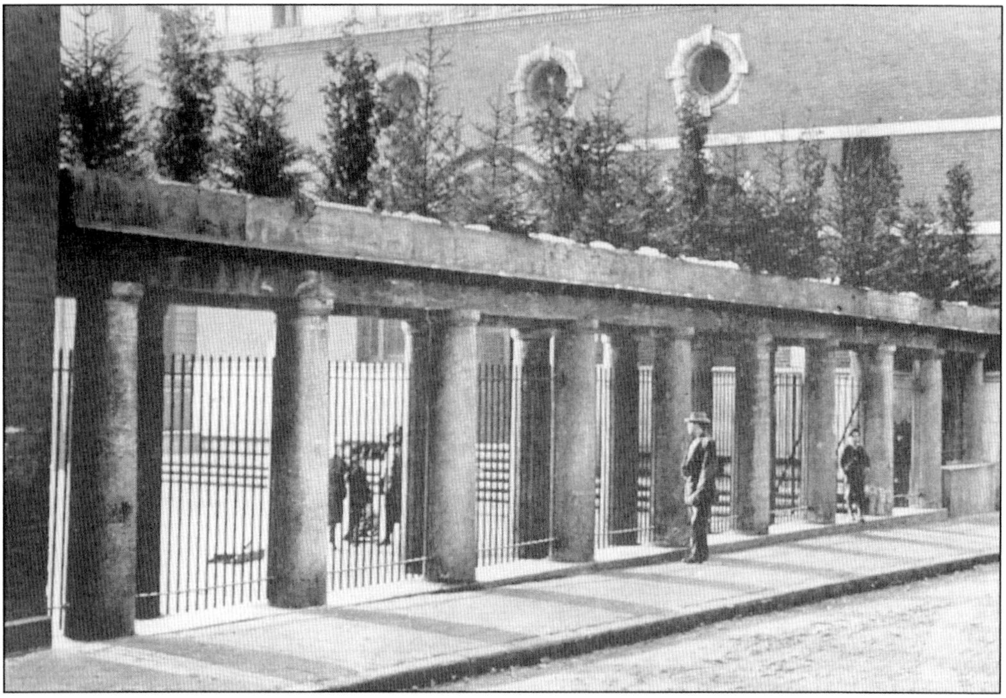

The Prince Street Playground was an open area that allowed children to play away from traffic in the street. A pergola of Doric columns separated the playground from the roadway, and fir trees were added along the top for greenery.

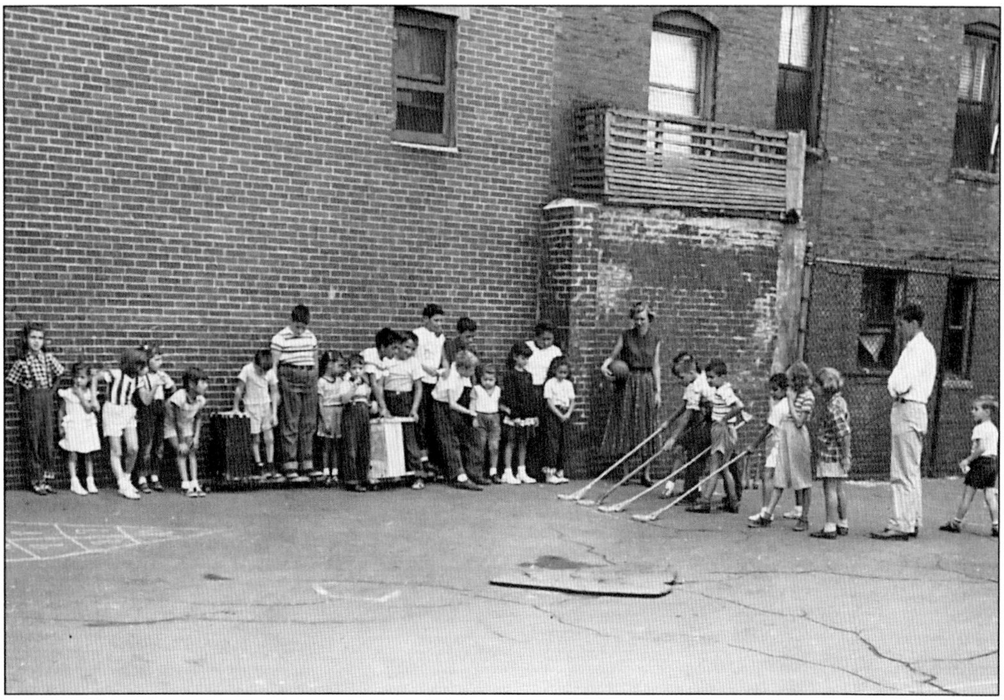

Children play shuffleboard at the North Bennett Street Playground in the mid-1950s. (Courtesy of Pizzaria Regina North End)

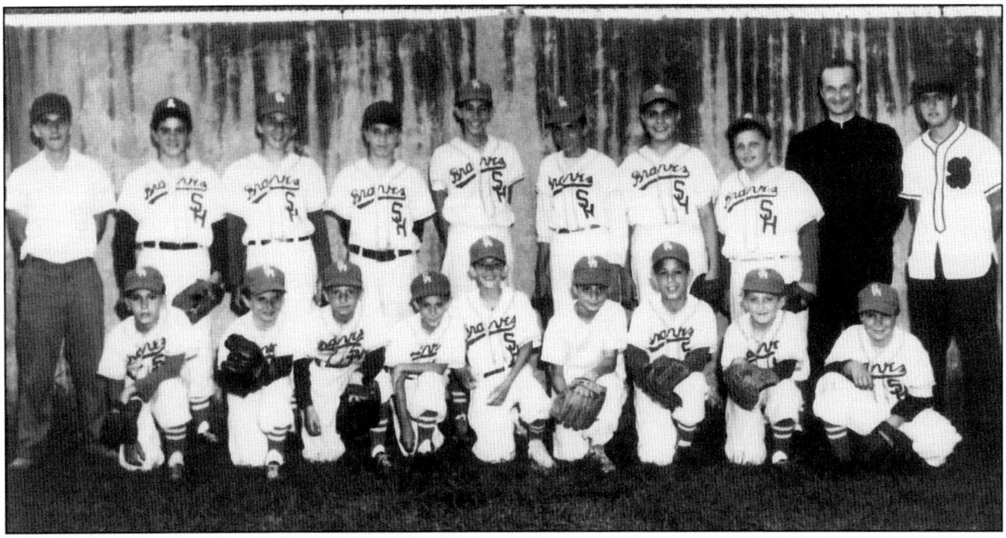

The Sacred Heart Braves were a baseball team made up of boys from the North End. From left to right are as follows: (front row) Dennis Lepore, Roger Ruggerio, Gaspar Ostuni, Vito Aluia, Charlie Marino, Steve Messina, John Sergi, Carmine "Tilly Rags" De Martino, and Mike Bono; (back row) Peter Carcia, William Demarco, Sal Carcia, Lenny Lepore, Sammy "Eight Ball" Marino, Domenic "Jr" Santoro, Anthony Pino, John Casali, Father Jerry from Sacred Heart Church, and Anthony Gaeta. (Courtesy of Vito Aluia)

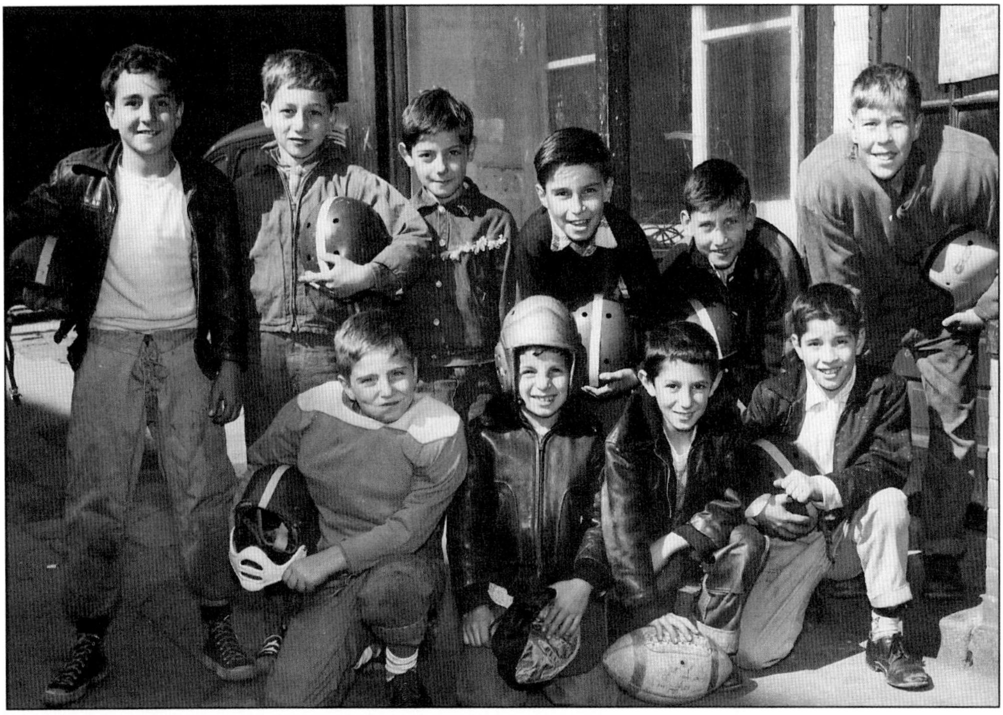

Neighborhood boys pose after having enjoyed a game of football in North Square. From left to right are as follows: (front row) Joe Palazzola, Frank Annese, Vito Aluia, and Paul Scola; (back row) Ritchie Longo, Anthony Indelicato, Donald Zona, Vinny D'Antonio, Albert Firicano, and Ralph Salvati. (Courtesy of Vito Aluia)

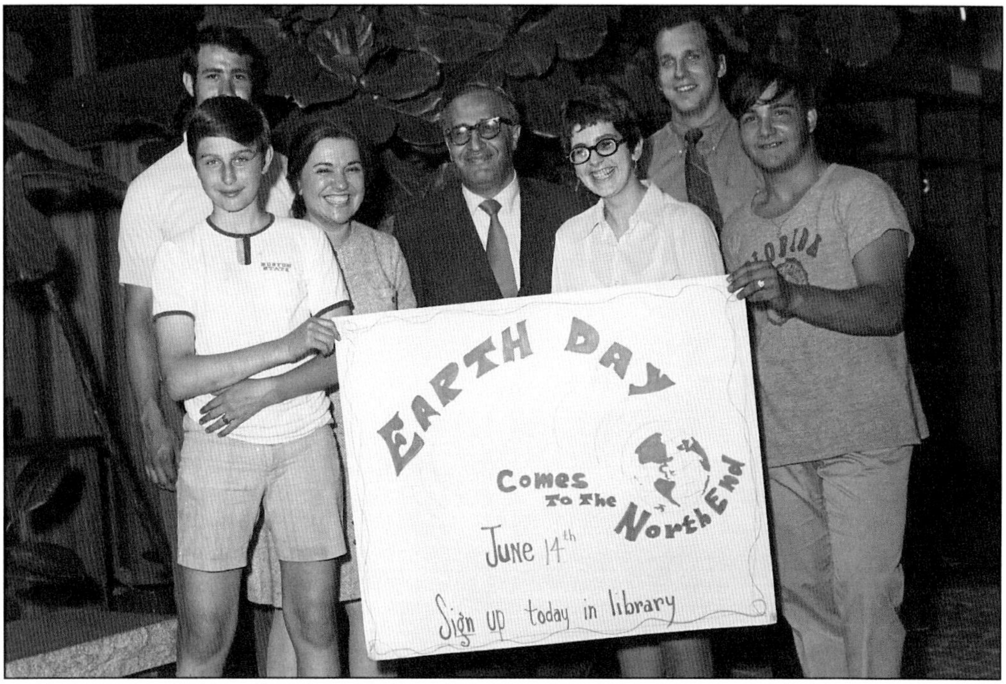

Earth Day was celebrated in the North End on June 14, 1970. Participants hold a banner urging residents to sign up for activities at the North End Branch of the Boston Public Library. John Catilo is in the front on the right; in the rear are Robert La Rocco and Charlie Falco, director of the North End Little City Hall. (Courtesy of the BPL)

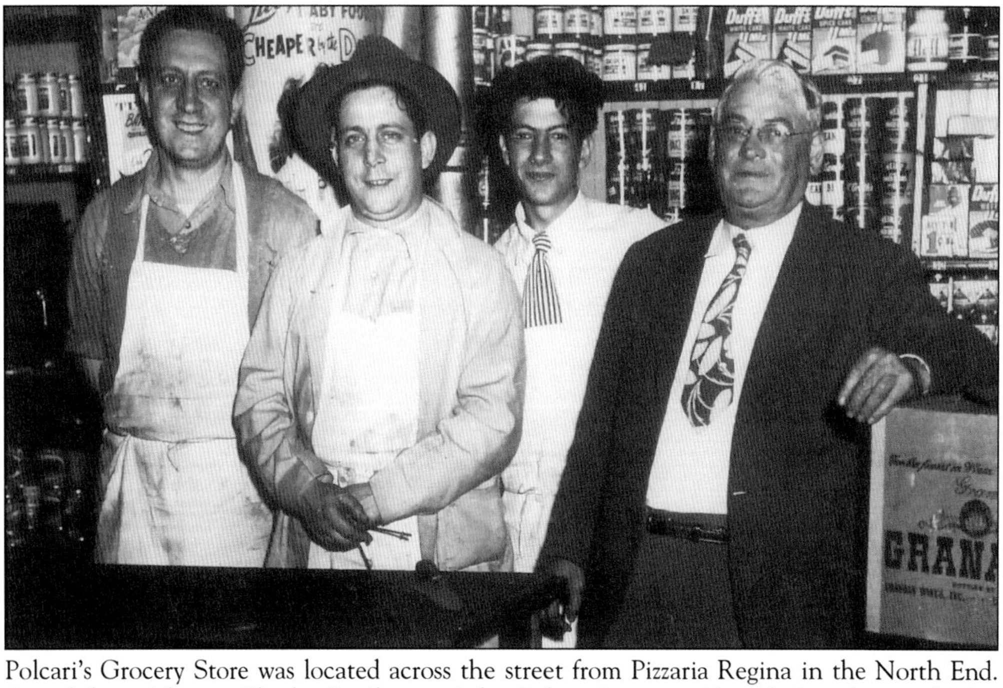

Polcari's Grocery Store was located across the street from Pizzaria Regina in the North End. From left to right are Charles Bevilacqua, John Polcari Jr., an unidentified worker, and John Polcari Sr. (Courtesy of Pizzeria Regina North End)

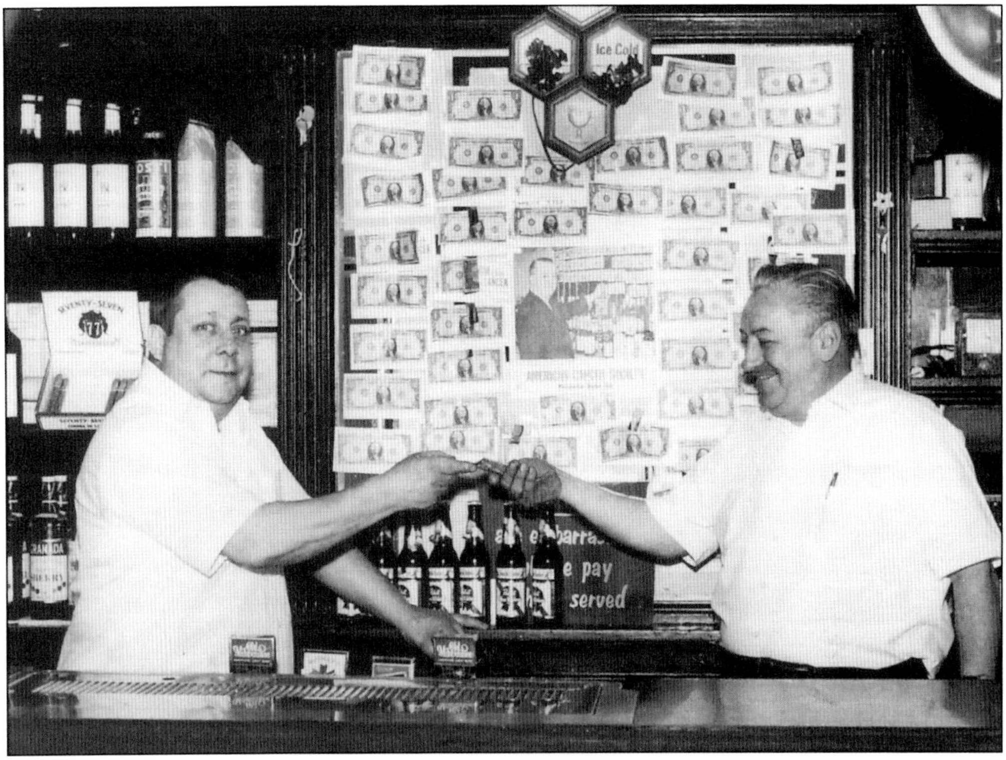

Polcari's annually raised money for the American Cancer Society from patrons who often became more generous as closing time approached. Holding a contribution are Domenic Sammarco (left) and Anthony Polcari. (Courtesy of Pizzeria Regina North End)

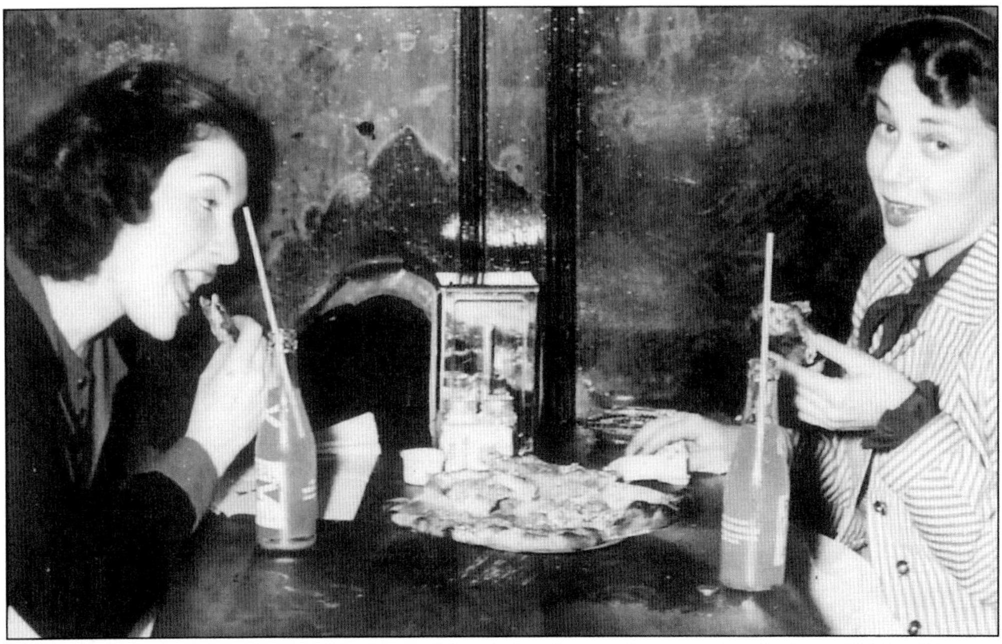

A small cheese pizza and a bottle of ice cold soda has been a favorite lunch since 1926 at Pizzeria Regina. Believe me! (Courtesy of Pizzeria Regina North End)

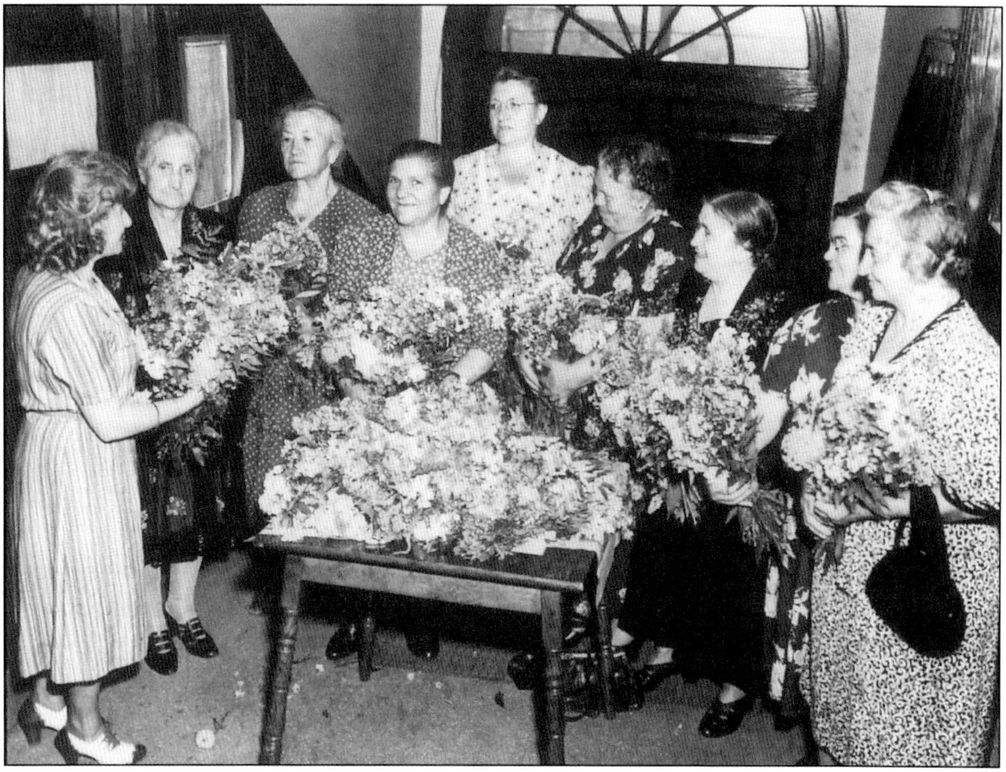

The Grandmother's Club poses in the lobby of the North End Union in the late 1950s. What grandmother doesn't deserve a bouquet of flowers? (Courtesy of Pizzeria Regina North End)

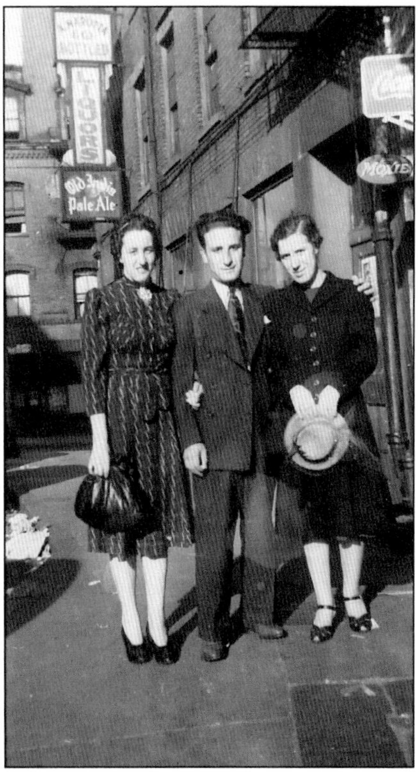

Standing in North Square in the late 1940s are Kay Scola (left), Leo Romano, and his sister, Mary Della Soccorsa Aluia. (Courtesy of Vito Aluia)

Seven

The Feasts

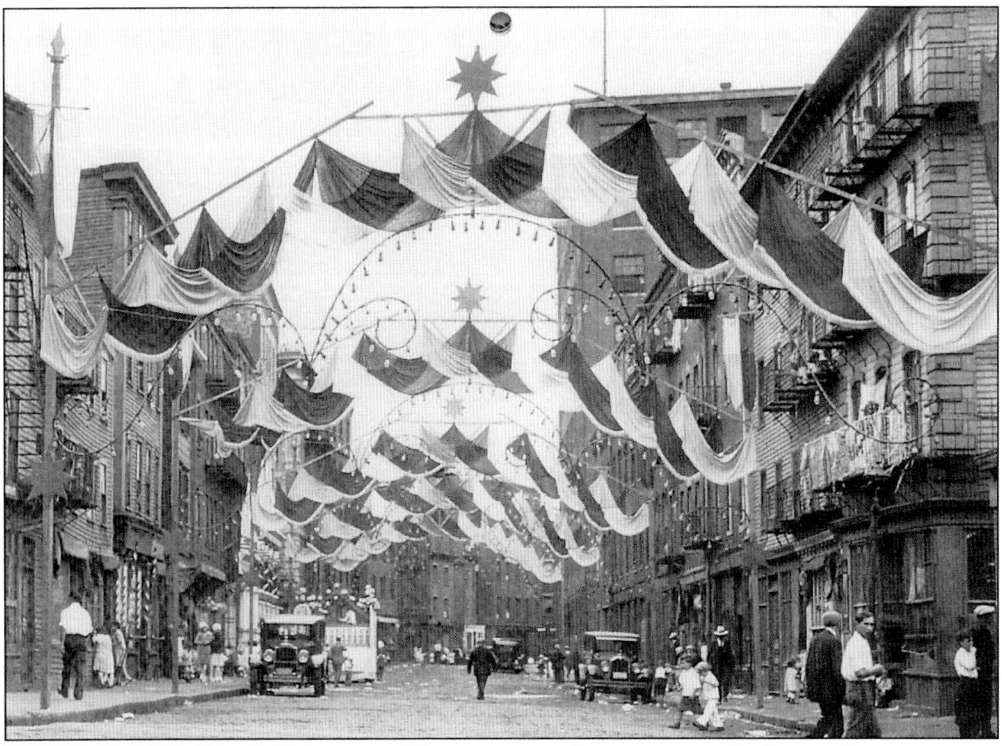

The feasts, or feste, began at the turn of the century and were organized to honor the patron saint of social clubs. In the 1930s, electric lights for the Fishermen's Feast were strung on arches with decorative bunting above North Street, shown here looking from Fleet Street. The evening was one of both reverence and merriment, but the morning presented street cleaners with a massive clean up. (Courtesy of the BPL)

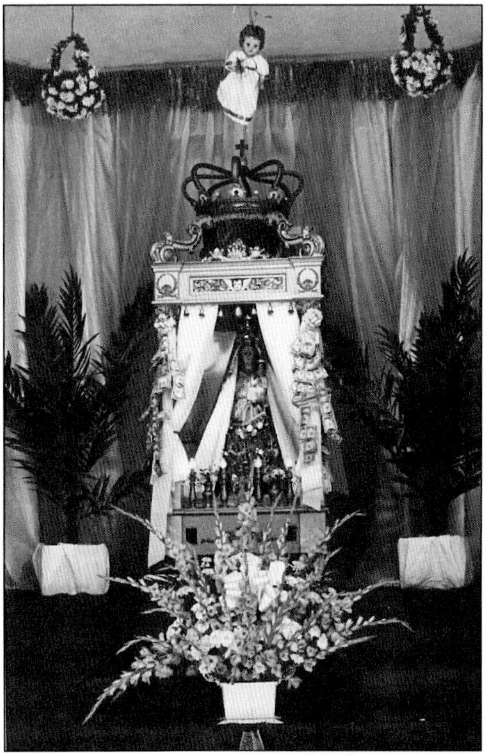

Statues of saints, bedecked with ribbons, were kept in shrines, and donations for the charitable acts of the society were pinned to the ribbons. An angel hovers above the saint while it awaits a procession through the streets of the North End. (Courtesy of the BPL)

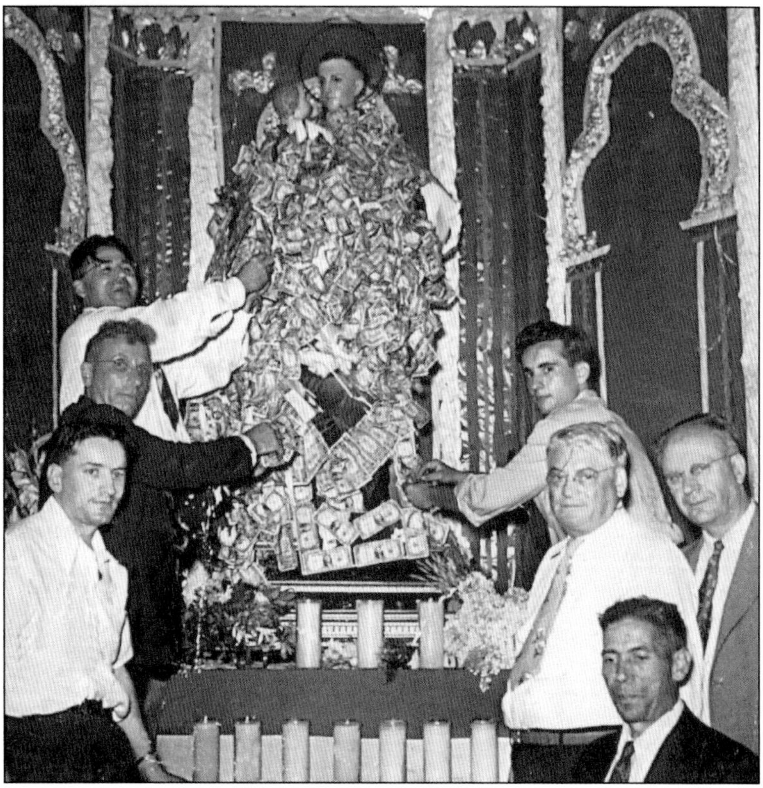

Members of the Society of Saint Anthony pin contributions to ribbons bedecking his statue in the mid-1950s. (Courtesy of Pizzaria Regina North End)

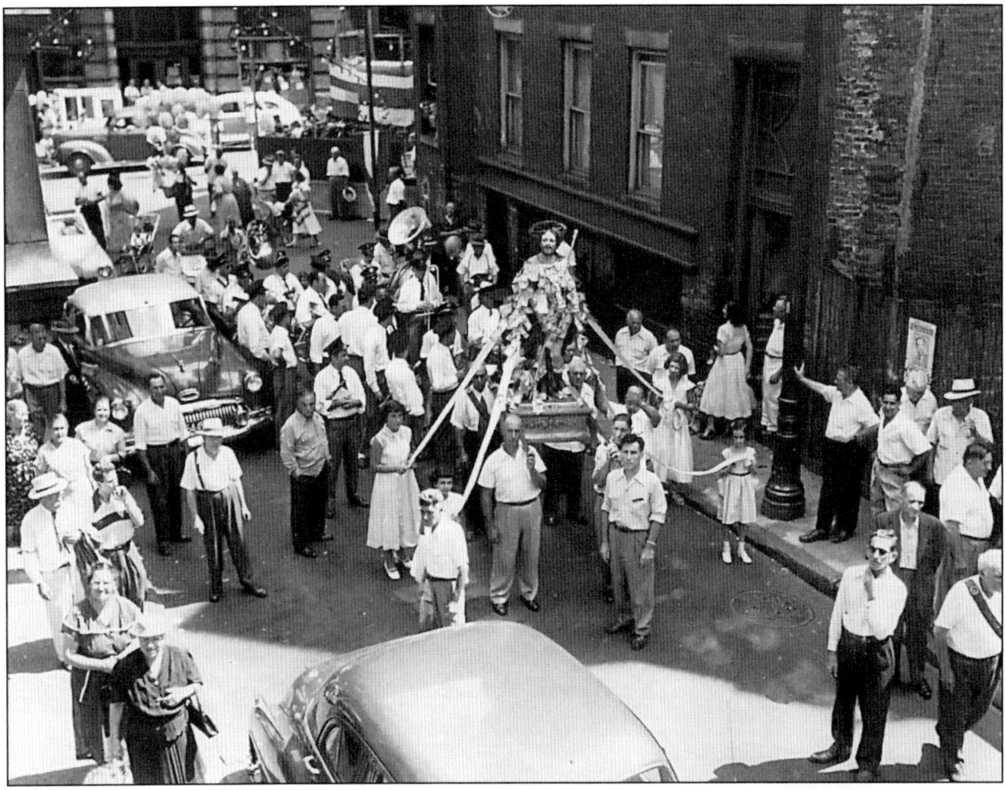

The Feast of Saint Joseph is celebrated on March 19; here the feast is celebrated with a procession through the North End in the 1940s. (Courtesy of Pizzeria Regina North End)

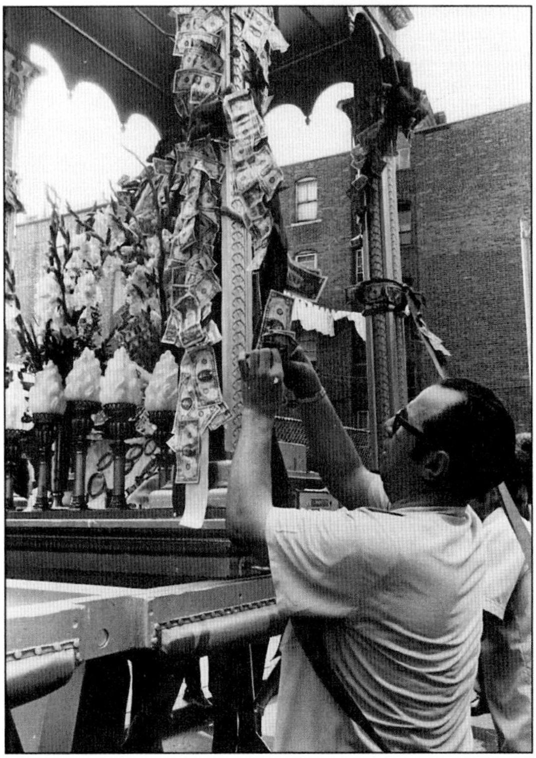

As the statues of the saints are carried through the streets, the procession is often halted to allow contributions to be pinned to ribbons cascading from the shrine. (Courtesy of the BPL)

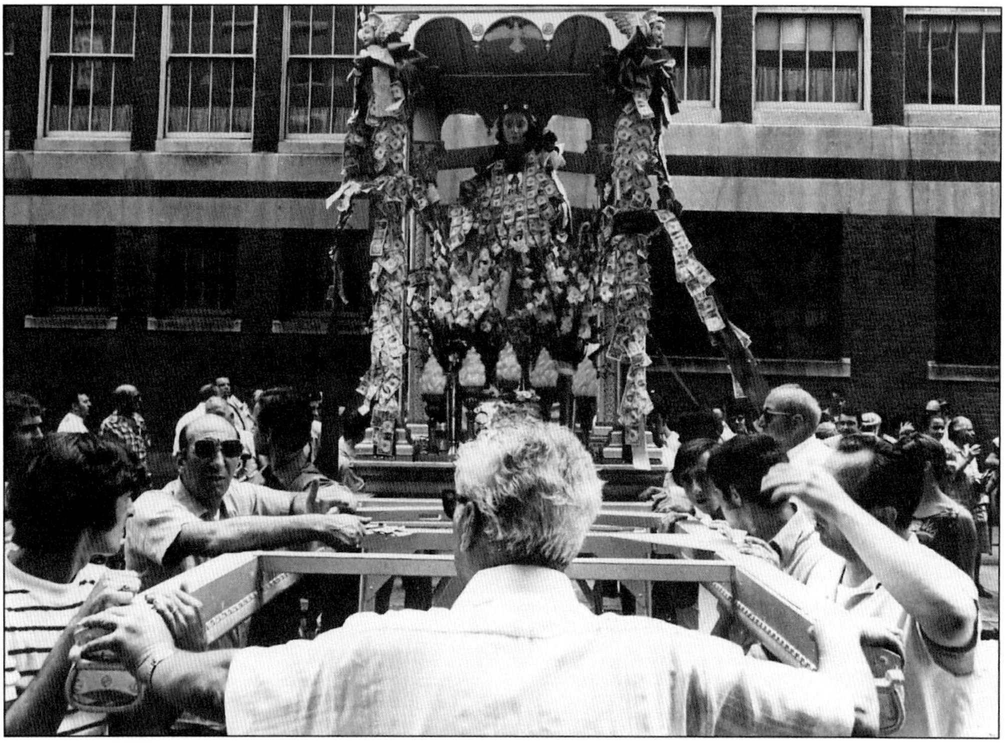

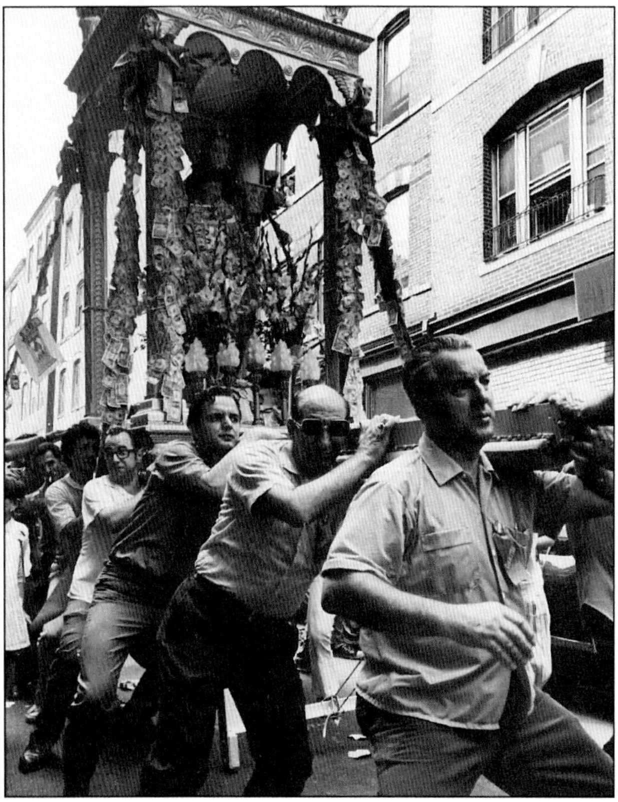

The statue of Saint Agrippina di Mineo is halted in front of the house-shrine of Saint Joseph on Charter Street. It is a tradition that the procession is halted as it passes before every society where a statue of a saint is housed. (Courtesy of the BPL)

Men bear the shrine housing the statue of Saint Agrippina di Mineo during the feast in 1971. (Courtesy of the BPL)

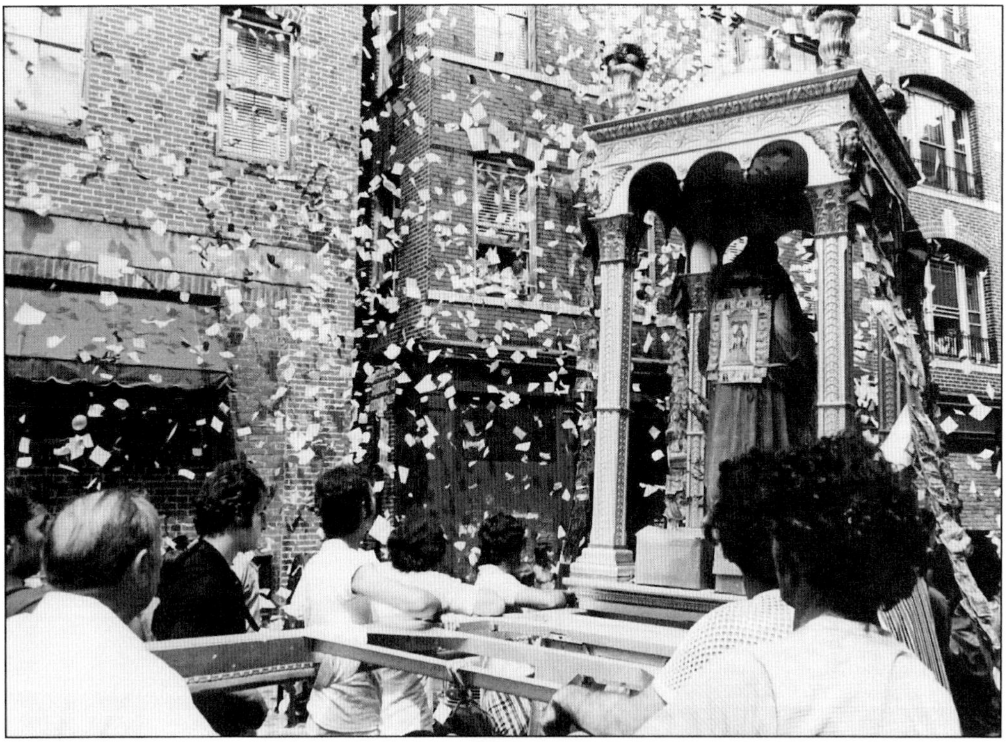

Confetti is showered upon the procession of the statue of Saint Agrippina di Mineo by people watching from windows or fire escapes high above the street. (Courtesy of the BPL)

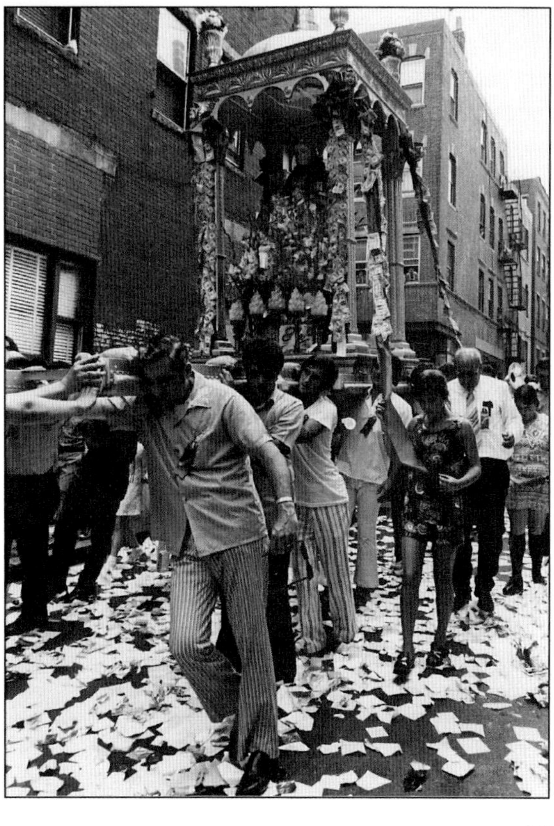

Men bear the saint's shrine during the street procession, while young girls hold the ribbons to which they will pin contributions received along the way. (Courtesy of the BPL)

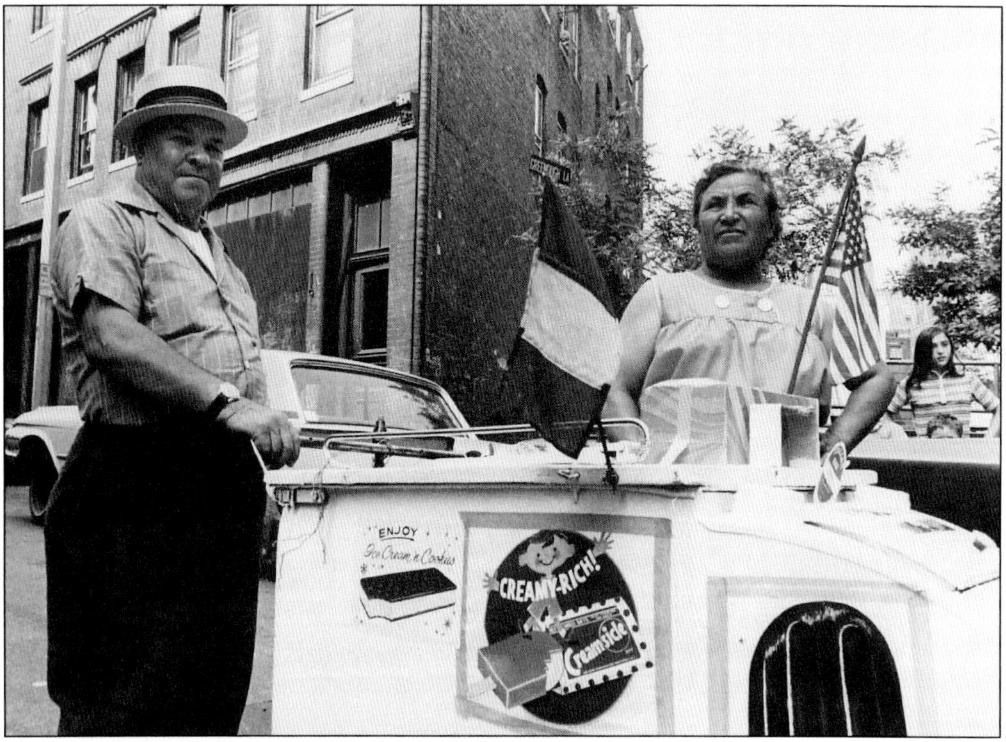

A couple offers creamsicles to feast-goers opposite Greenough Lane from an ice cream wagon proudly displaying the flags of both the United States and Italy. (Courtesy of the BPL)

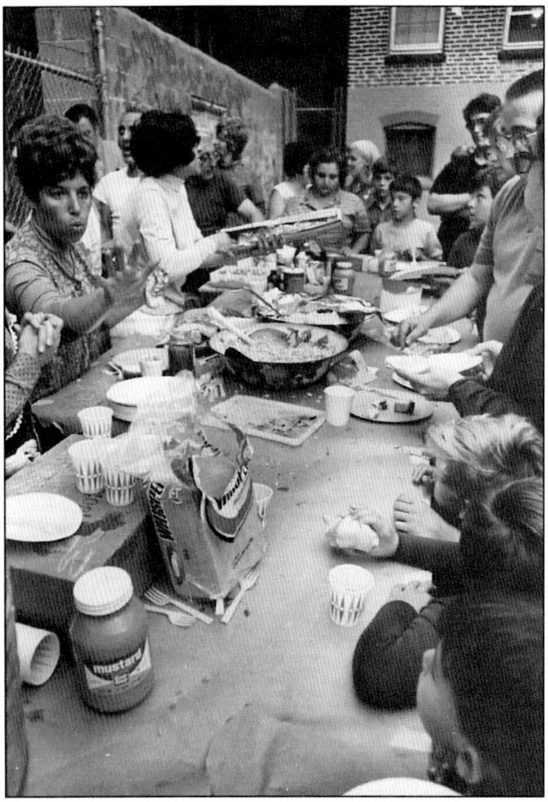

Residents of the North End offer "feast food" such as sausage and pepper subs, fried calamari, fried dough, pizza, and other typical street fare to those attending the feasts. (Courtesy of the BPL)

Eight

The Great Molasses Flood

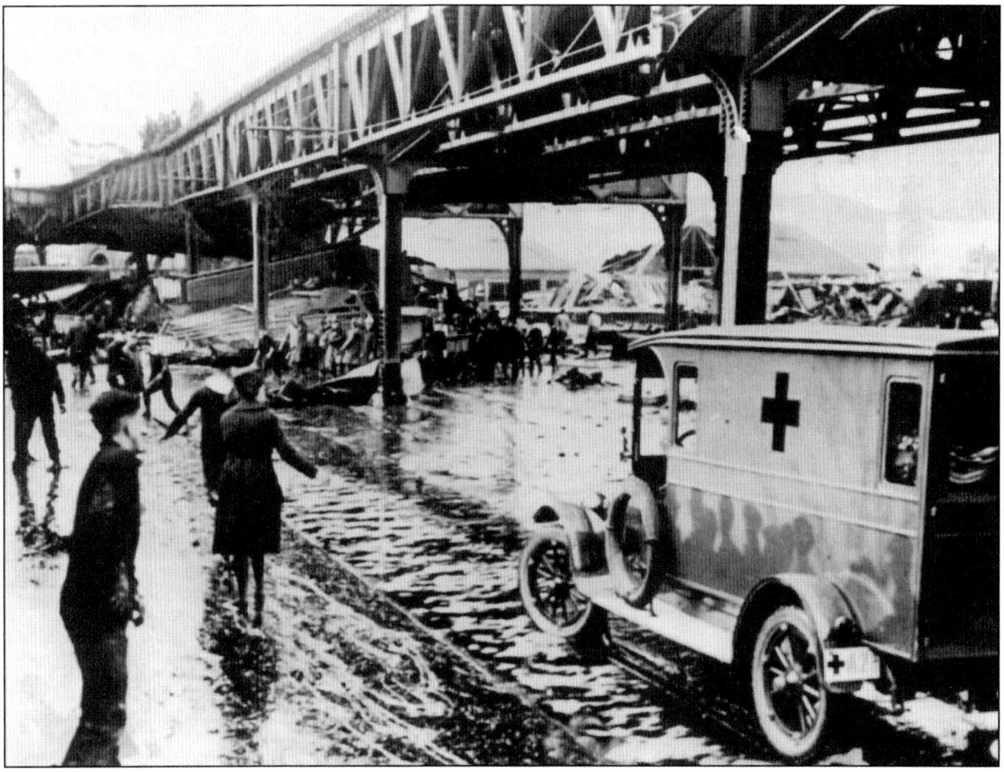

On January 15, 1919, at 12:30 pm, the greatest molasses flood in history took place in the North End. The tracks of the Elevated Railway that connected South Station and North Station along Commercial Street buckled with the impact of the molasses flood that cascaded from an elevated storage tank of the United Liquor Company. A Red Cross ambulance arrives at the scene of the disaster as people scramble to assist those who were swept into the debris and find the twenty-one people who were killed by the two million gallons of molasses. (Courtesy of *The Boston Globe*)

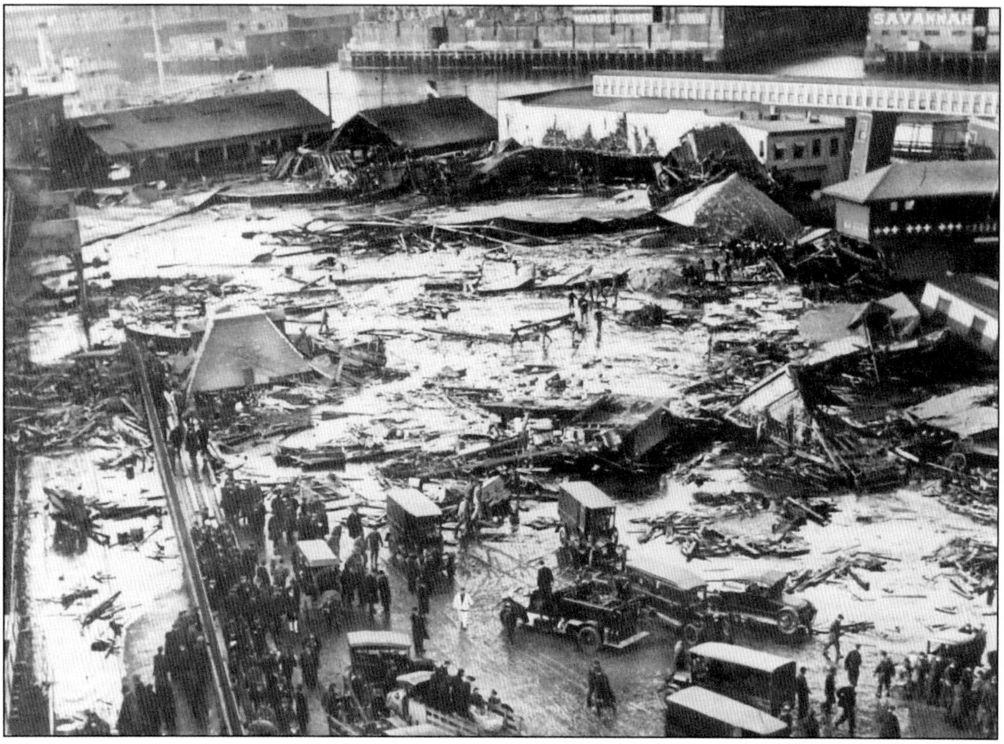

The area across from Copp's Hill became a tangled wreck of wood-framed sheds and buildings, iron fences, and debris that was swept toward the edge of the Charles River by the force of the cascading molasses. (Courtesy of *The Boston Globe*)

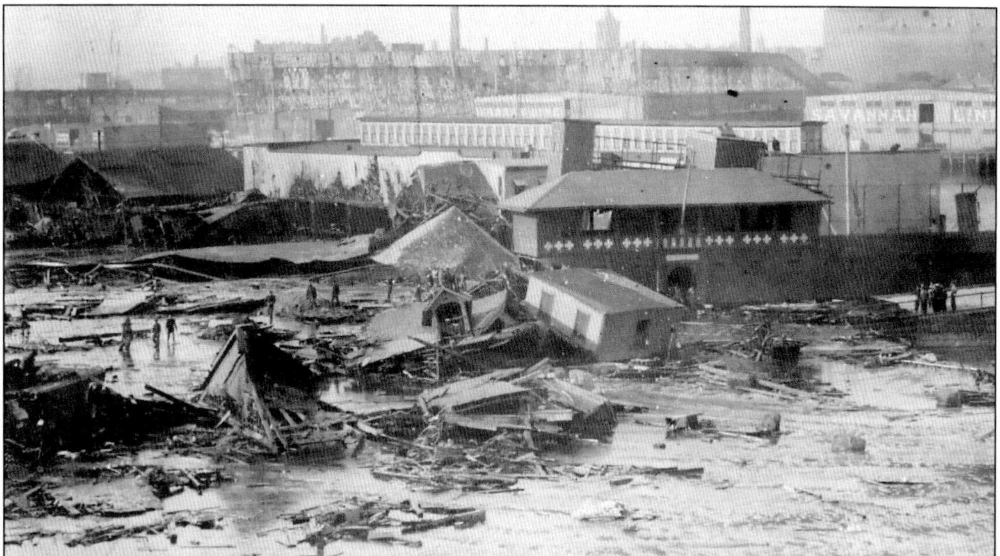

A close-up of the wreckage shows the remains of wood-framed buildings that were literally pushed as far as they would go. The molasses drenched the area and took weeks to clean up. The wharfs on the Charlestown side of the Charles River can be seen in the distance. (Courtesy of *The Boston Globe*)

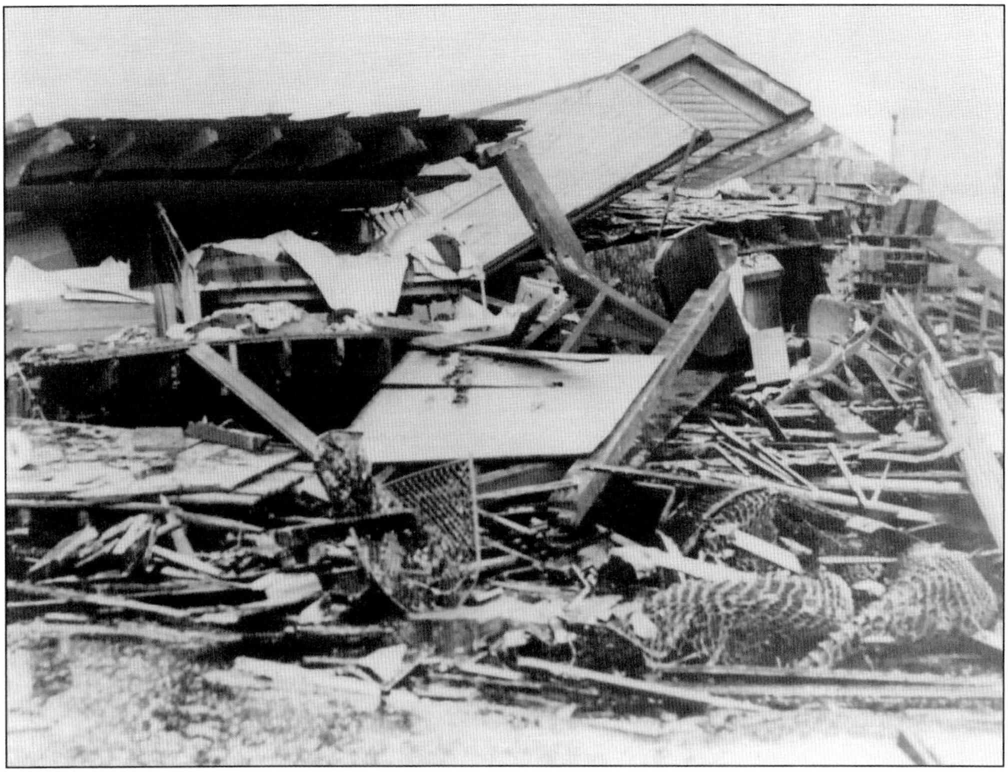

Wood, wire, metal, and everything else that was in the path of the molasses flood created mountains of debris. (Courtesy of *The Boston Globe*)

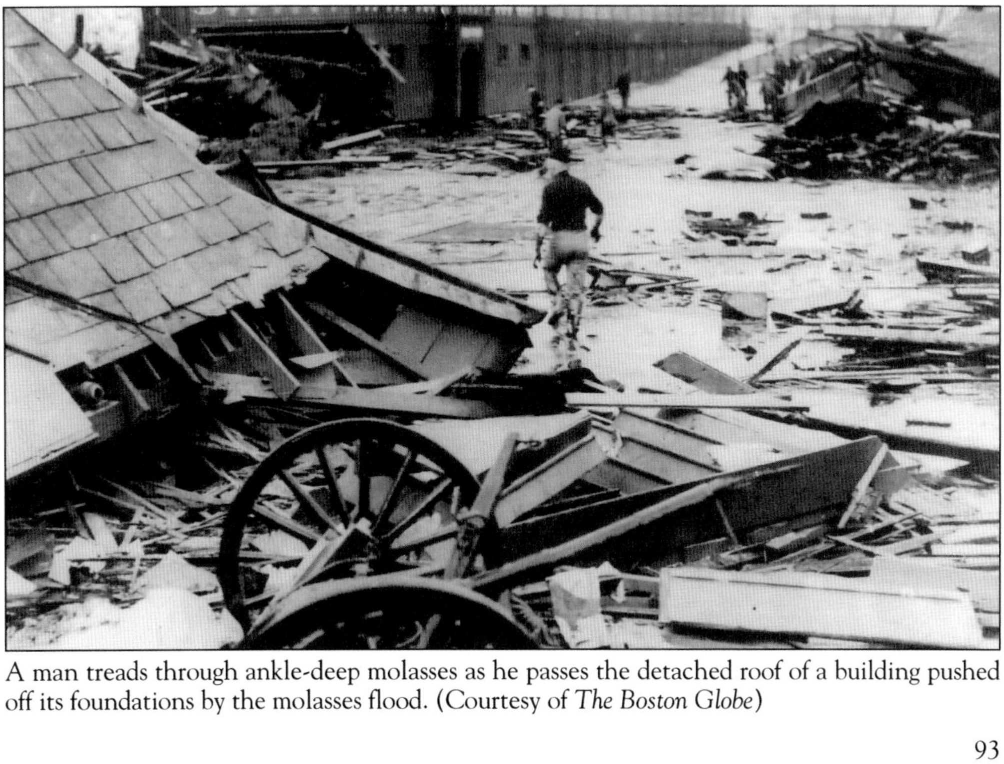

A man treads through ankle-deep molasses as he passes the detached roof of a building pushed off its foundations by the molasses flood. (Courtesy of *The Boston Globe*)

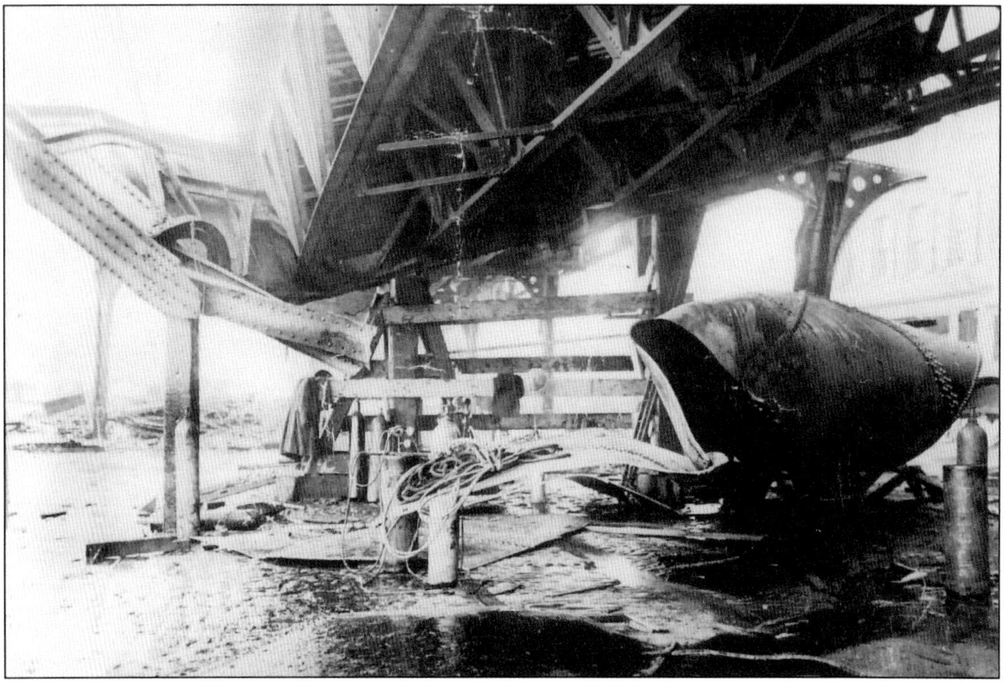

A crumpled iron support of the elevated tracks along Commercial Street give an example of the force of the molasses flood. It took hundreds of workmen working around the clock for a week to clear the wreckage. (Courtesy of *The Boston Globe*)

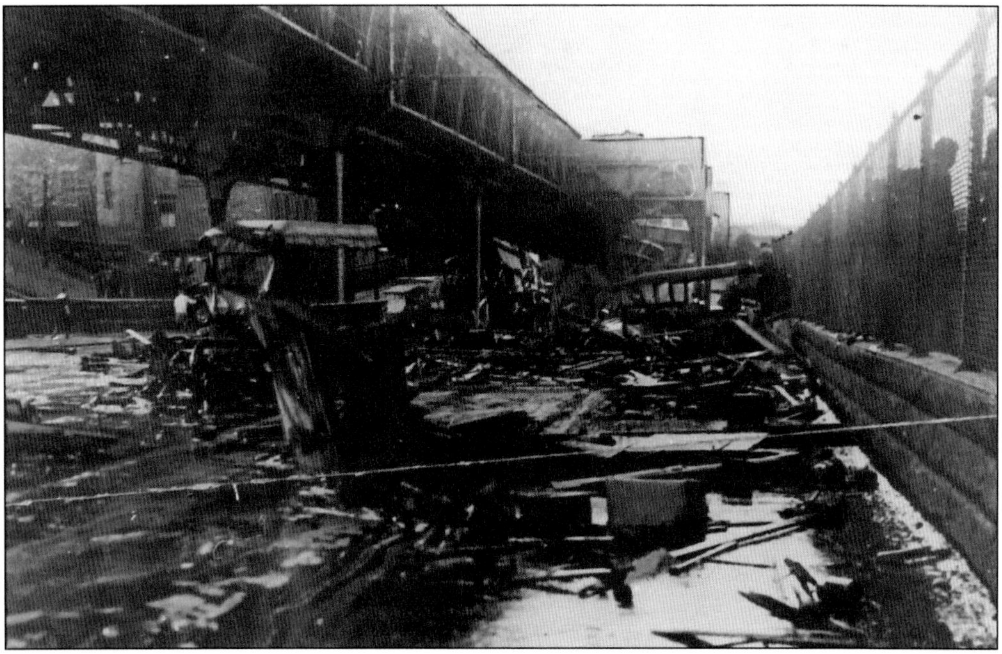

Looking toward North Washington Street, Commercial Street was strewn with debris and molasses the afternoon of the flood. People lined the fence on the right looking, as if in a daze, at the devastation. On the far left can be seen the wall of the park on Copp's Hill. (Courtesy of *The Boston Globe*)

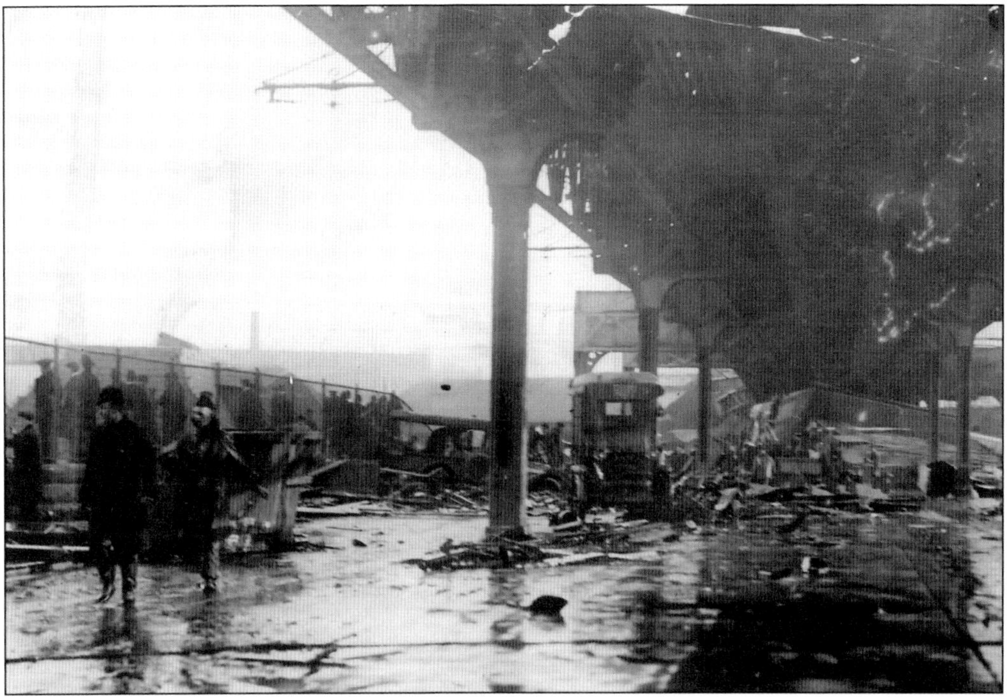

Looking down Commercial Street, spectators on the left stare at the debris under the elevated tracks. (Courtesy of *The Boston Globe*)

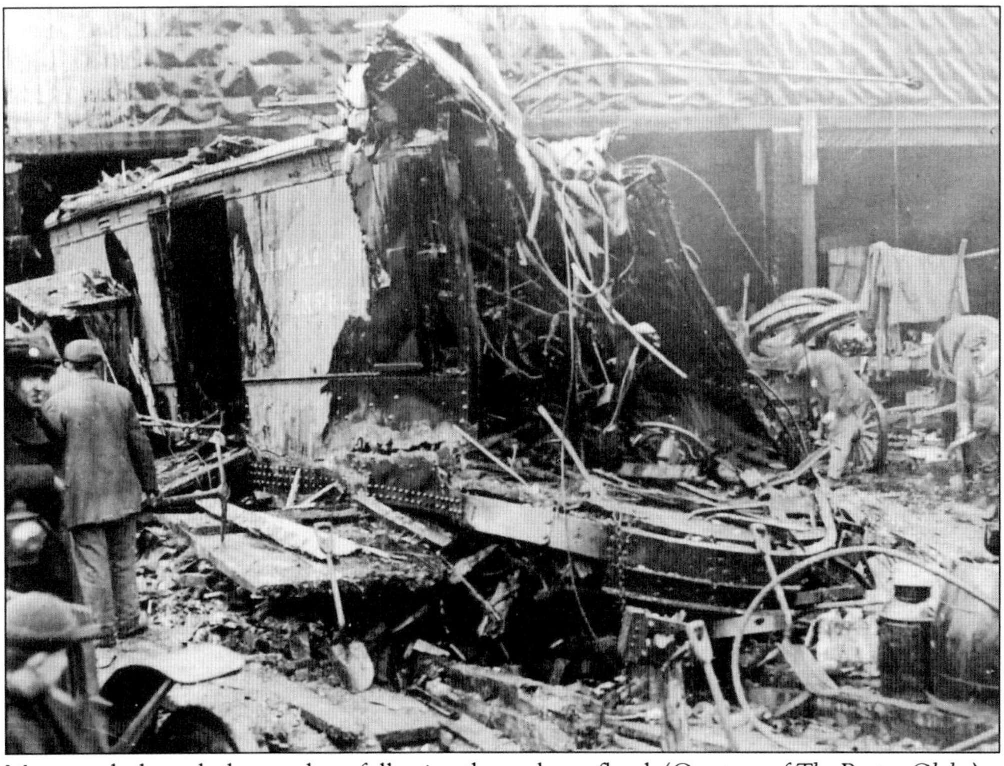

Men search through the wreckage following the molasses flood. (Courtesy of *The Boston Globe*)

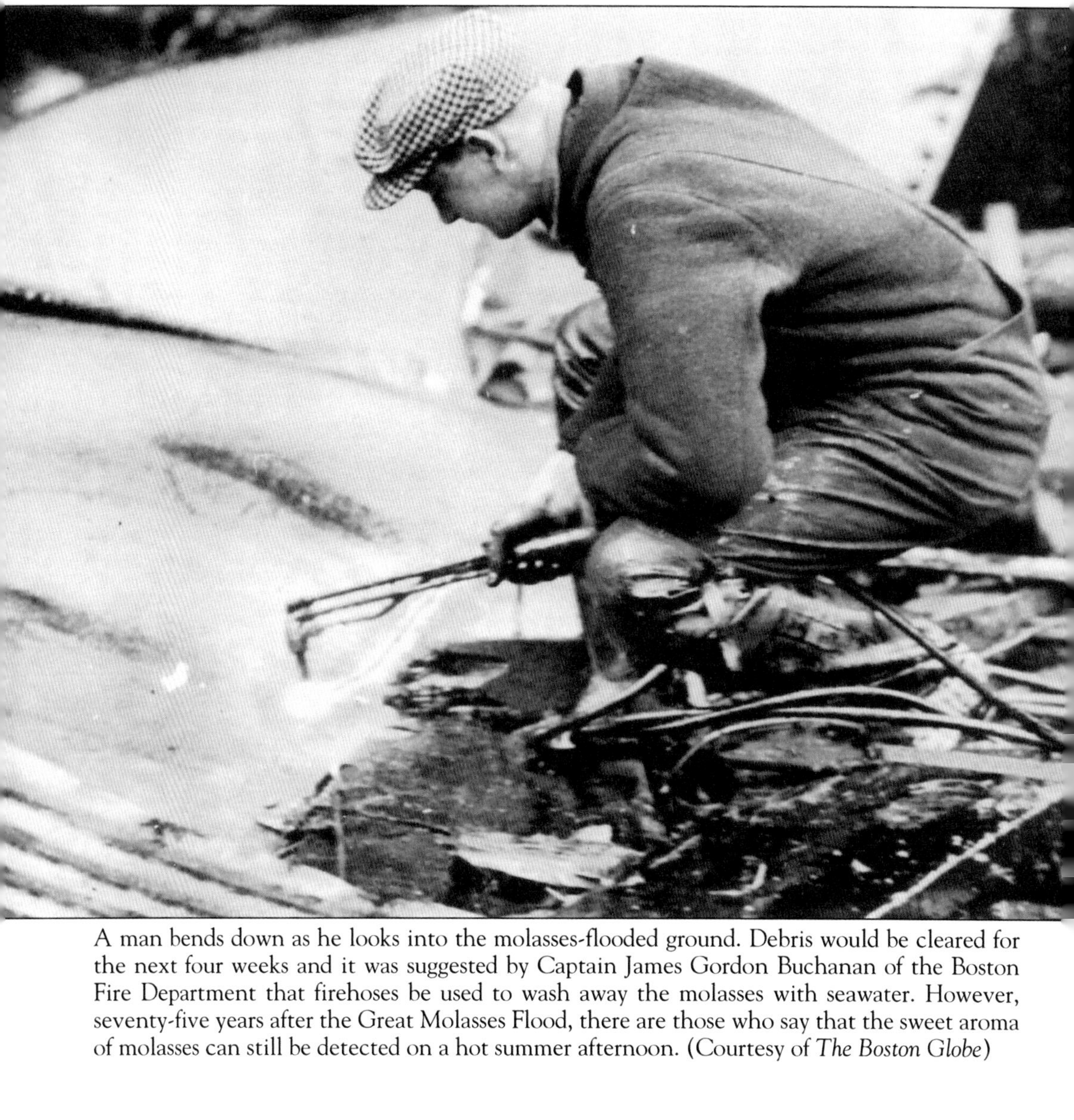

A man bends down as he looks into the molasses-flooded ground. Debris would be cleared for the next four weeks and it was suggested by Captain James Gordon Buchanan of the Boston Fire Department that firehoses be used to wash away the molasses with seawater. However, seventy-five years after the Great Molasses Flood, there are those who say that the sweet aroma of molasses can still be detected on a hot summer afternoon. (Courtesy of *The Boston Globe*)

Nine

Transportation

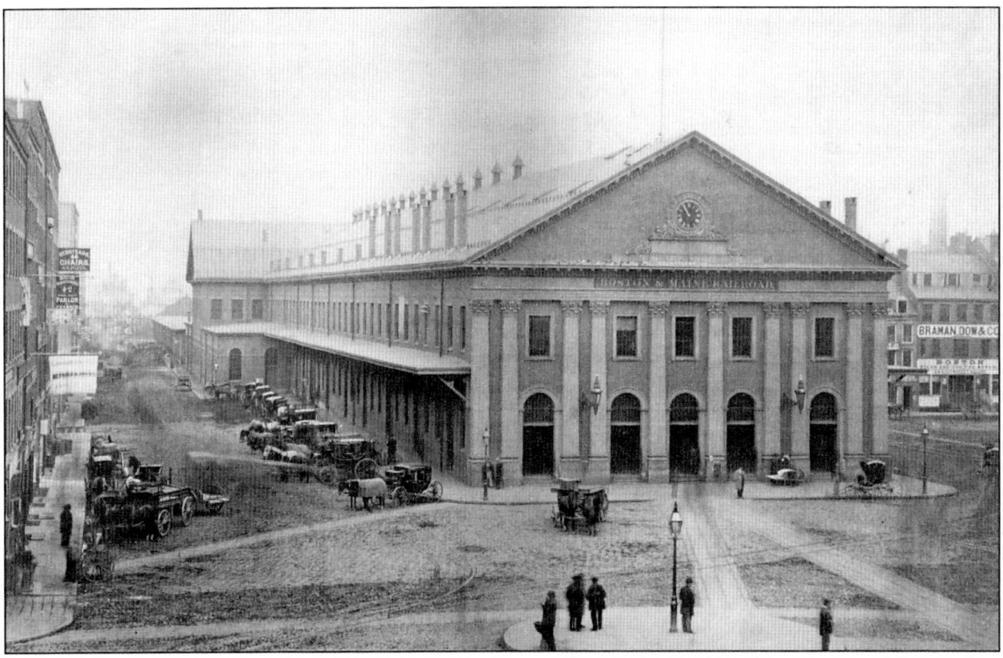

The Boston and Maine Railroad terminus, an elegant Greek Revival building, was in Haymarket Square. Hacks (or cabs) are waiting for passengers on the left. (Courtesy of the BPL)

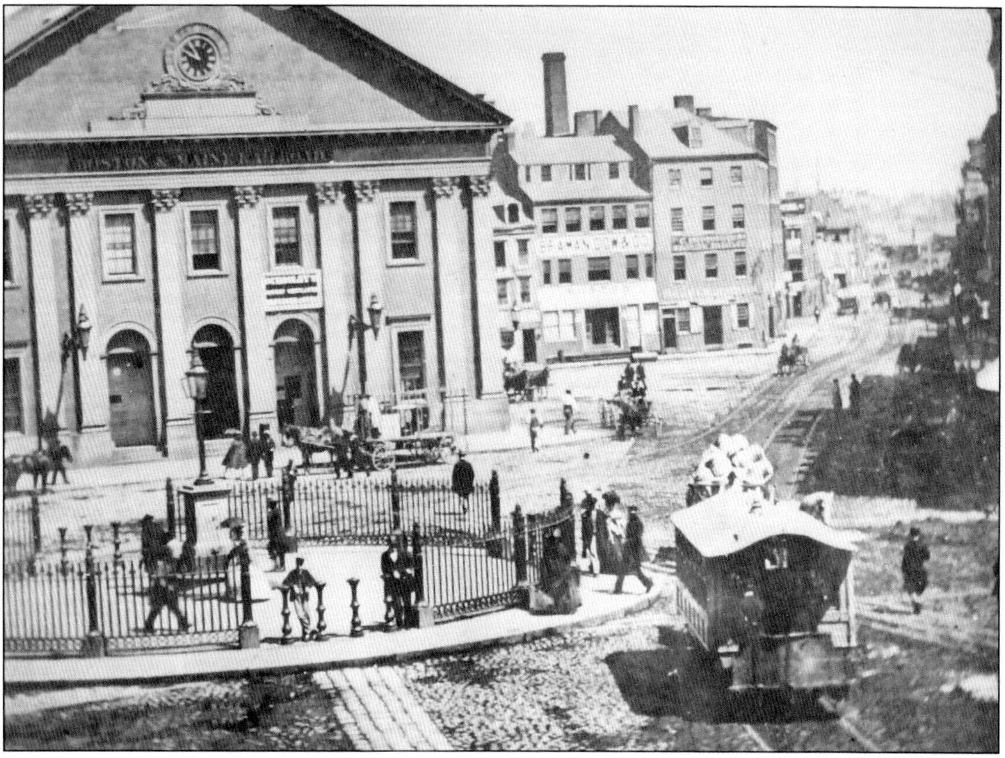

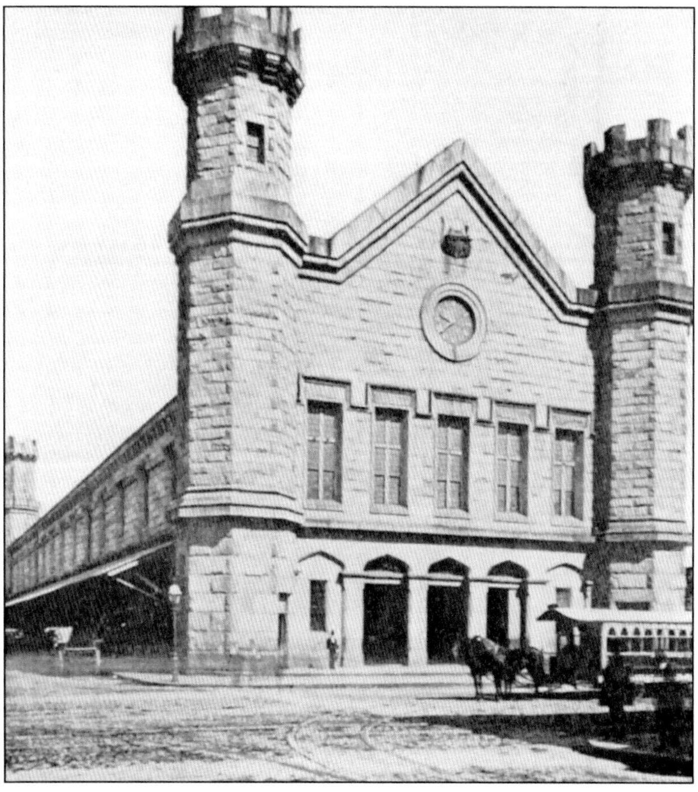

In front of the Boston and Maine Railroad terminus was a circular cast-iron fenced enclosure with a gas lamp in the center. A horse-drawn streetcar passes on the right. (Courtesy of Vito Aluia)

The Fitchburg Railroad Station was on Causeway Street and connected Boston with Fitchburg, Massachusetts, via the Hoosic Tunnel route. A superb granite depot, it was designed by George Dexter and built in 1847.

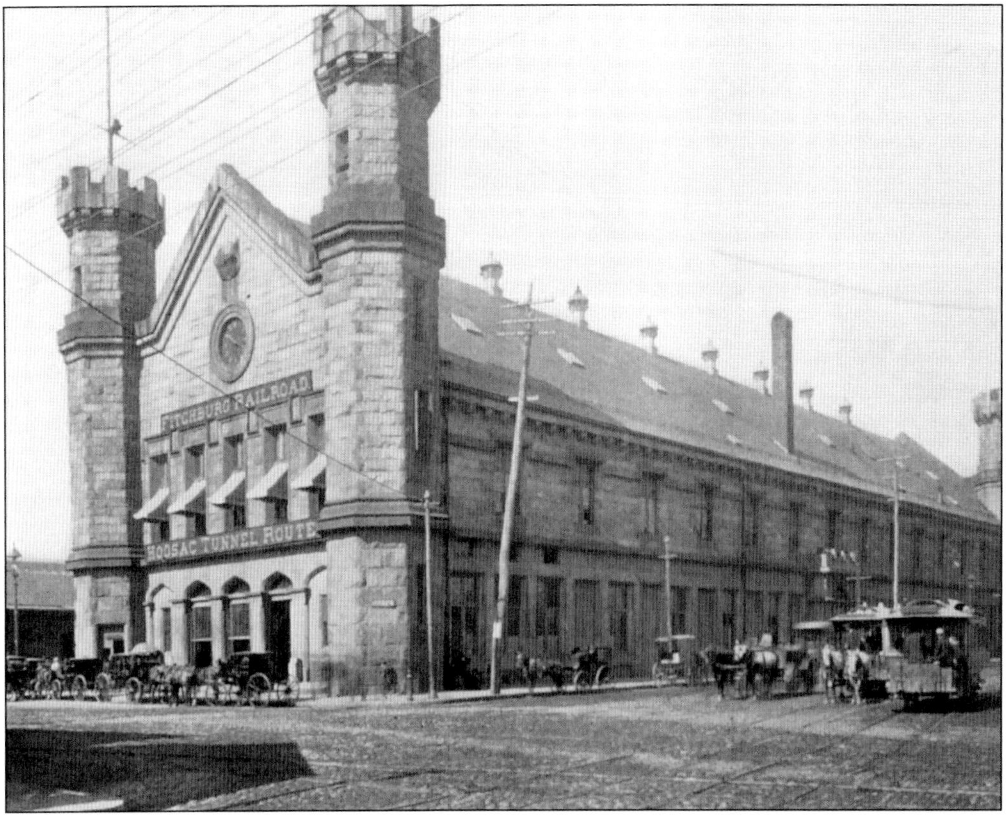

Though built as a railroad terminus, the Fitchburg Railroad Depot was used as a concert hall when Jenny Lind, the "Sweedish Nightingale," came to Boston. The overselling of tickets meant that hundreds had to be turned away; however, to please her audience (and save the head of the promoter), Jenny Lind sang from one of the crenelated towers to the rapture of her admirerers and the relief of the promoter.

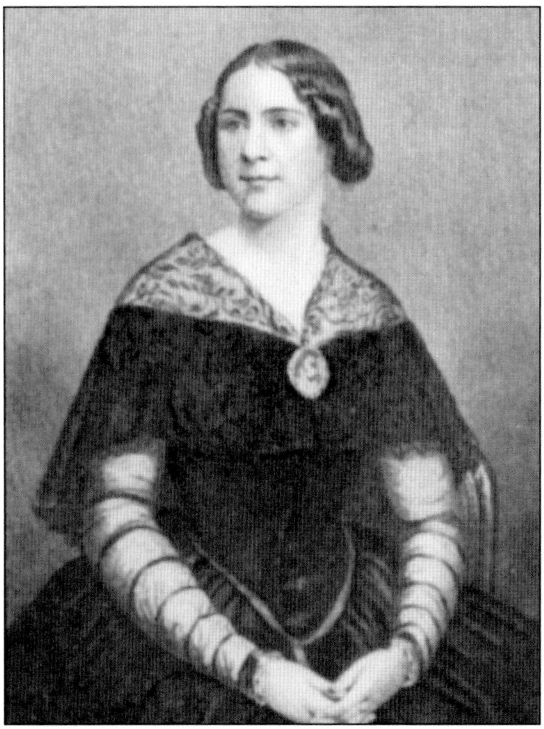

Jenny Lind was brought to America in 1850 by Phineas T. ("P.T.") Barnum and dubbed the "Sweedish Nightingale." It was said that she "had almost unlimited execution, sang with great earnestness, and did everything in a highly finished broad style." She later married her accompanist, Otto Goldschmidt, at the home of Samuel G. Howe on Louisburg Square in 1853.

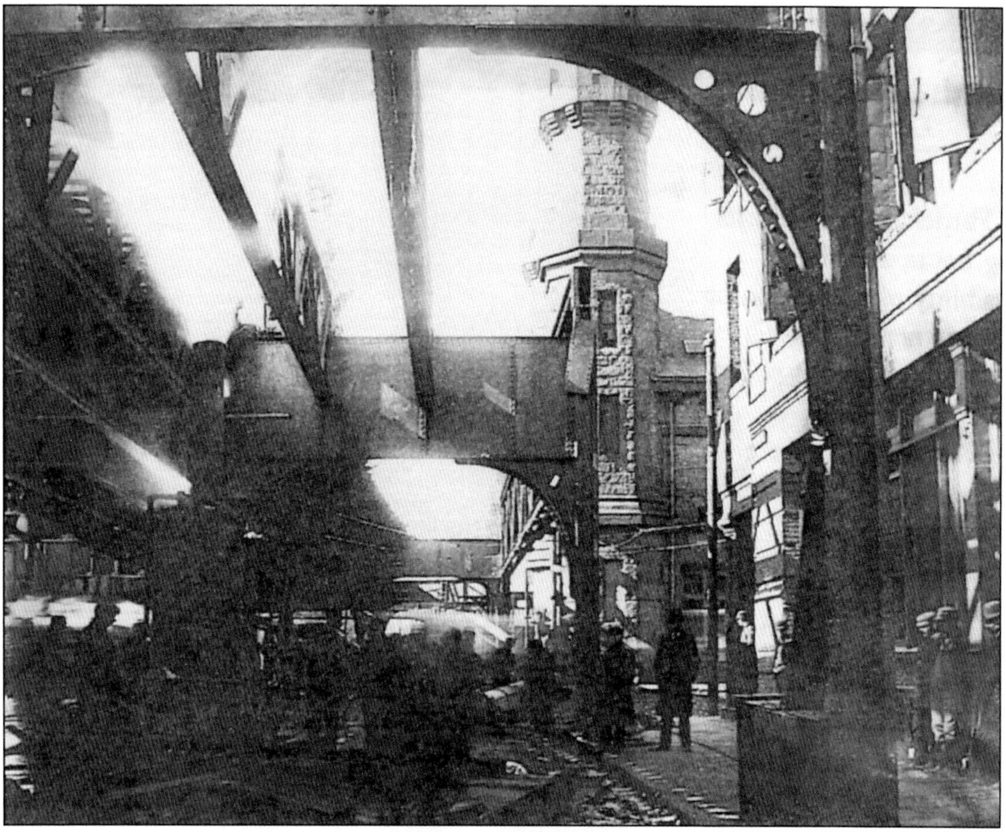

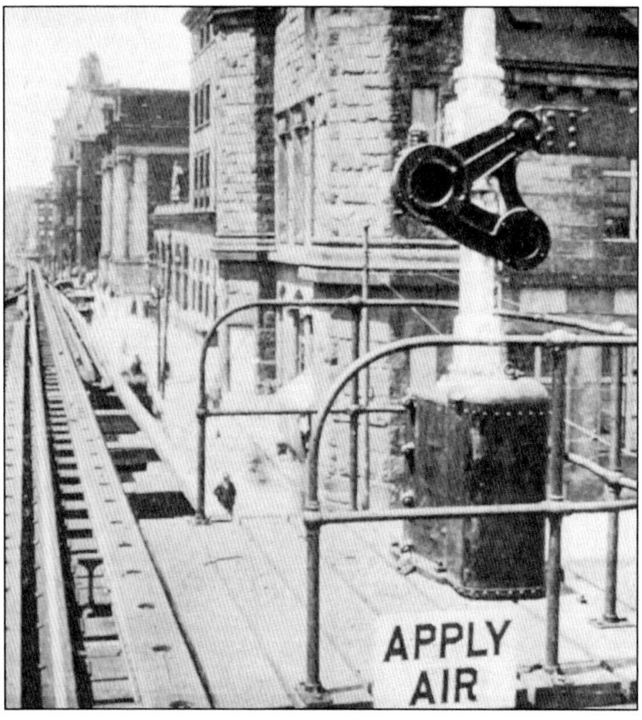

By the turn of the twentieth century, the Elevated Railway was being built to connect Roxbury and Charlestown. The support structure at North Station on Causeway Street is shown here being erected. One of the crenelated towers can be seen on the right; ironically, the tower from which Jenny Lind sang was saved when the depot was demolished, and was later erected in Truro on Cape Cod as a memorial to her.

A signal would alert trains on the Elevated Railway to either stop or proceed on the precarious bend of the tracks at North Station. No other noise can imitate the squealing of the wheels as the train snaked along the double curve of the railroad at this point.

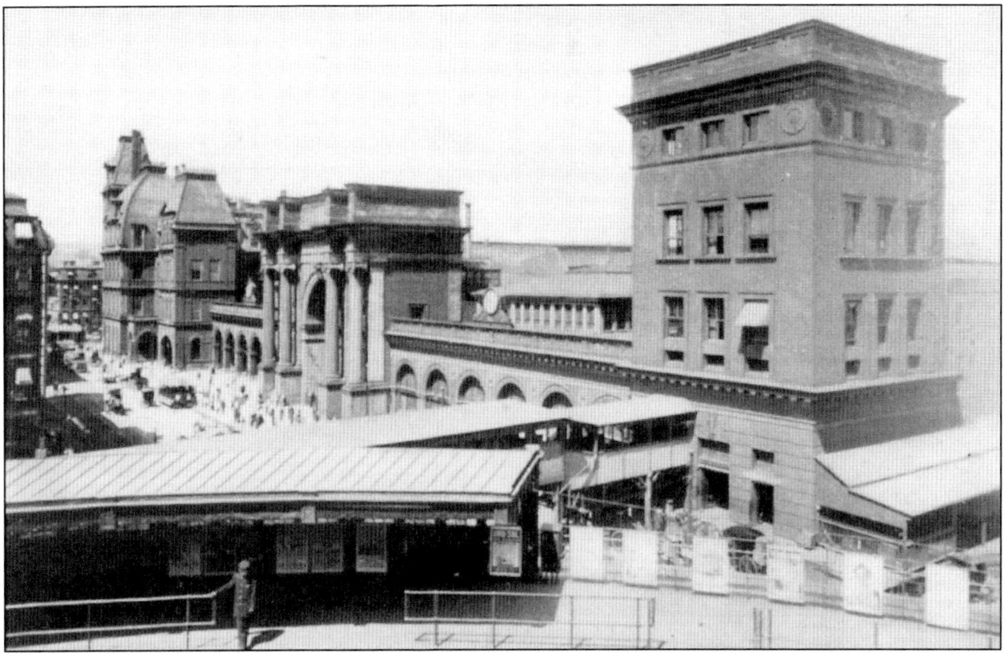

North Station, dubbed "Union Station," was built in 1893 on Causeway Street to the west of the Fitchburg Railroad Depot. A massive structure that was designed by Shepley, Rutan, and Coolidge, it was later replaced by the Boston Garden, which had an entrance for passengers using the trains at North Station.

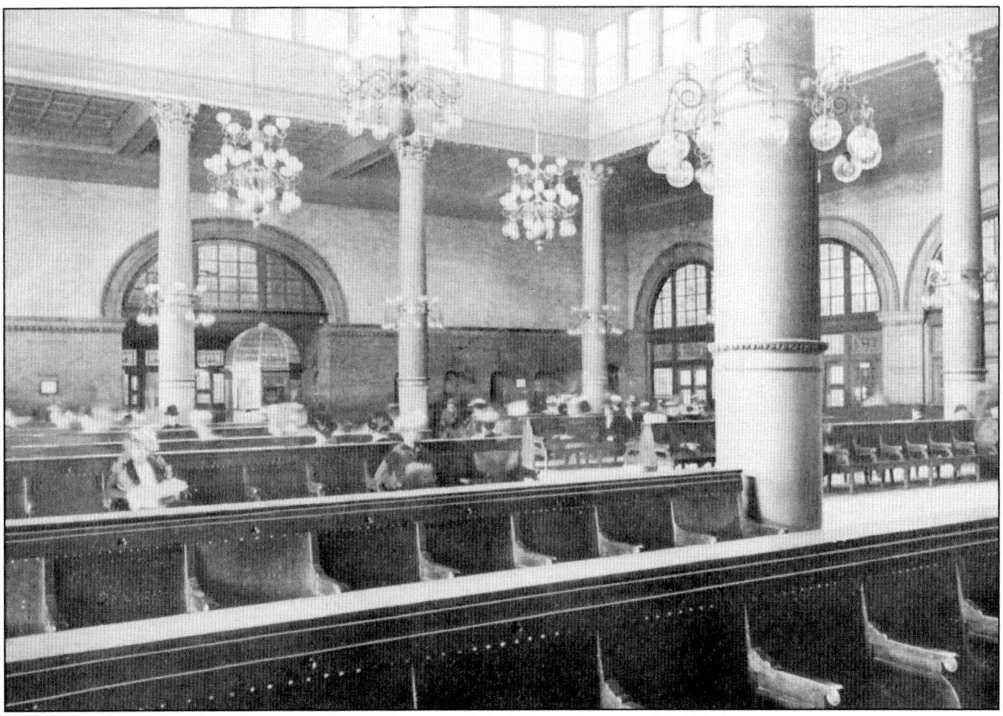

The main waiting room at North Station had leather-upholstered oak benches for passengers awaiting their trains.

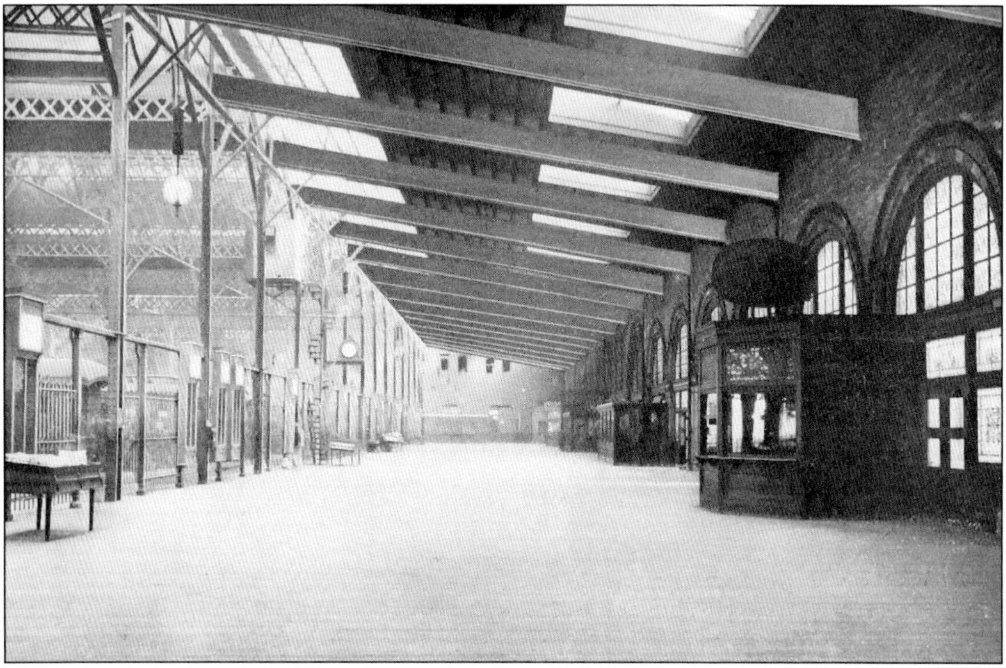

The midway at North Station was a sweeping wood floor that led from the waiting room to the platform where passengers boarded their train.

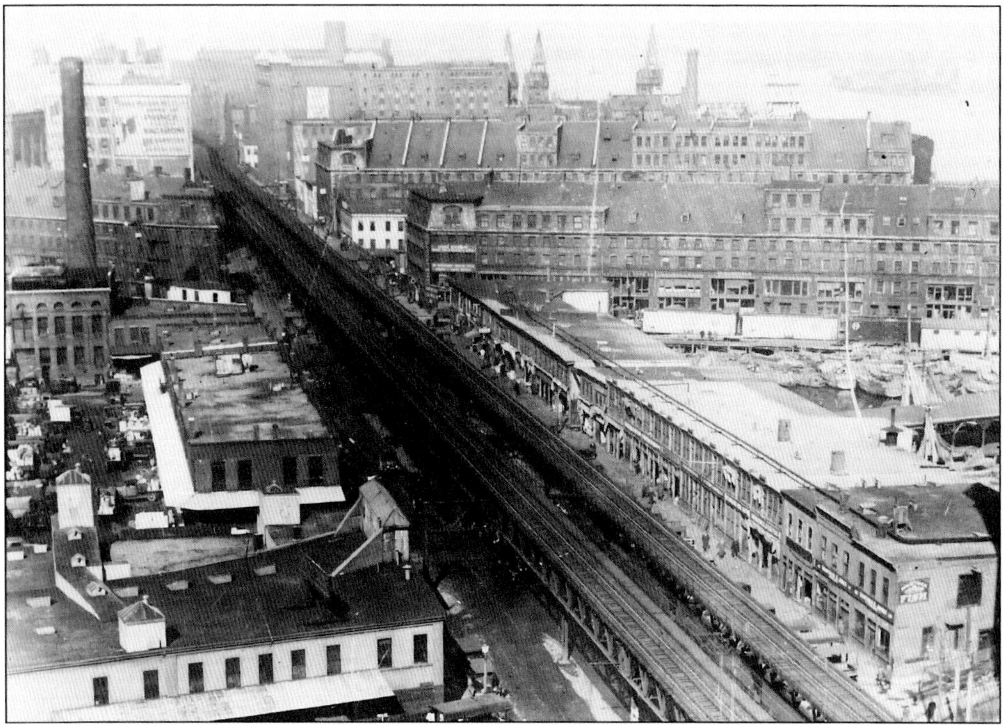

The Elevated Railway had a spur that connected South Station and North Station via Atlantic Avenue and Commercial Street in the North End. This double-tracked line went through the densely populated North End until the time of World War II. (Courtesy of Vito Aluia)

Ten

A Branch of the Library

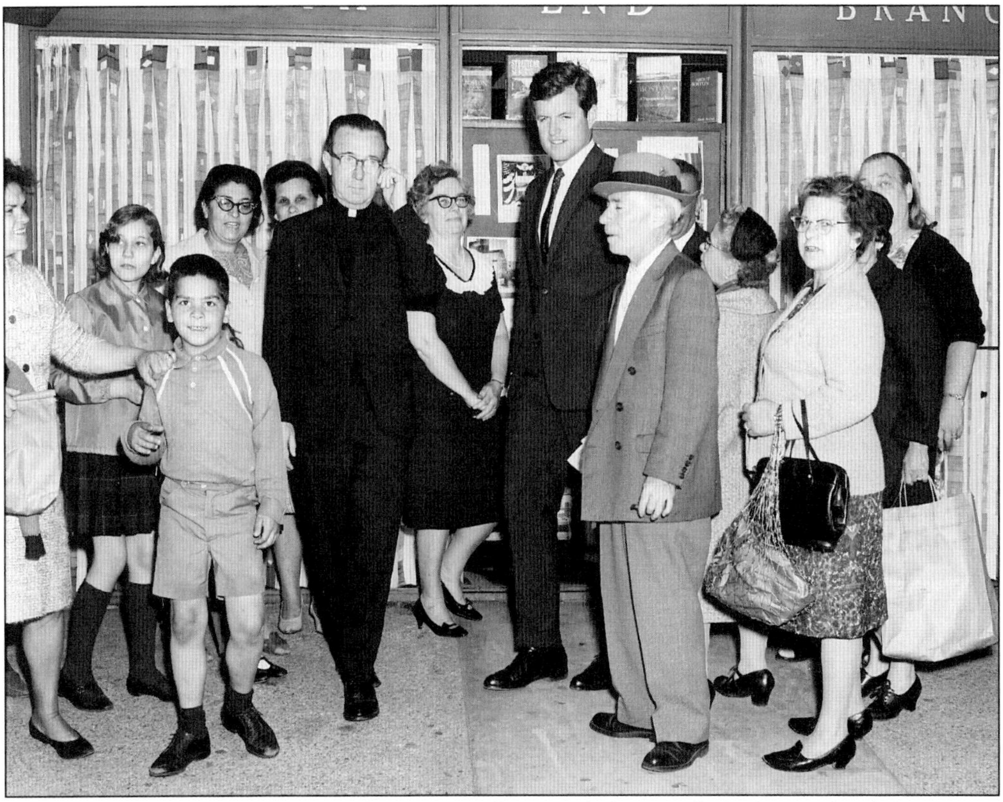

On June 1, 1967, Senator Edward M. Kennedy visited the North End Branch of the Boston Public Library to view an exhibit on the history of the North End. "Honey Fitz" (his maternal grandfather), Mayor John F. Fitzgerald, and Rose Fitzgerald Kennedy (his mother) were born in the North End and were once parishioners of Saint Stephen's Church on Hanover Street. Greeting Senator Kennedy are Reverend Sullivan of Saint Stephen's Church and Librarian Mrs. Geraldine Herrick. (Courtesy of the BPL)

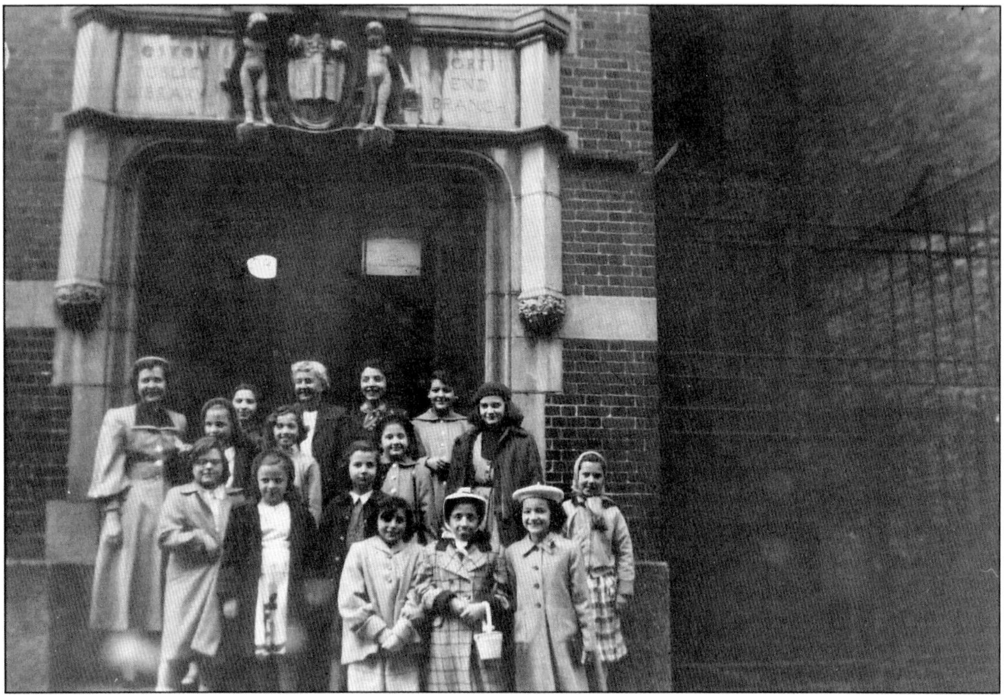

A group of young girls pose on the steps of the old library on North Bennet Street. The library building was originally the First Methodist Church, but was later the Portuguese church of Saint John the Baptist at 3A North Bennet Street. Standing on the steps with the girls are Miss Ellen Peterson and Miss Dorothy Becker. (Courtesy of the BPL)

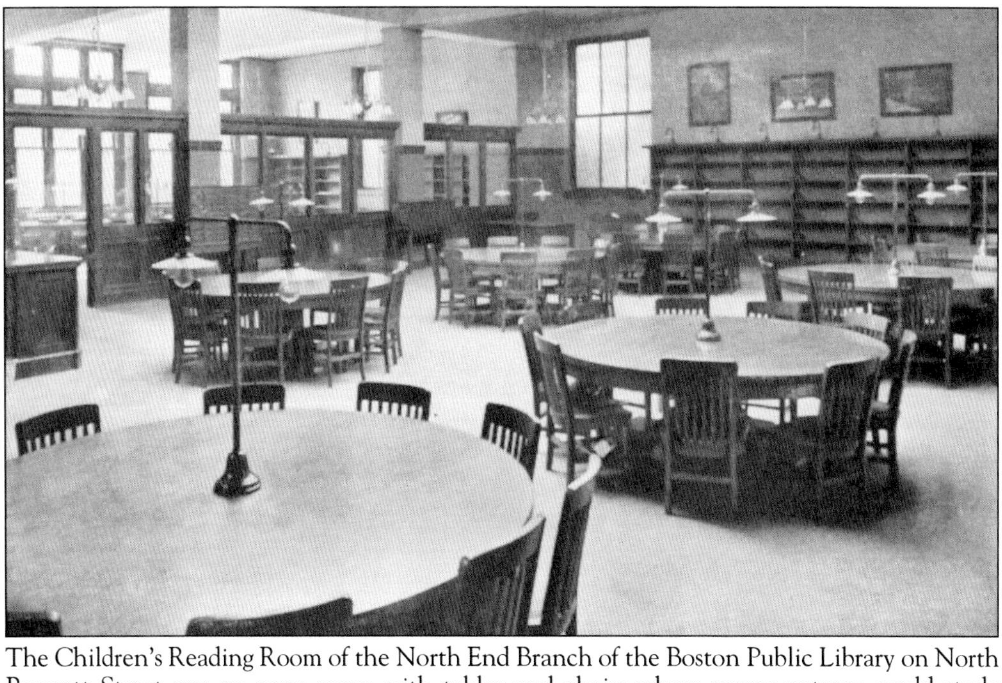

The Children's Reading Room of the North End Branch of the Boston Public Library on North Bennett Street was an open room with tables and chairs where young patrons could study after school.

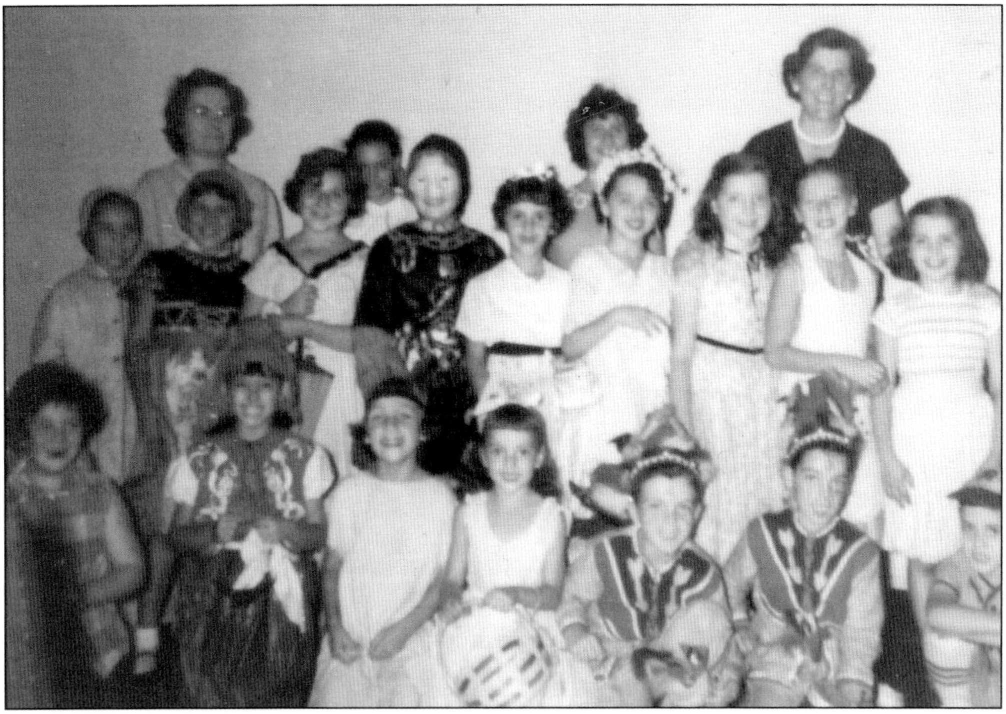

The Summer Reading Club in 1955 had an "End of Summer" party at the library. (Courtesy of the BPL)

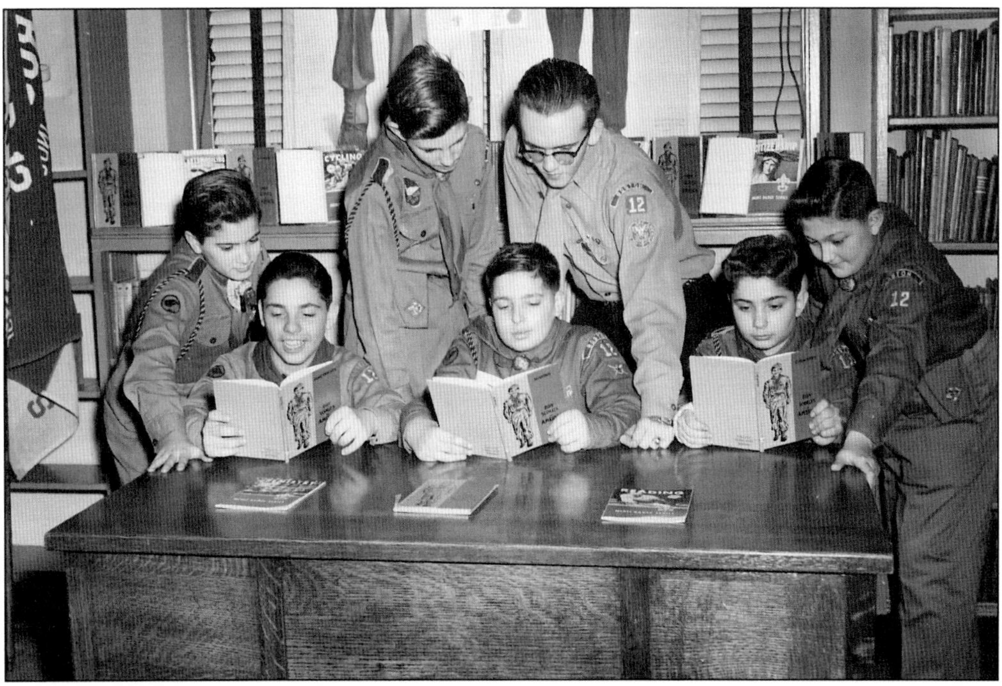

Boy Scouts had a corner of the library where they could study for merit badges, which included chemistry, reading, and citizenship. The troop in the North End was formed in 1916 and is considered one of the first inner-city troops. (Courtesy of the BPL)

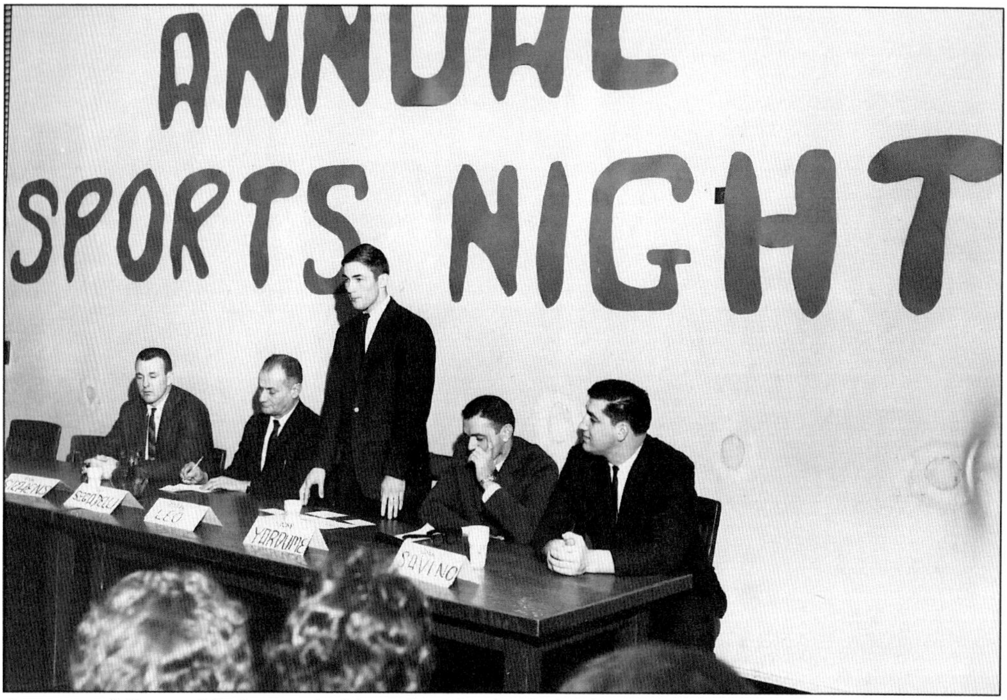

An annual Sports Night was held at the North End Library. Here, ? Leo is applauded by the audience as Messrs. Stephens, Segadelli, Yardume, and Savino sit at the head table. (Courtesy of the BPL)

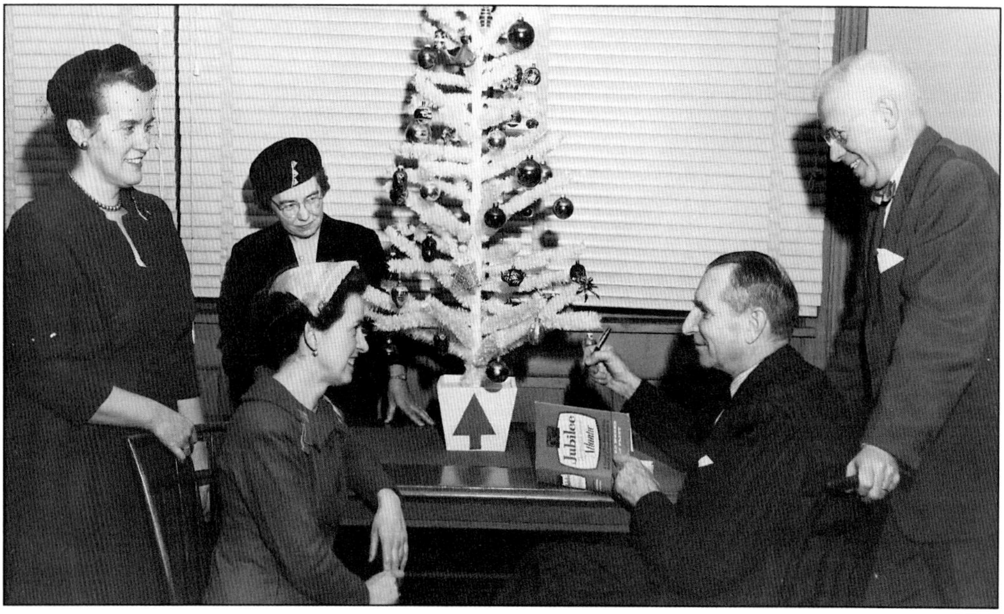

During Christmas, 1957, Miss Pietrina Maravigna presented a copy of the book *Jubilee—One Hundred Years of the Atlantic Monthly* and *The Italians in America* to the North End Library. From left to right are Emily Flint (assistant editor of the *Atlantic Monthly* and co-editor of *Jubilee)*, Librarian Geraldine Herrick (standing), Miss Maravigna, Edward Weeks (co-editor of *Jubilee)*, and Milton Lord (director of the Boston Public Library). (Courtesy of the BPL)

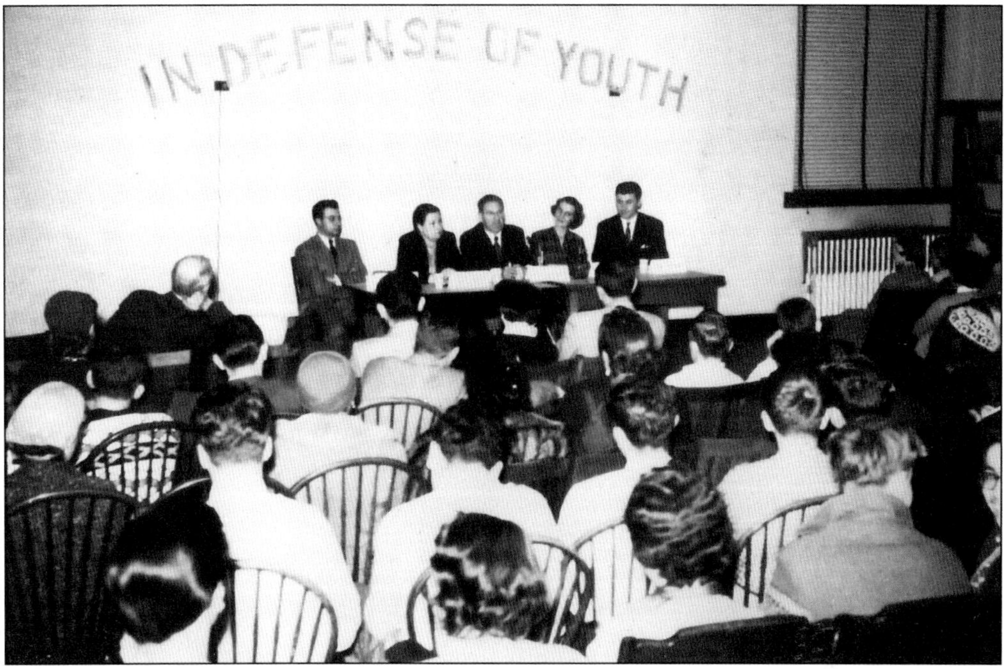

The program "In Defense of Youth" was held at the North End Library in 1957. Concerned about the future of the youth of Boston, these panel discussions would be held at various branch libraries to include a wider audience. (Courtesy of the BPL)

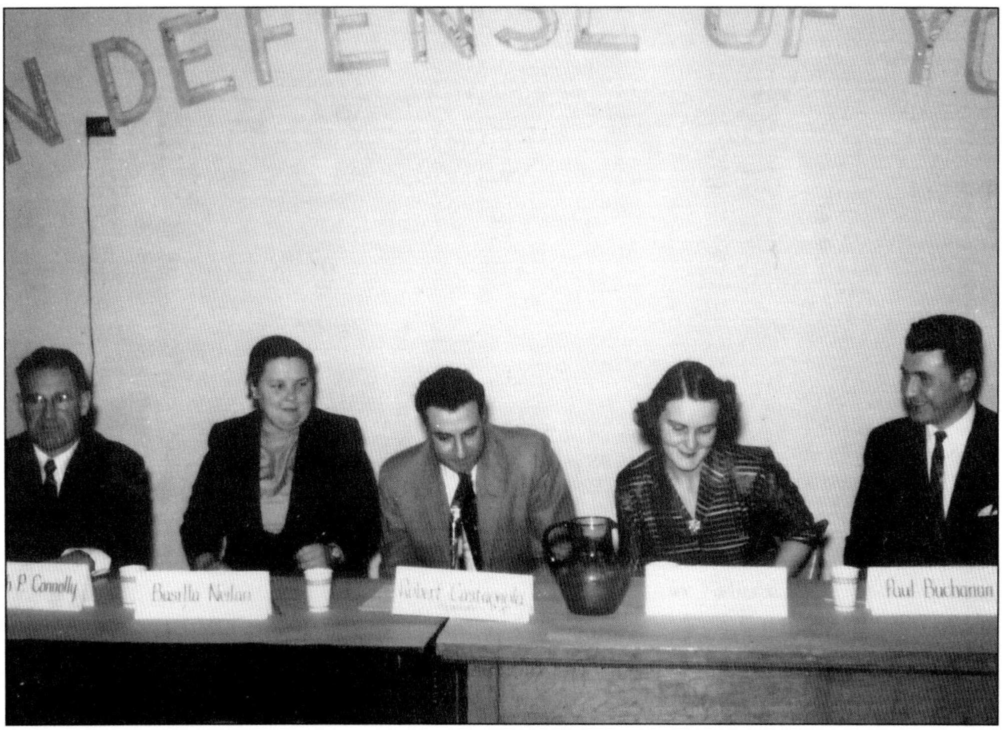

Participating in the program were Joseph P. Connelly, Basilla Neilon, Robert Castugnola, Jane Manthorne, and Paul Buchanan. (Courtesy of the BPL)

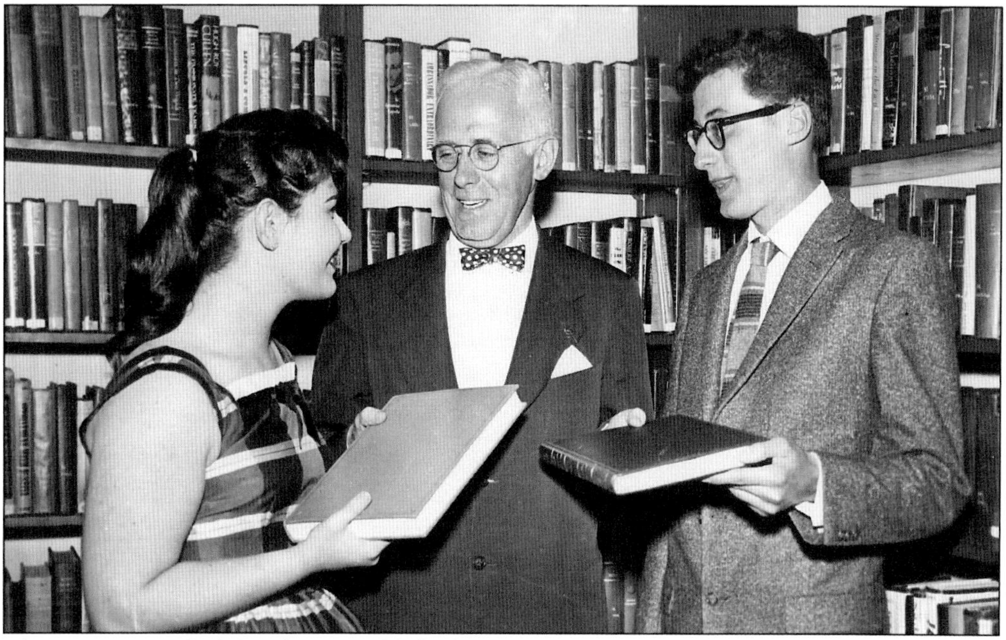

The Mary U. Nichols Fund was established in 1949 "for the purchase of books of lasting value which are awarded annually to the North End boy and girl who have done the best work in English during their senior year in high school." Milton Lord, director of the Boston Public Library, is shown here awarding the Nichols Book Prize in 1958 to Sandra De Luca and Anthony Segadelli. (Courtesy of the BPL)

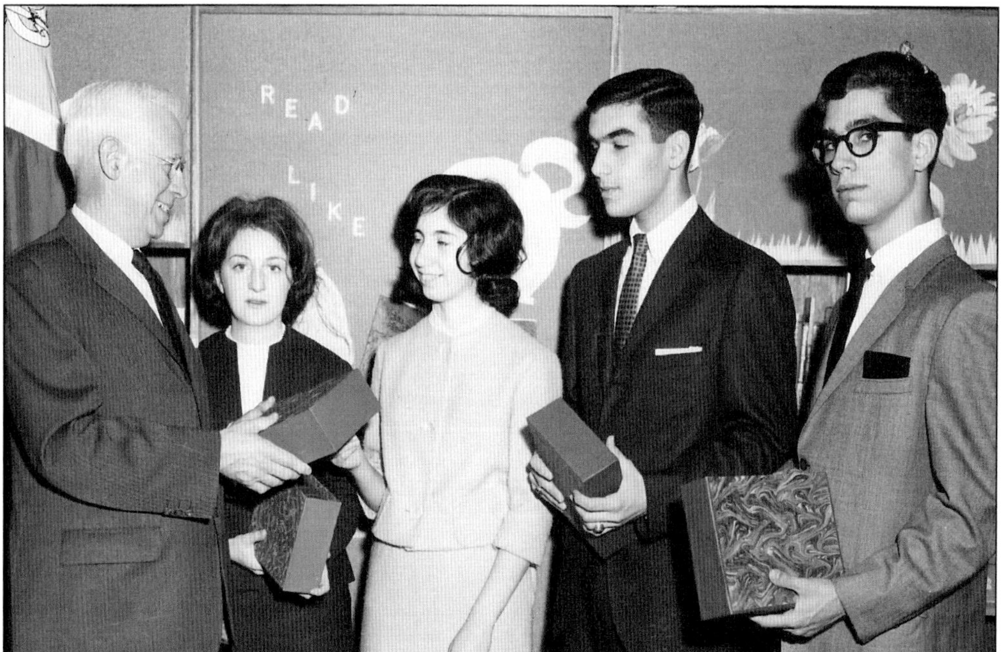

On May 5, 1965, Milton Lord presented books to the winners of the Nichols Book Prize for 1964 and 1965 to Roberta Lombardozzi (1964), Angela and Robert Dello Russo (1965), and Domenic Stagno (1964). (Courtesy of the BPL)

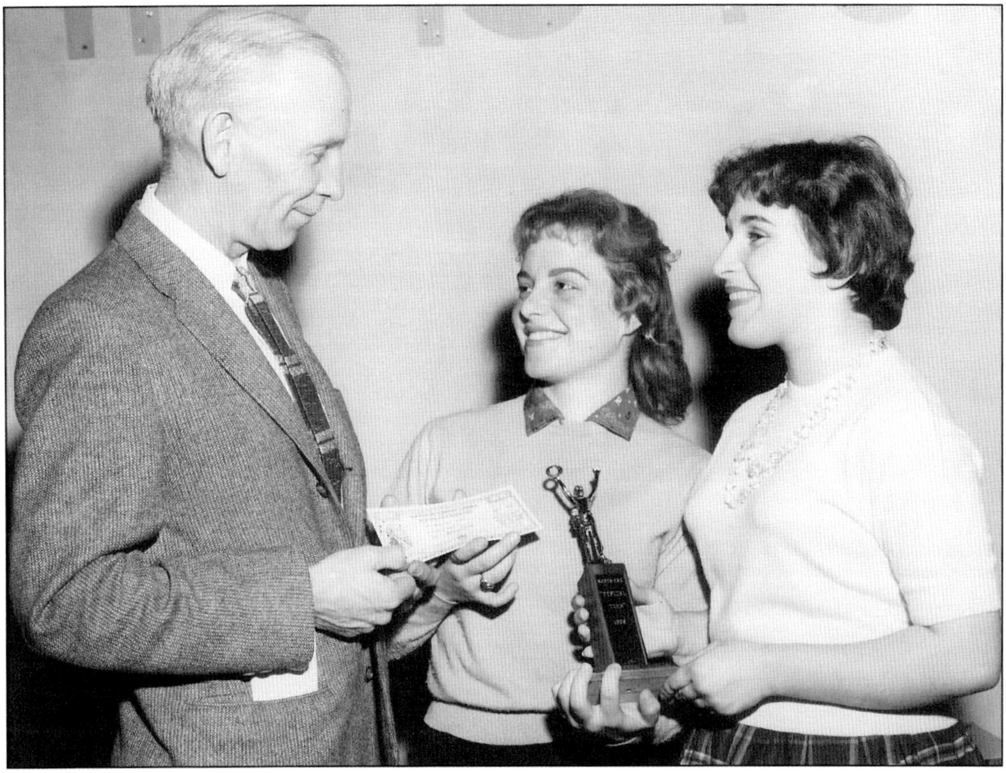

Mr. Frank Haney of the North End Union presents a savings bond and a trophy to Patricia Adrianee and an unidentified girl. (Courtesy of the BPL)

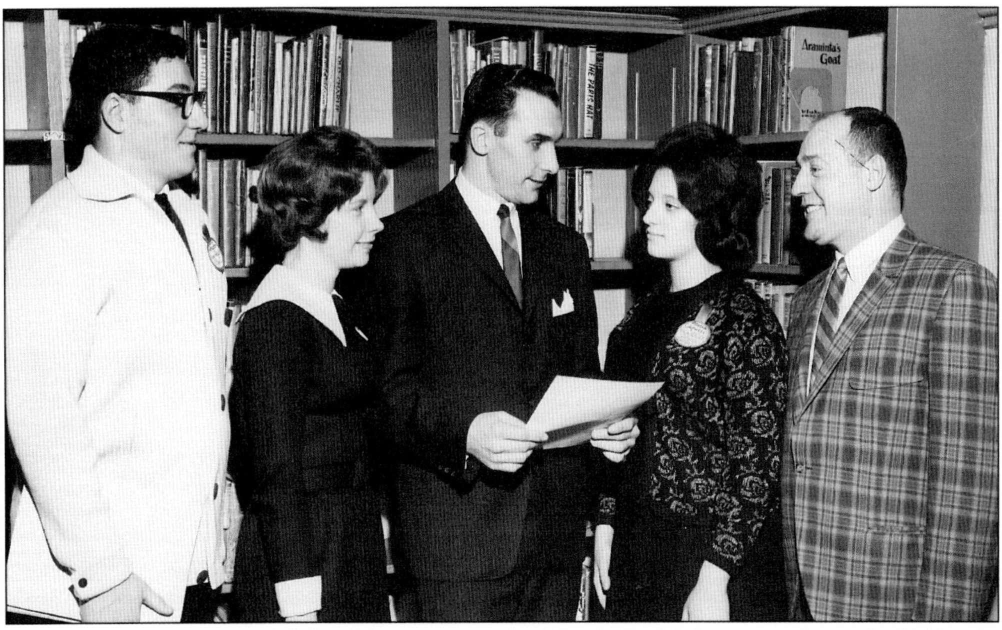

Members of the Young Adults Group met at the North End Library in the early 1960s. As role models for other neighborhood students, they were an important feature of the forums "In Defense of Youth." (Courtesy of the BPL)

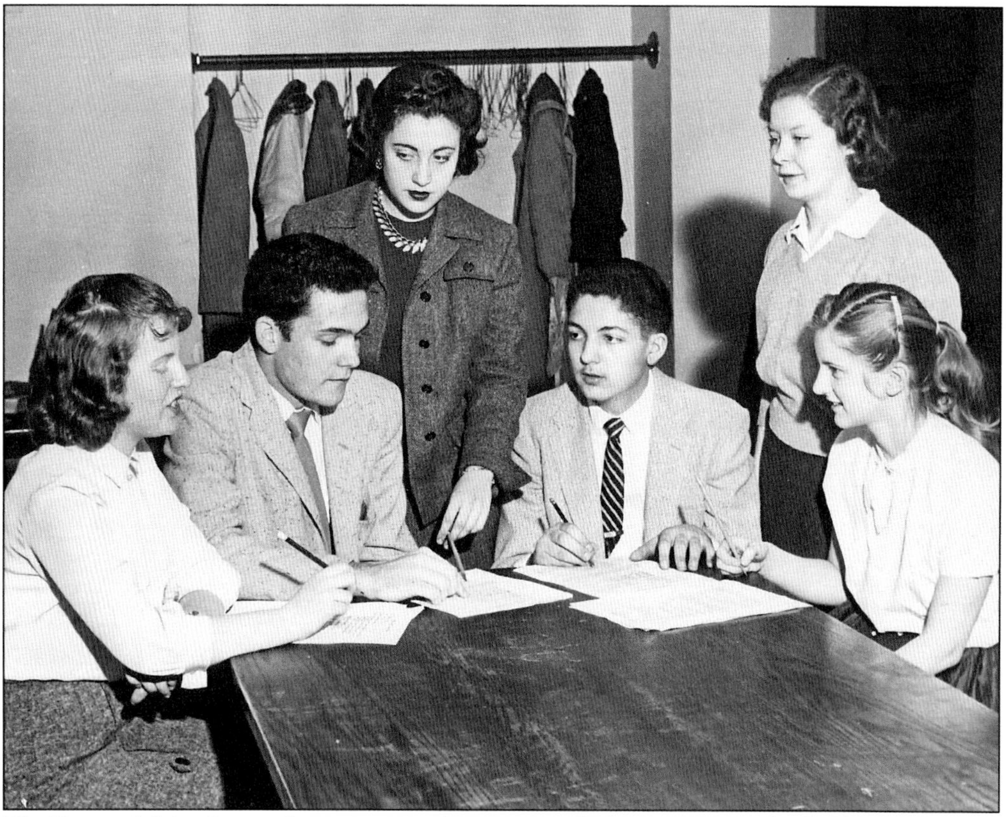

The Young Adults Group plans an musical evening with Danny Kaye, to be held at the Copley Square Library. (Courtesy of the BPL)

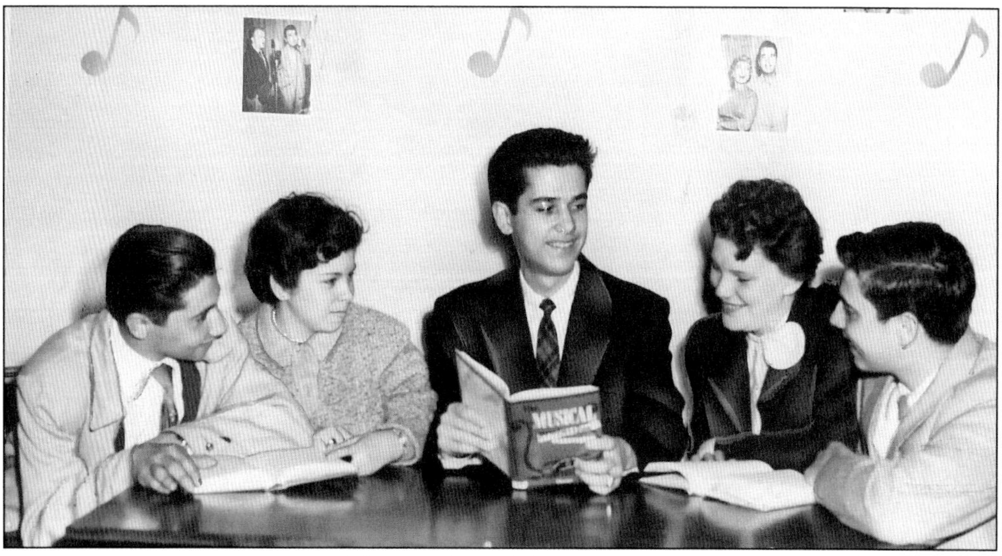

These musically aware young adults are, from left to right, Carmine De Cristoforo, Patricia Sasso, Bernard De Sinone, Emily Salvati, and Robert Church. (Courtesy of the BPL)

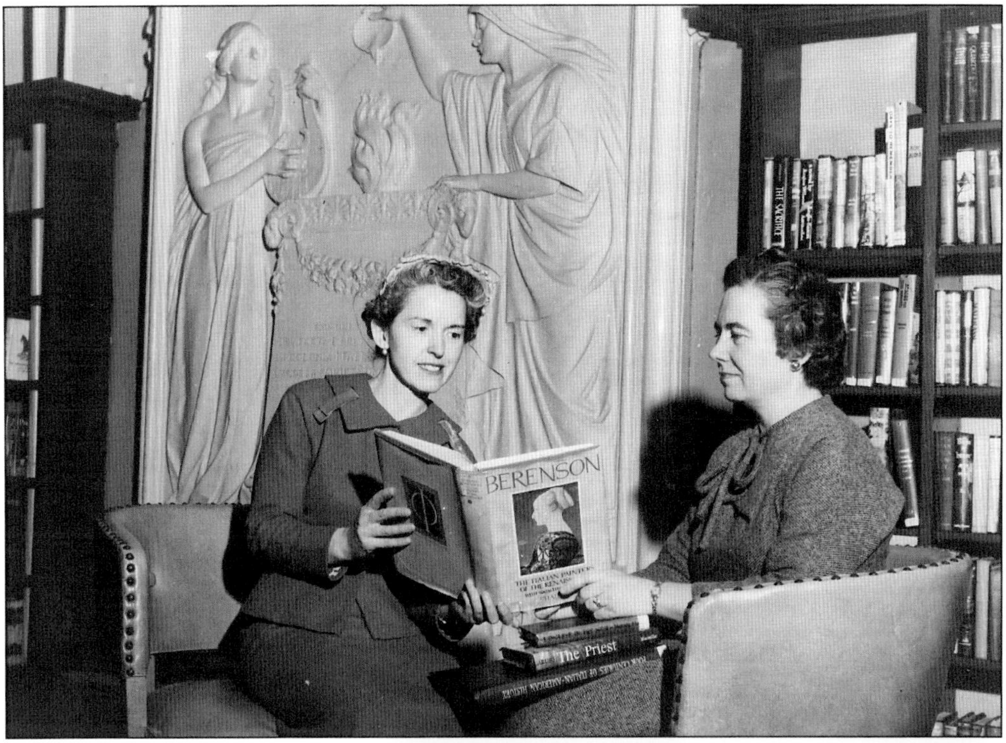

Miss Pietrina Maravigna and Geraldine Herrick discuss the book *Berenson*, which Miss Maravigna had just donated to the North End Library. (Courtesy of the BPL)

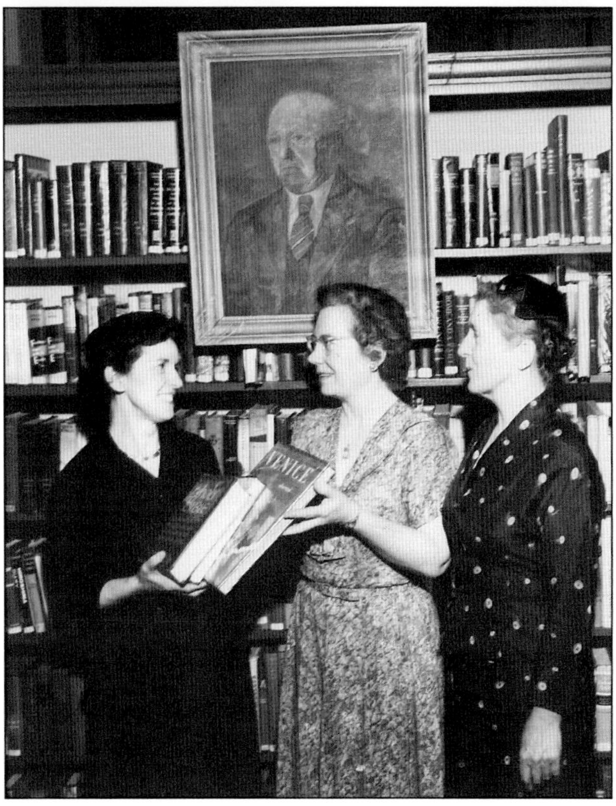

The Misses Pietrina and Maria Maravigna with Geraldine Herrick, branch librarian, hold a recently donated set of books in 1959. Behind them is a portrait of Mr. Maravigna, painted by his daughter Maria. (Courtesy of the BPL)

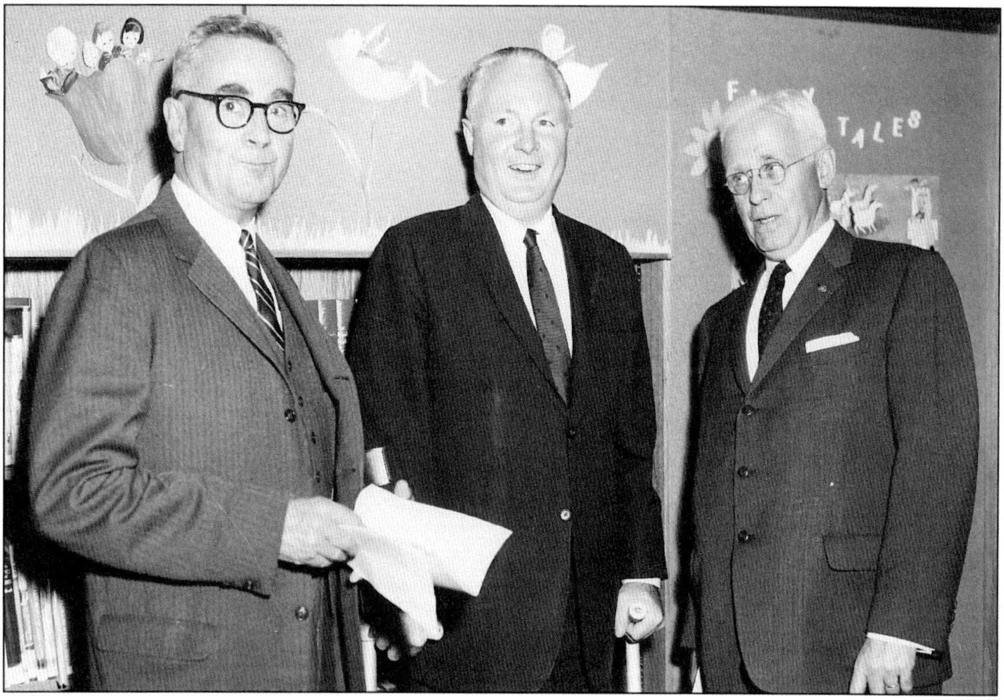

On May 5, 1965, the North End Branch of the Boston Public Library was visited by, from left to right, Augustin Parker (president of the Board of Trustees of the Boston Public Library), City of Boston Mayor John F. Collins, and Milton Lord (director of the Boston Public Library). (Courtesy of the BPL)

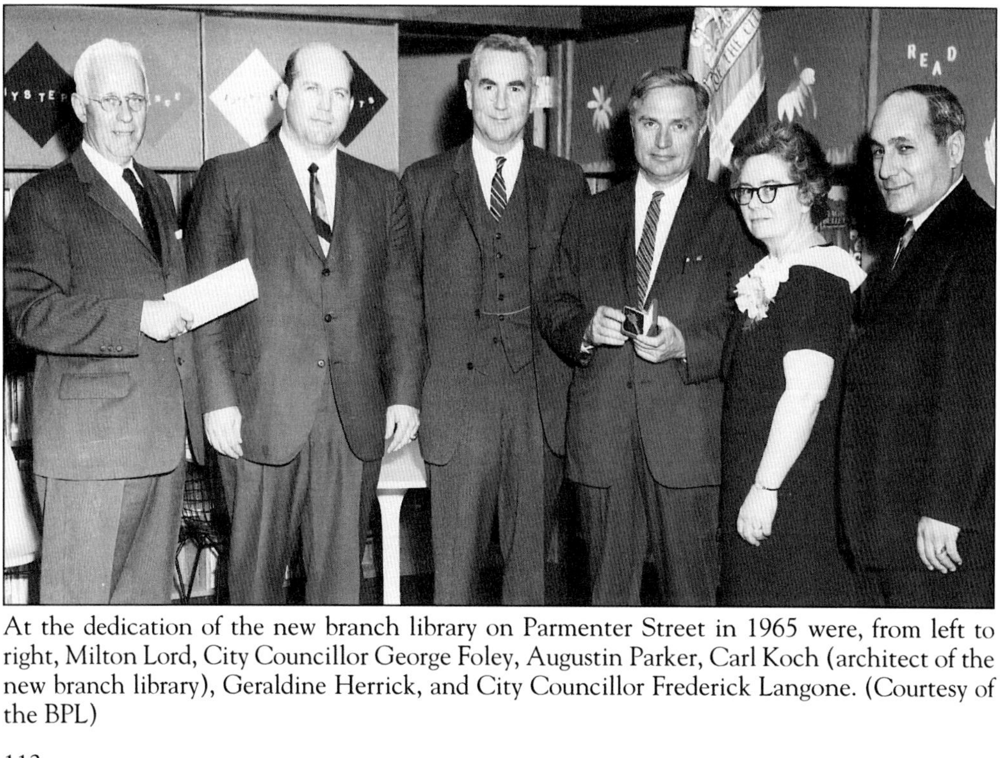

At the dedication of the new branch library on Parmenter Street in 1965 were, from left to right, Milton Lord, City Councillor George Foley, Augustin Parker, Carl Koch (architect of the new branch library), Geraldine Herrick, and City Councillor Frederick Langone. (Courtesy of the BPL)

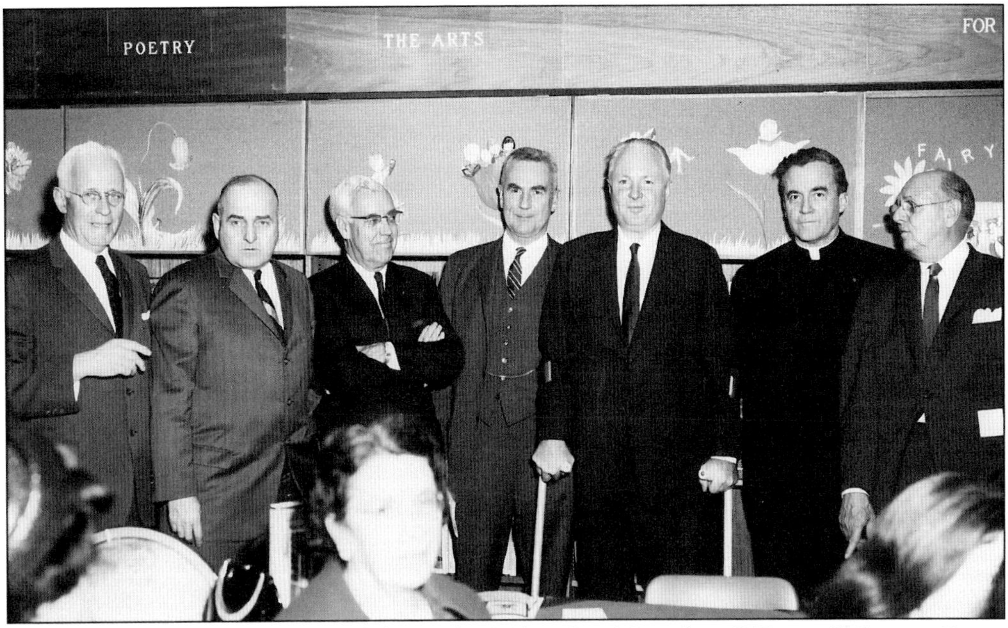

Also at the dedication were, from left to right, Milton Lord, Lenahan O'Connell, Esquire, Erwin Canham, Augustin Parker, Boston Mayor John Collins, Monsignor Edward Murray, and Sidney Rabb. (Courtesy of the BPL)

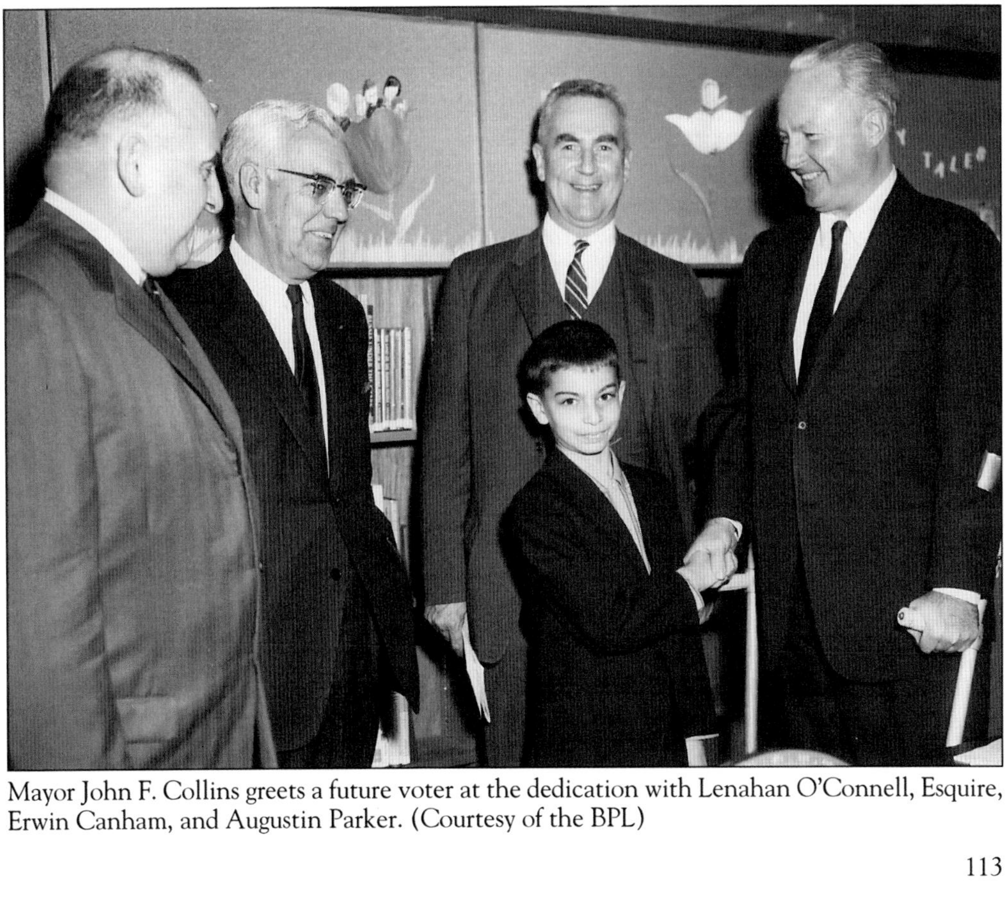

Mayor John F. Collins greets a future voter at the dedication with Lenahan O'Connell, Esquire, Erwin Canham, and Augustin Parker. (Courtesy of the BPL)

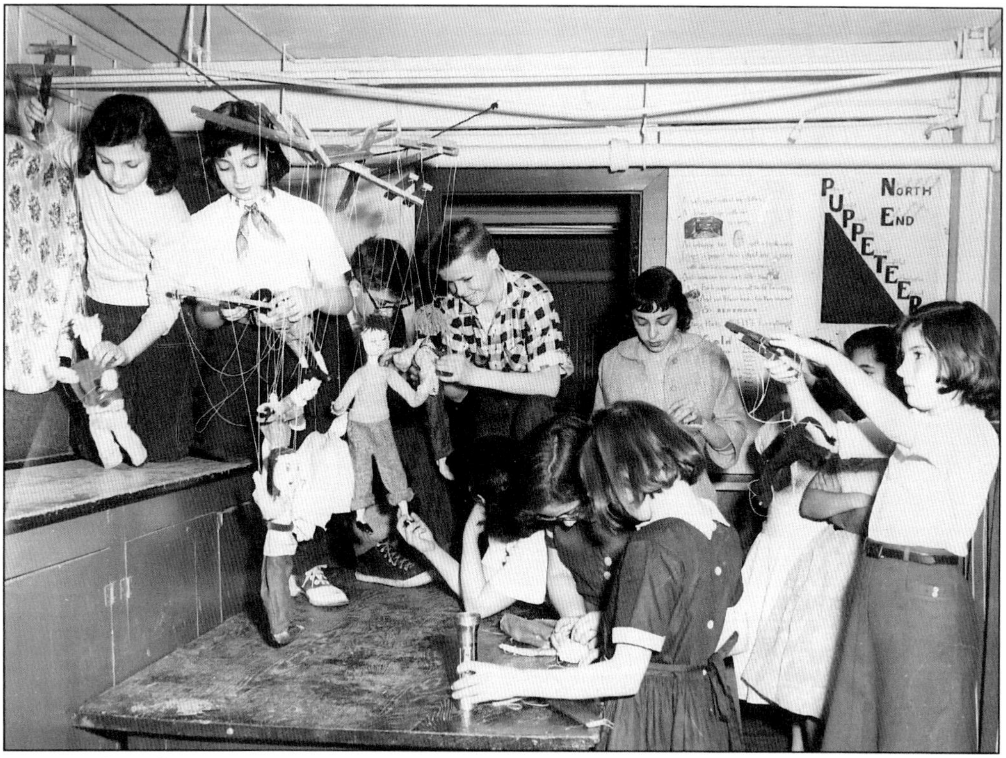

The North End Puppeteers were formed in 1946 at the North End Branch of the Boston Public Library. Here members of the group prepare to present a puppet show in the basement of the North Bennett Street branch. (Courtesy of the BPL)

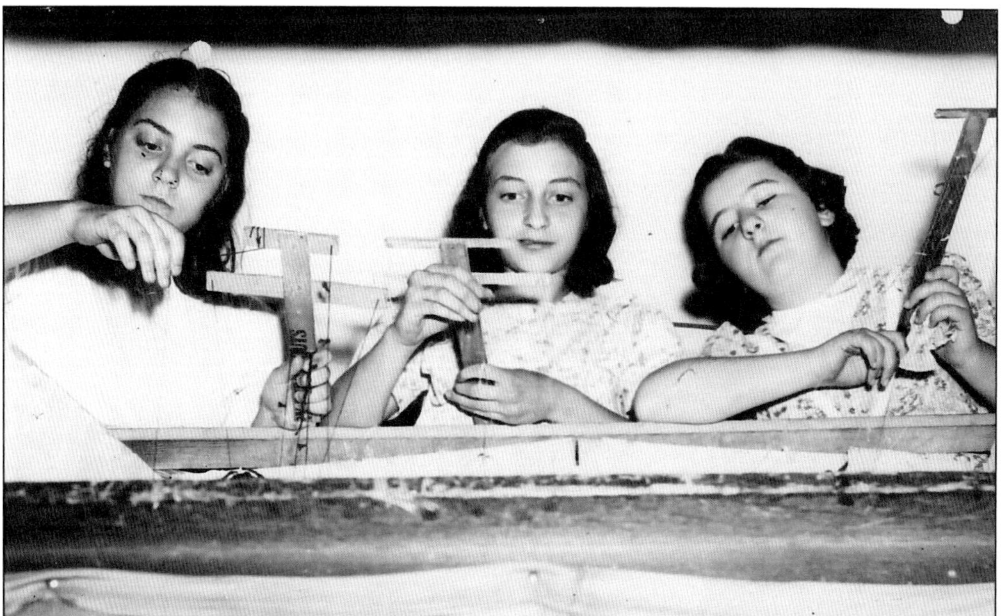

Three friends combine dexterity and skill as they manipulate their puppet's strings from above the stage. (Courtesy of the BPL)

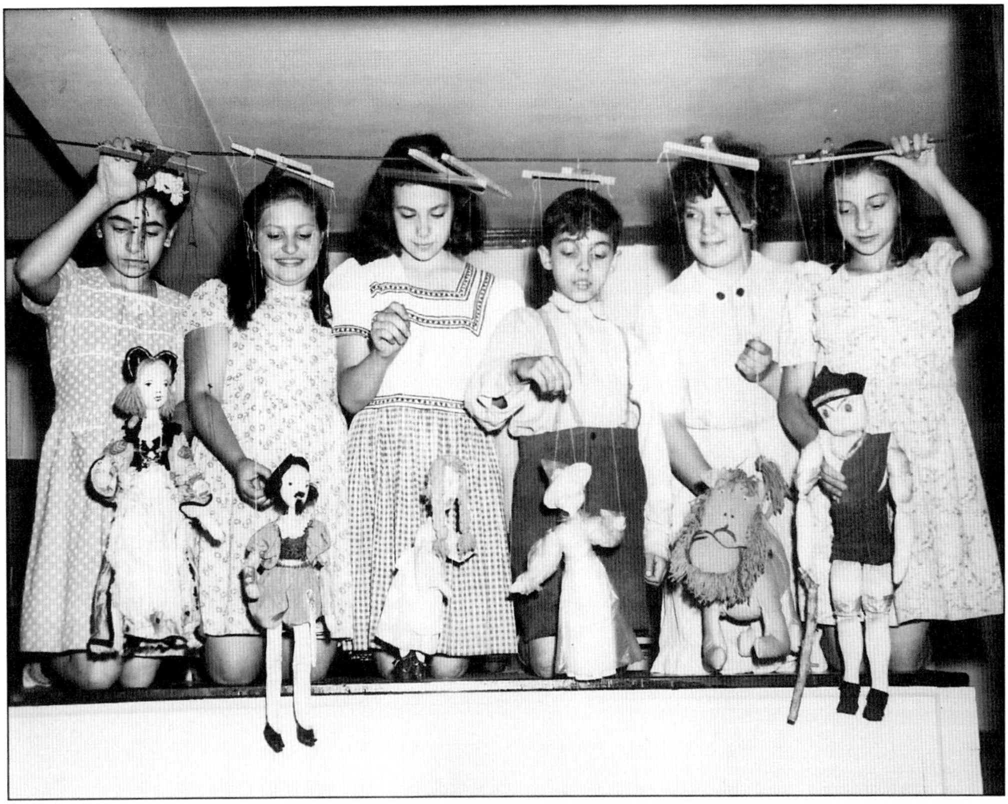

Puppets were handmade by the children, and occasionally by their parents, after the play to be presented was chosen. Here these "master puppeteers" show their characters. (Courtesy of the BPL)

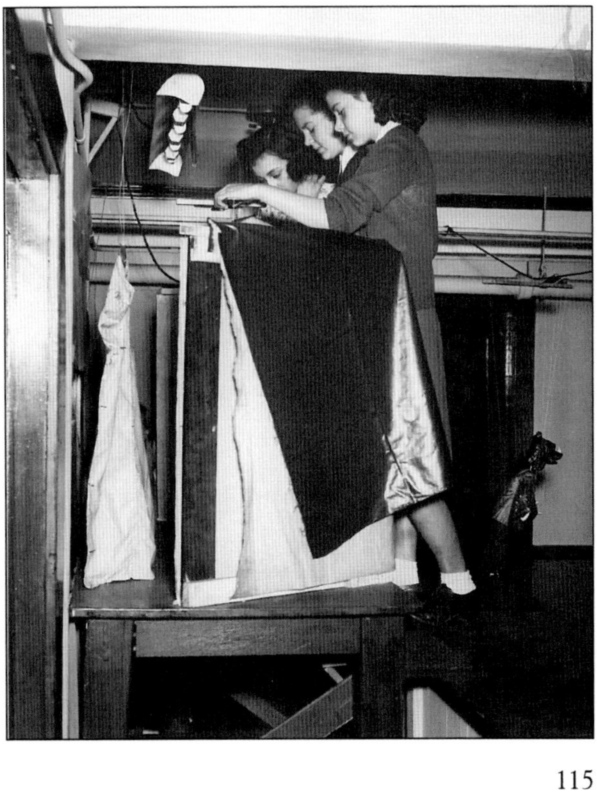

A puppet stage can be a fascinating place behind the scenes. These three friends seem to be enjoying the delight their puppets are creating in the audience. (Courtesy of the BPL)

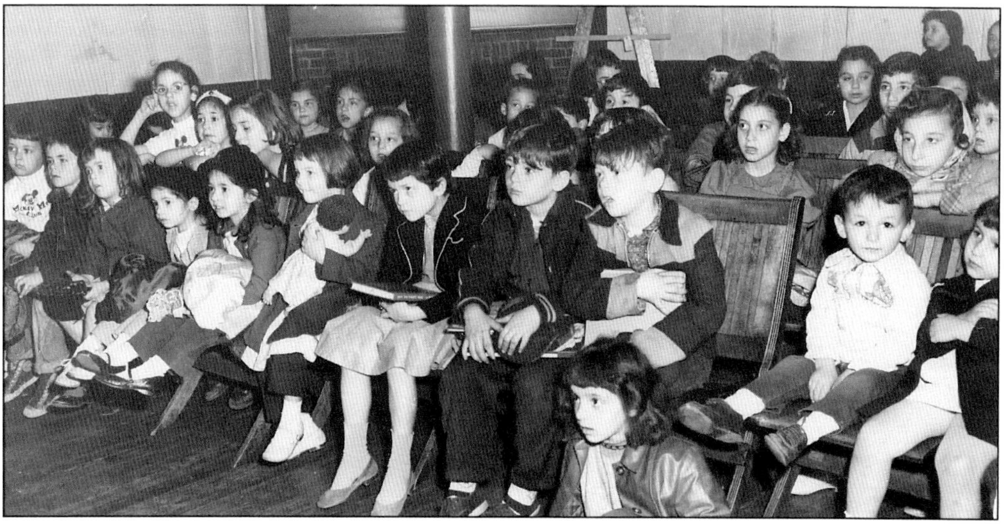

This audience eagerly awaits a puppet show in the early 1960s at the North Bennett Street library. These shows included perennial favorites such as *Pinocchio* and *Hansel and Gretel*. (Courtesy of the BPL)

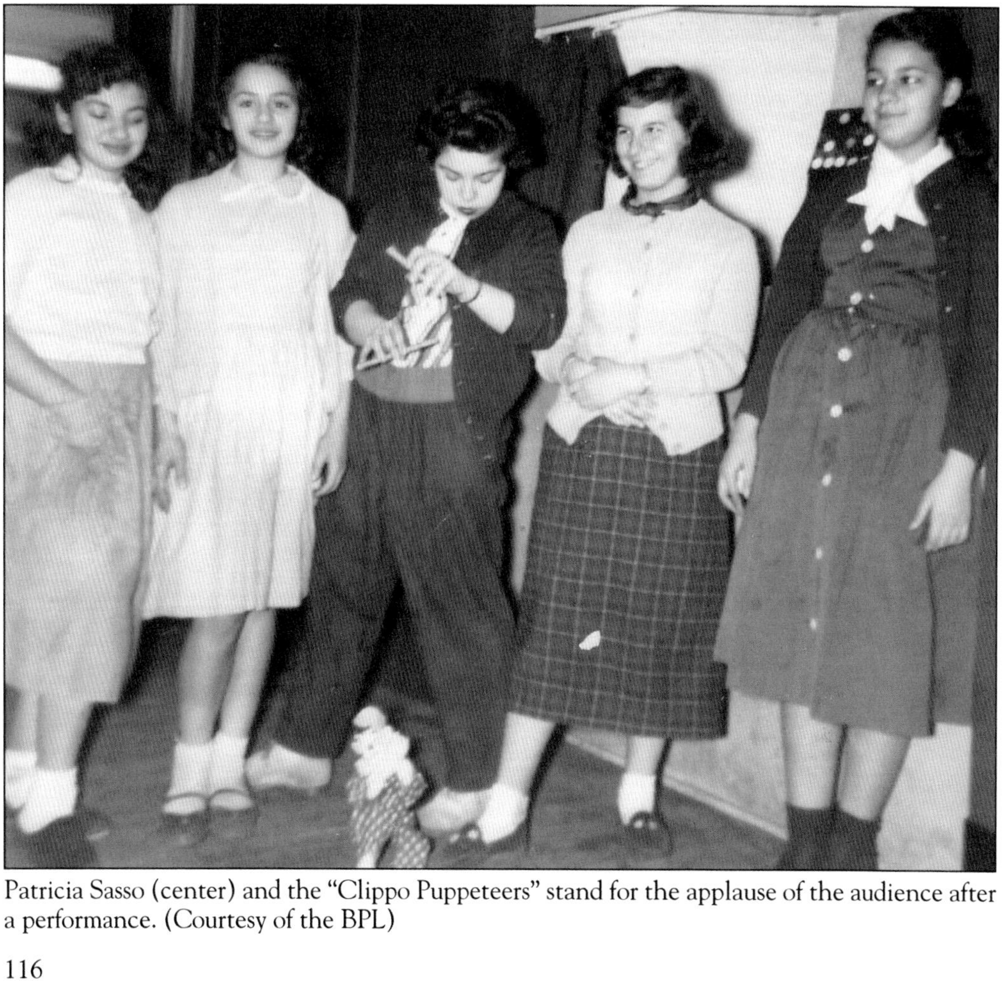

Patricia Sasso (center) and the "Clippo Puppeteers" stand for the applause of the audience after a performance. (Courtesy of the BPL)

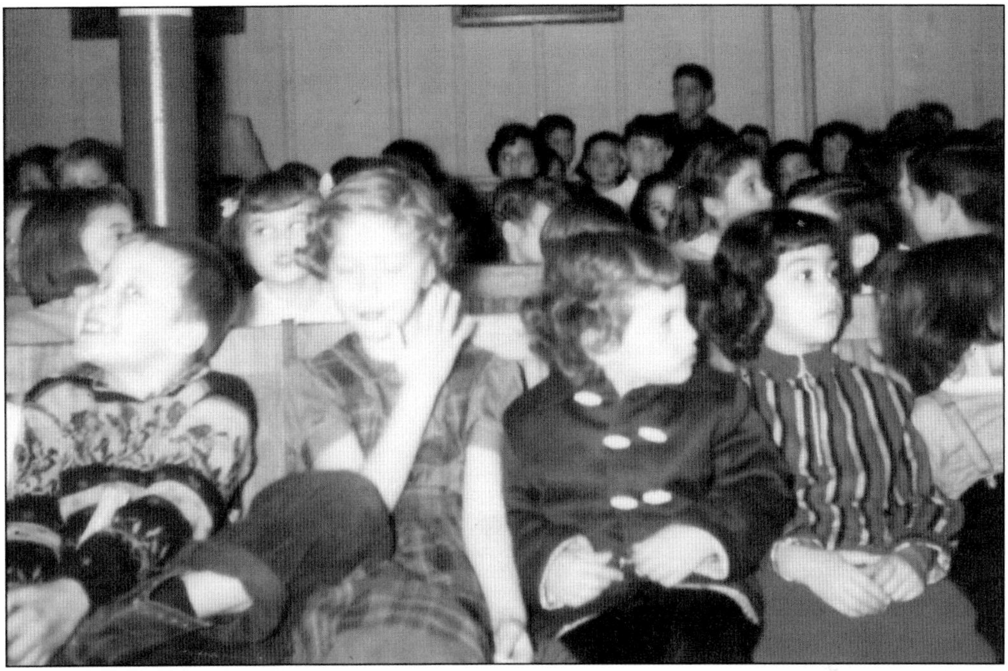

A mesmerized audience of children stare intently as the puppets act out a play. The delight and merriment of these children can be seen in their eyes! (Courtesy of the BPL)

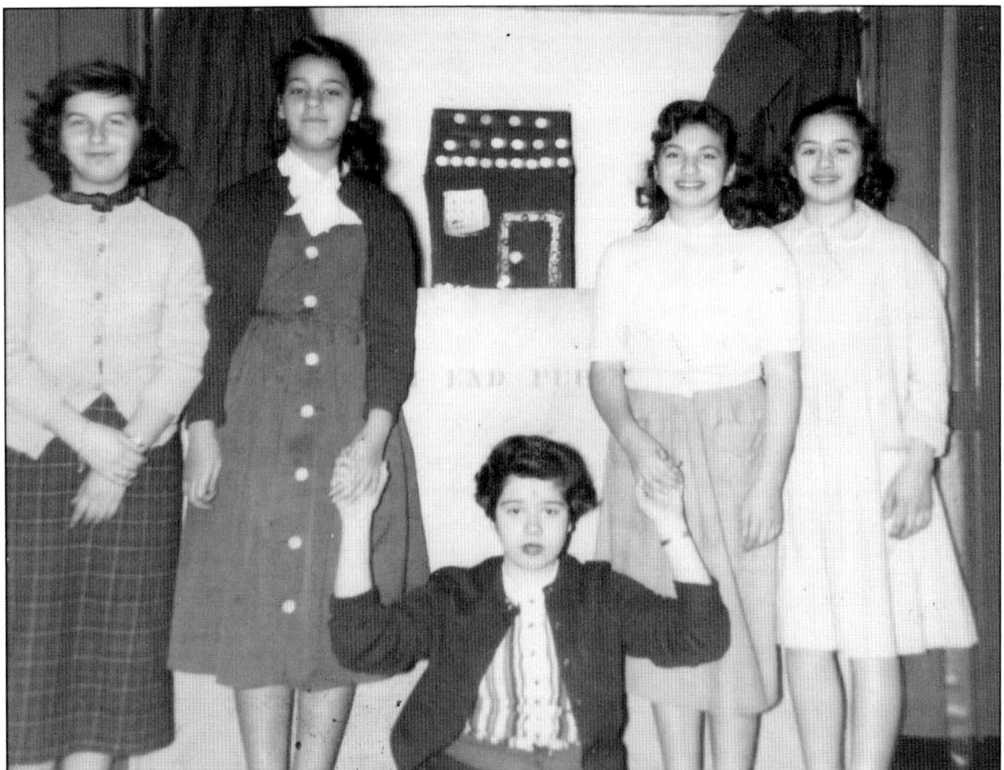

Patricia Sasso takes a bow with her "Clippo Puppeteers." (Courtesy of the BPL)

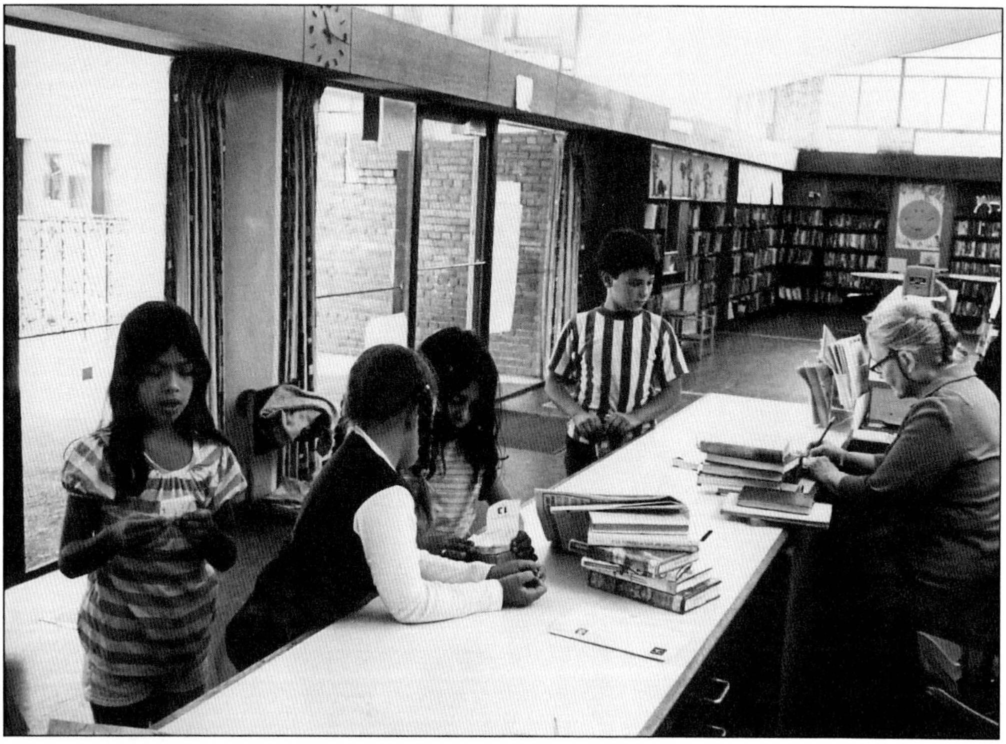

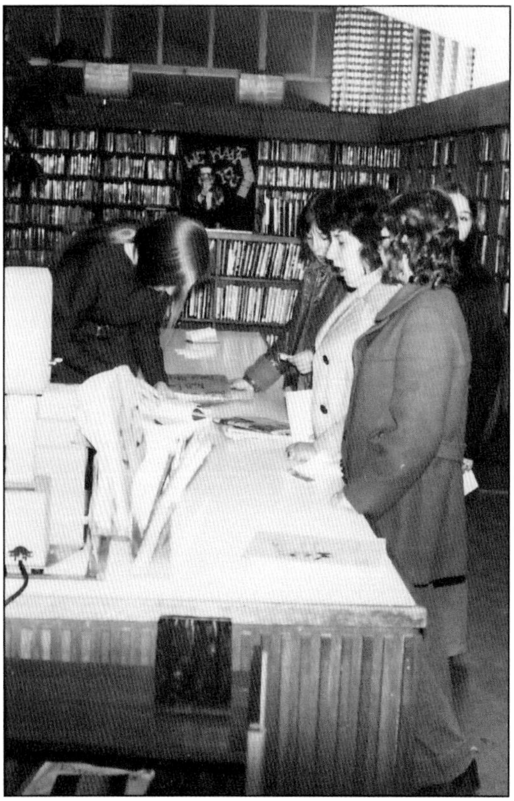

Children check out books from the library in 1971. (Courtesy of the BPL)

In the fall of 1965, three girls check out books from the freshly stacked library shelves, which were filled prior to the library's dedication on May 5, 1965. (Courtesy of the BPL)

Various activities were planned for neighborhood residents, among them "Hair and Makeup Styles." An instructor described and demonstrated various hairstyles to the young ladies in the audience that they could try at home. (Courtesy of the BPL)

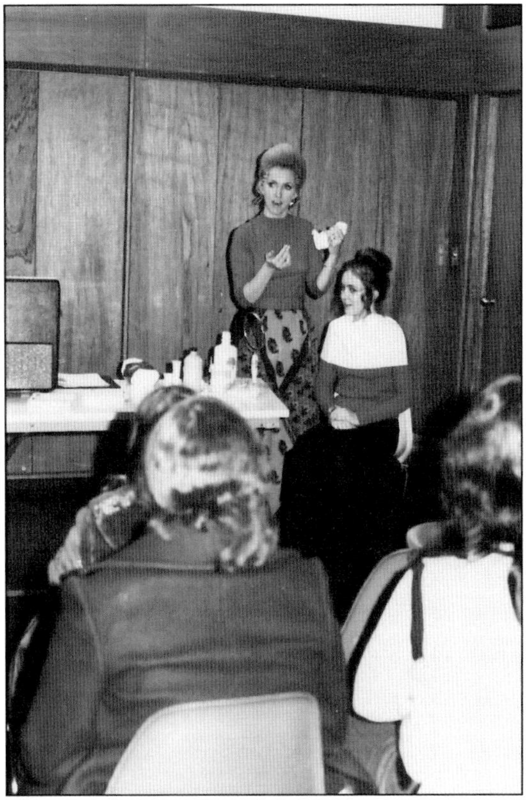

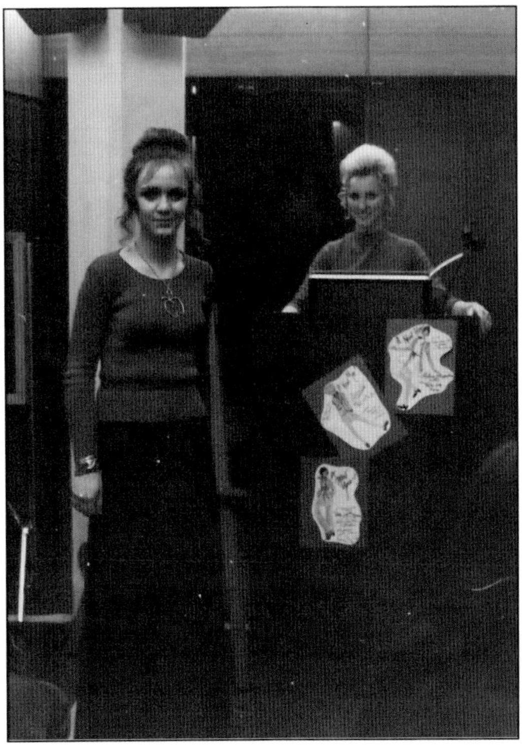

A beaming instructor proudly stands behind a young lady who models her "hip" new hairstyle, which looks remarkably like the instructor's, for the audience. (Courtesy of the BPL)

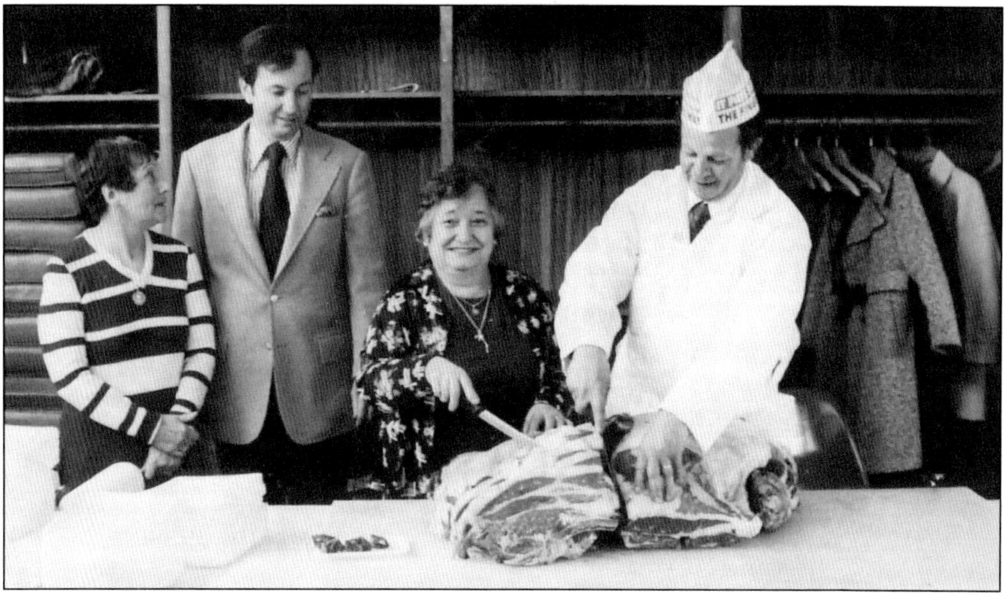

A popular "Tuesday Topics" lecture was "Make No Mis Steaks" when a meat cutter from the First National Supermarket demonstrated different cuts of meat for an eager audience in 1976. From left to right are Anna Repucci, Ted Harrigan (of the First National Supermarket), Josephine Tranquillo, and Vincent Strazzulo (of the First National Supermarket). (Courtesy of the BPL)

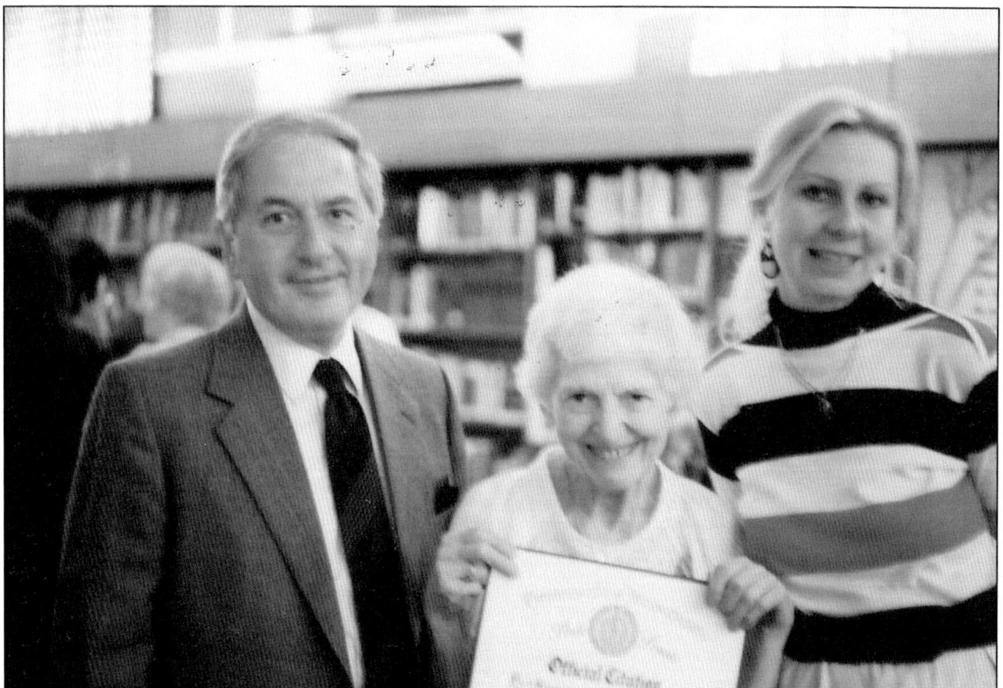

At the 40th anniversary of the Nichols Award in 1988, Miss Pietrina Maravigna was presented with a citation for her efforts on behalf of the North End Branch of the Boston Public Library. On the left is Guy Beninati and Branch Librarian Janet Buda. (Courtesy of the BPL)

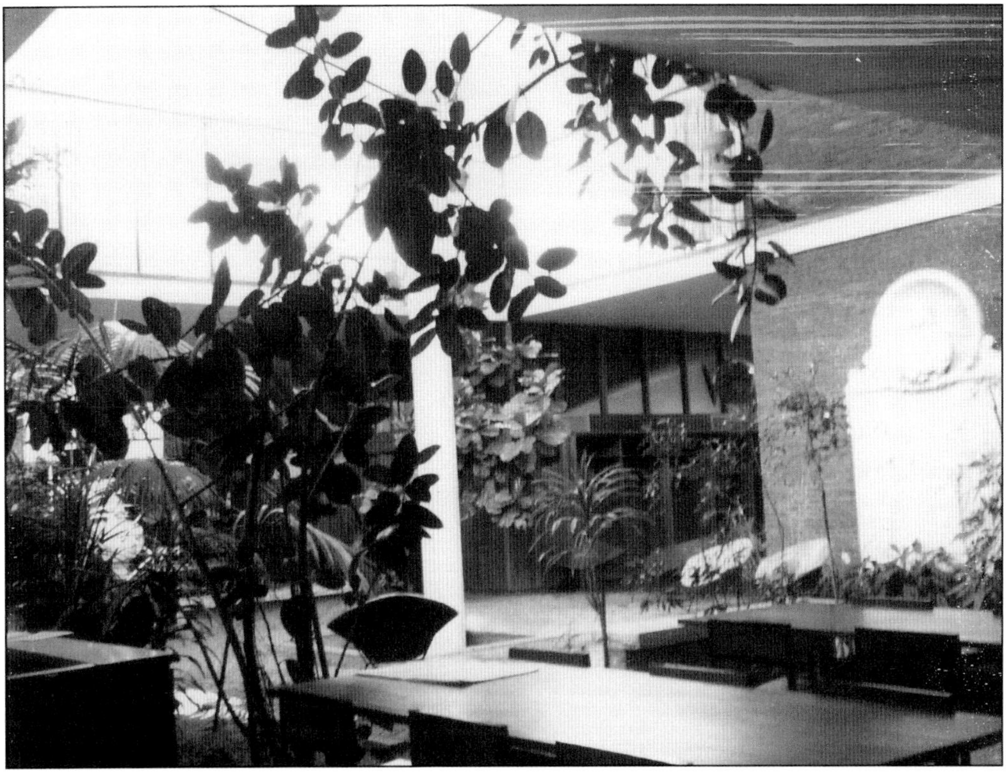

The center of the Parmenter Street branch library has a courtyard with lush tropical plants that thrive in the sun-filled area. A white marble tablet commemorating Christopher Columbus is mounted on the brick wall, and a water-filled pool creates a Mediterranean-inspired garden that is charming all year long. (Courtesy of the BPL)

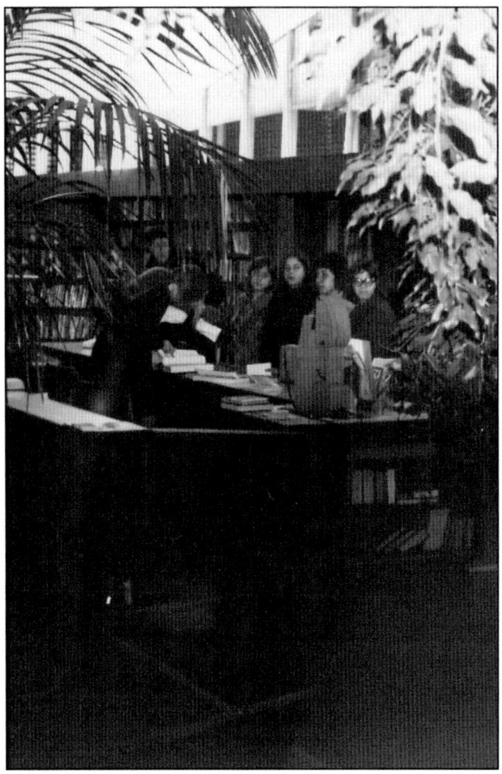

Book check-out is seen through the palm fronds and lush tropical plants that thrive in the courtyard of the library. (Courtesy of the BPL)

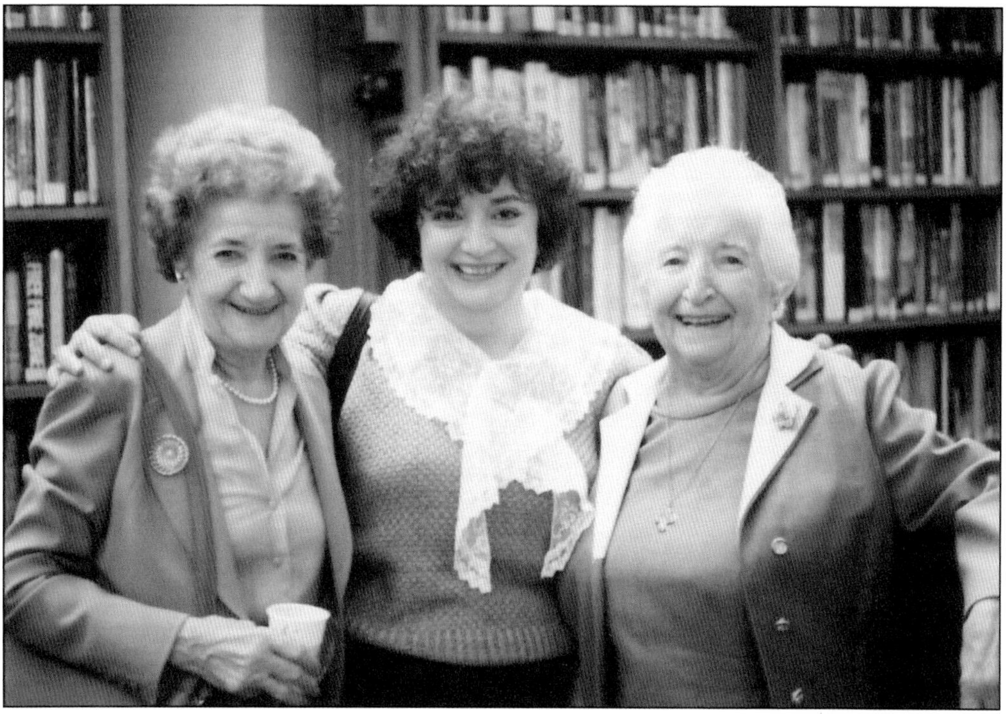

Three friends pose following the Nichols Award Program in 1988. (Courtesy of the BPL)

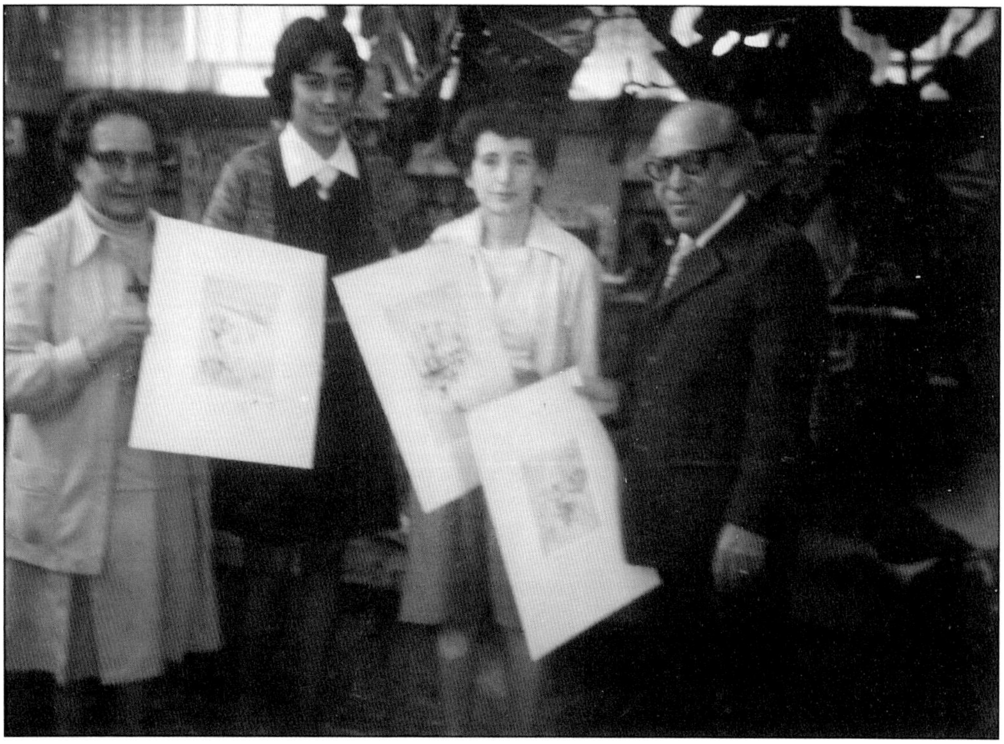

In November of 1976, there was a presentation by Peter Tardo to Sister Mary Pierzozzi, Paula Jocline, and Rhoda Blacker. (Courtesy of the BPL)

NORTH END BRANCH
of the
BOSTON PUBLIC LIBRARY
cordially invites you to attend
the first annual awarding of the
MARY U. NICHOLS BOOK PRIZES
on
Thursday evening, June 2, 1949
at eight o'clock

3A North Bennet Street
Boston, Massachusetts

ELLEN C. PETERSON
Branch Librarian.

This invitation was for the first Nichols Book Prize, given annually to a student in the North End who excelled in English in their senior year in high school. The fund was established in 1949 in honor of Mary U. Nichols, a former librarian at the North End Library. (Courtesy of the BPL)

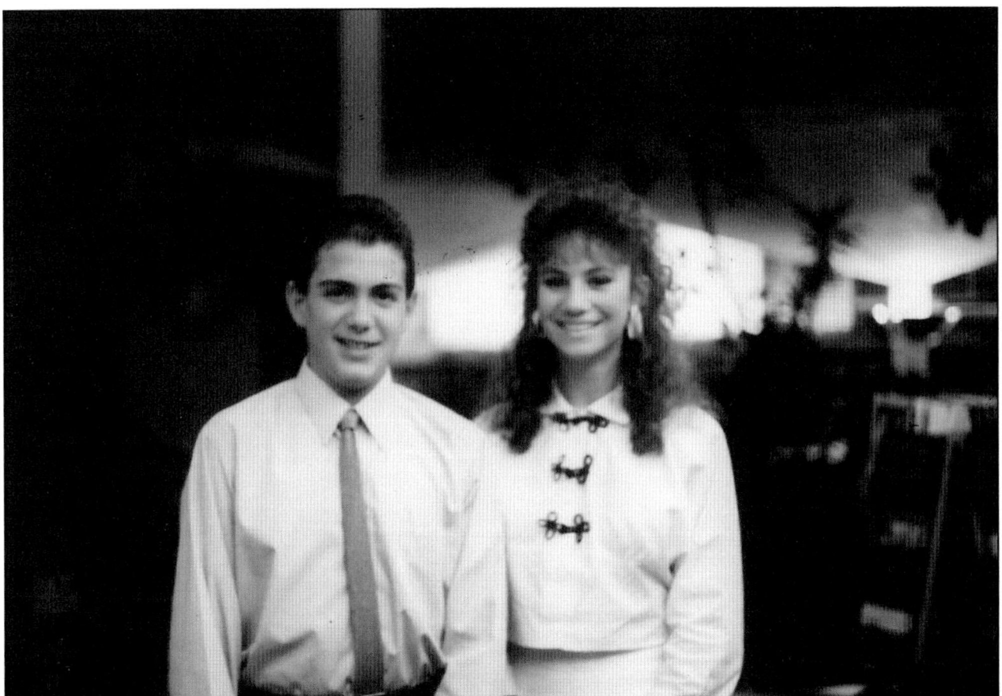

The winners of the 1988 Nichols Book Prize were Laureen Murphy and Joseph Bova. (Courtesy of the BPL)

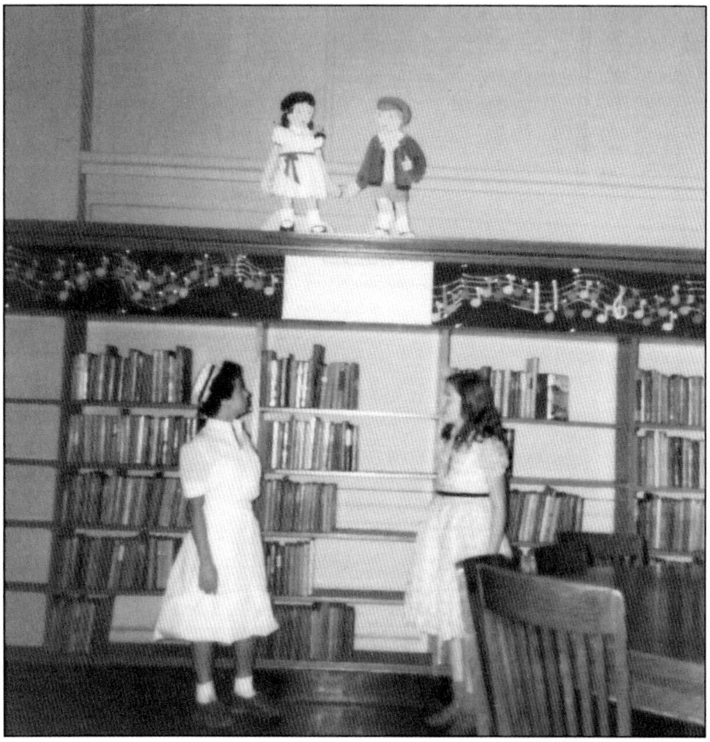

Santina Coco and Loretta Mancini are shown here standing in the Children's Room of the library in 1955. (Courtesy of the BPL)

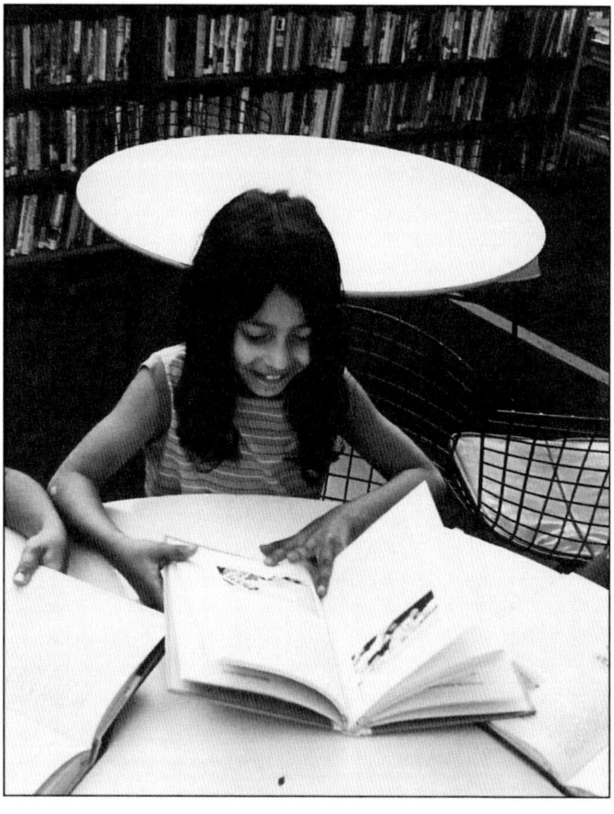

A young lady looks through one of thousands of books available at the North End Branch of the Boston Public Library. (Courtesy of the BPL)

The ever-generous Pietrina Maravigna has made it a custom to present books to the North End Library at Christmas. Accepting the gift of a book is Geraldine Herrick, branch librarian. (Courtesy of the BPL)

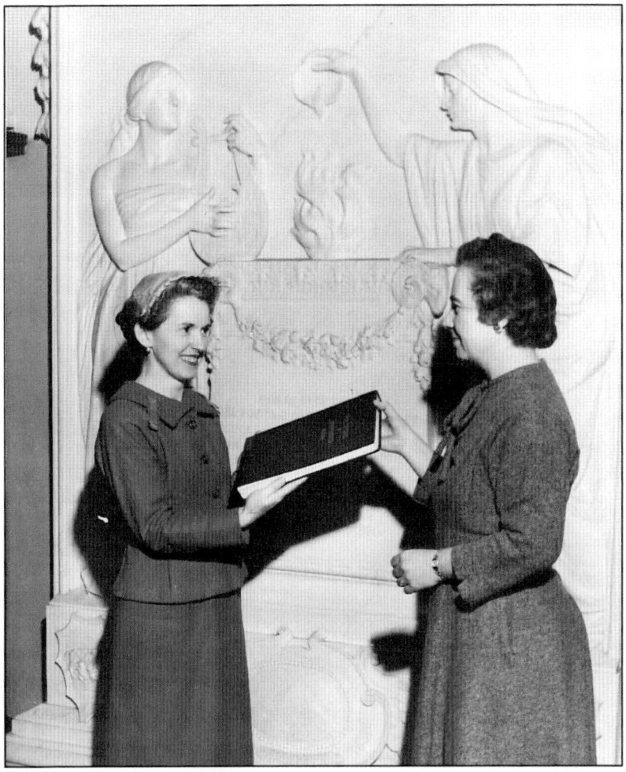

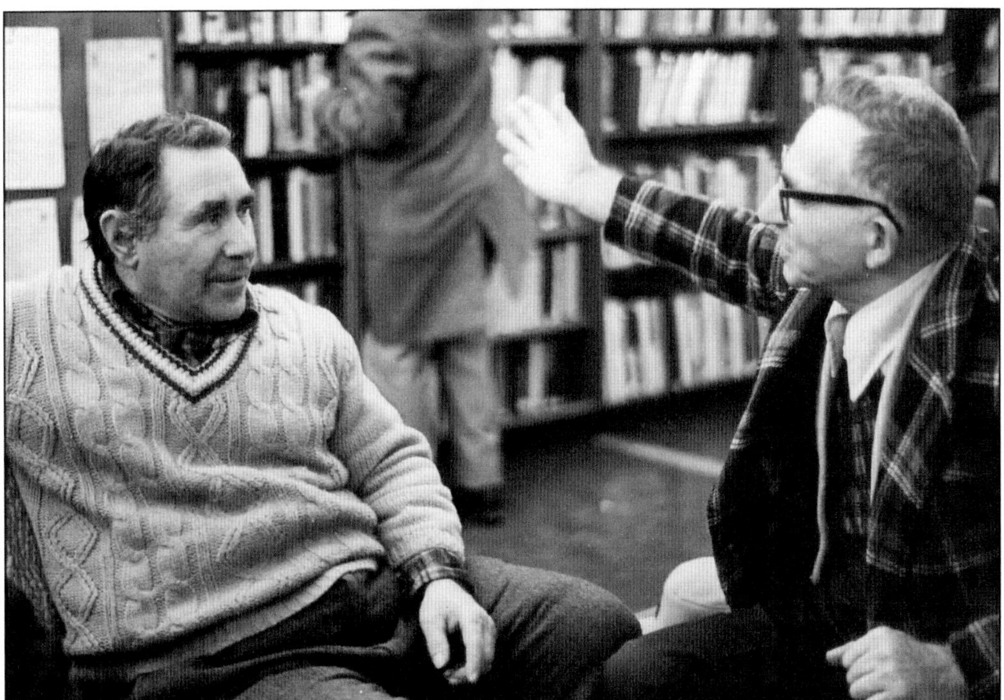

Two neighbors discuss the latest news in the sun-filled courtyard of the North End Library. (Courtesy of the BPL)

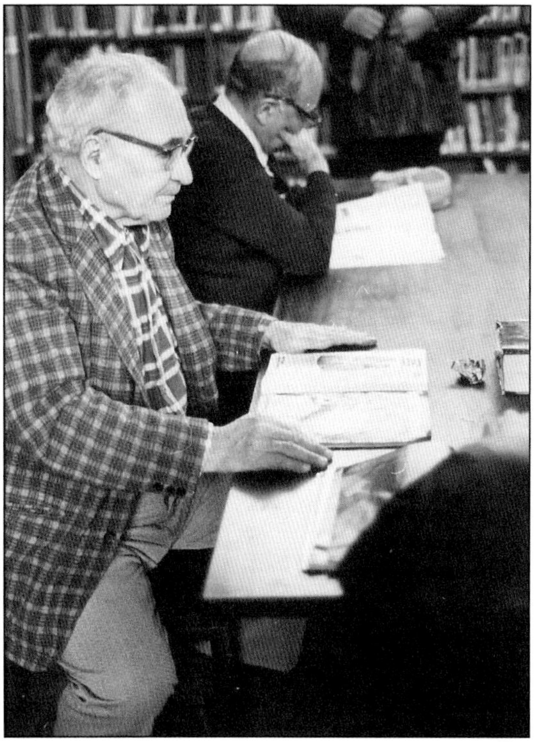

The North End Library is used by different age groups for different things, but whether it's to read books and newspapers, plot investments, or catch up on neighborhood news, all are assured of getting a friendly welcome by the staff. (Courtesy of the BPL)

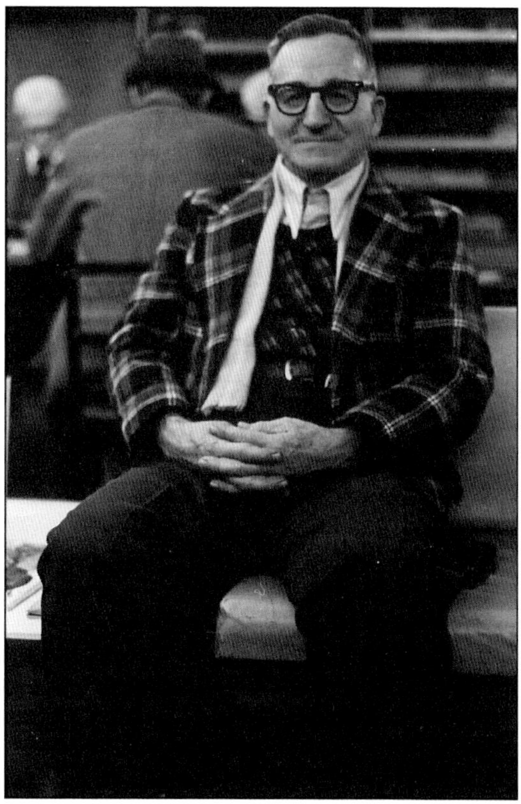

Retired, but not forgotten, this man was a regular library patron in the 1970s. (Courtesy of the BPL)

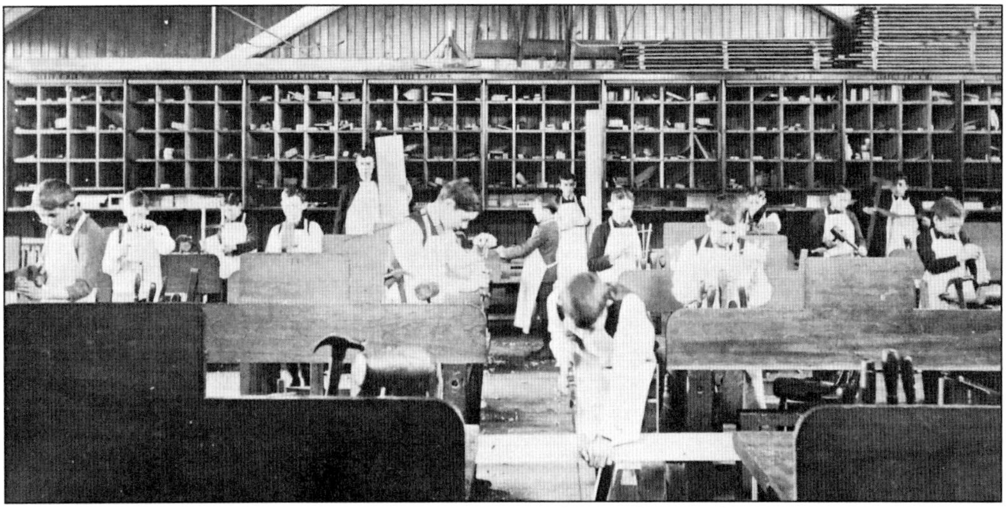

This turn-of-the-century photograph of a carpentry class at the North Bennett Street Industrial School shows students at their shop benches. Gustaf Larsson had introduced Sloyd, a method of training from Sweden, and it became popular throughout the city. Today the school offers various courses including bookbinding, watch and jewelry repair, and a course in fine cabinetmaking. (Courtesy of the BPL)

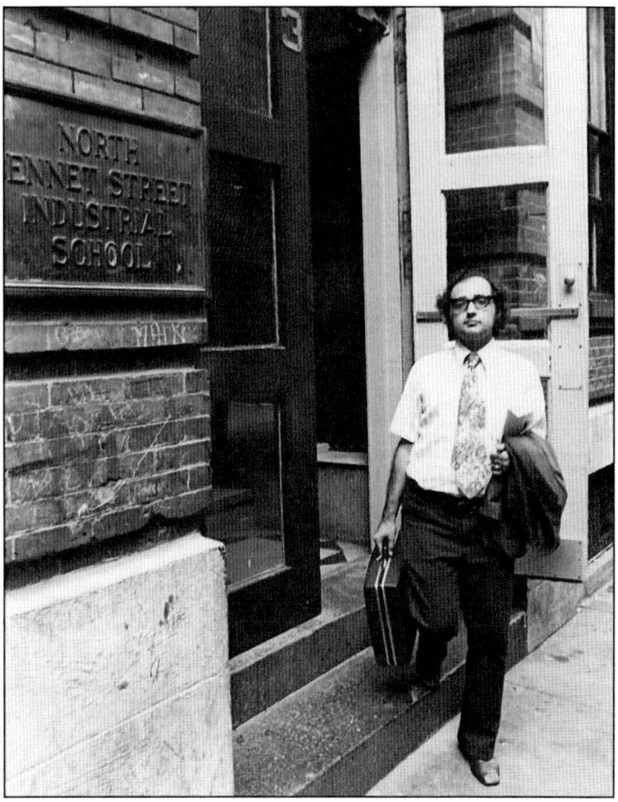

Walter Bacigalupo, assistant to the director of the North Bennett Street Industrial School in 1971, leaves by the front door after a long day at work. (Courtesy of the BPL)

Acknowledgments

I wish to thank Janet Buda, Branch Librarian of the North End Branch of the Boston Public Library, for encouraging me to write this pictorial history of the North End of Boston. Her generosity in contributing her time and photographs has made this book a fascinating spectrum of the oldest neighborhood of Boston.

I would also like to thank the following for their continued support and encouragement: Daniel J. Ahlin, Vito Aluia (for generously loaning photographs from his personal collection), Anthony Bognanno, Paul and Helen Graham Buchanan, Gerard Cronin (*The Boston Globe*), Dexter, Joseph and Mildred Carvotta Giannelli, Edward W. Gordon, James Z. Kyprianos, Jonathan T. Melick, Stephen and Susan Paine, Fran Ross of Pizzeria Regina North End, Dennis Ryan, Anthony and Mary Mitchell Sammarco, Gilda Sammarco, Rosemary Sammarco, the late Luigi and Rose Giannelli Sammarco, Sylvia Sandeen, Robert Bayard Severy, William Varrell, and my ever-patient editor, Jamie Carter.